Visible Women

Visible Women:
Tales of Age, Gender and In/Visibility

By

Christine Bell

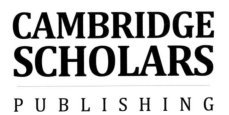

CAMBRIDGE
SCHOLARS
PUBLISHING

Visible Women: Tales of Age, Gender and In/Visibility,
by Christine Bell

This book first published 2012

Cambridge Scholars Publishing

12 Back Chapman Street, Newcastle upon Tyne, NE6 2XX, UK

British Library Cataloguing in Publication Data
A catalogue record for this book is available from the British Library

ISBN (10): 1-4438-3631-1, ISBN (13): 978-1-4438-3631-9

This book is dedicated to my mother, Dora Bell,
who did not have the chance to become an 'older woman'

TABLE OF CONTENTS

LIST OF PHOTOGRAPHS

ACKNOWLEDGEMENTS

My heartfelt and grateful thanks go to my seven wonderfully visible co-researchers, Alison, Cindy, Jane, Lynn, Marie, Sara and Val. Without them this work would not have been possible and they all contributed generously with their time, energy, openness, trust and humour.

David Hutchinson, my partner, has been an enormously important support in each step along the way and loyally read my every re-write.

Jane Speedy, professor, supervisor, guide and mentor through the narrative doctoral labyrinths for many years, has been a continuing inspiration and a generous, creative and very effective unstopper of blocks.

CHAPTER ONE

EXAMINING THE BONES

Reciter of bones, lover of poems –
memory has always been my long suit
(Itani, 2008: 280)

1.1 Why this exploration?

Rather than a complete invisibility of women
it is the distortion in their visibility
and the assumption of their derived identity and status ...
which ... occupy the attention ...

(Dube et al, 1986: xxiv)

This work is a subjective reflection on my membership of a group which I didn't ask to join, but became eligible for anyway. We're called 'older women' – and sometimes much less polite things. Whilst disliking the name-calling, I have been (mostly) sanguine about passing the various age milestones which apparently bring dismay for some in our 'group'. I am not, however, happy with the idea of quietly disappearing simply because of my age and gender.

There are many anecdotal stories about older women becoming invisible – often based on the experiences of well-known and apparently very visible women. There is very little in the way of theory or academic texts about this mythical 'invisible woman', but the wider media – newspapers, journals, radio, television, the internet, films and literary fiction – seem to carry frequent references to, and stories about, the invisibility of women over 50 (and sometimes even younger).

"We study things that trouble or intrigue us, beginning from our own subjective standpoints" (Hertz, 1997: xvii). What motivated me to start this exploration was indignation at the apparent acceptance of the 'fact' that we older women have become 'The Invisibles'. Nobody sees us any more – or so we are told – and we (pretty much) have to put up with it. That's how it is. Given that we have all – at whatever age, male as well as female - had experiences of being overlooked or apparently unseen, there is clearly some truth in these stories. But surely it must be a little more complicated than that? What are the other tales that might be told?

Coming to the world of academia late in life, with no first degree, I entered a wonderfully creative, taught, narrative doctoral programme at Bristol University at the age of 63, with what seemed like a clear idea of the aspects of professional life on which my dissertation research would be based. By the time I reached the stage of doing the research, aged 66, I was also moving from the world of relatively visible, self-employed, paid work into a way of living that is very different whilst potentially at least as interesting – if considerably poorer financially. My focus had shifted strongly away from my professional 'being' and towards whoever it might be that I was 'becoming'.

So I waited to see what would emerge. And there it was, all the time - what Hélène Cixous (2005: 184) calls *"the skin of the light"*; something that had been in my peripheral vision for a long time became, as I turned my gaze towards it, bigger and more colourful. It was my own story and that of many women I know – becoming older and still determined to be seen.   Jane Speedy, my very supportive supervisor (and the initiator of the narrative doctorate), laughed and said *"Thank goodness!"* and was enthusiastic about my laying aside what she called the *'worthy shoulds and oughts'* of my previous idea.

As I became more aware of the frequent media references to the apparent invisibility of older women, I initiated conversations and email correspondence with female friends and acquaintances of a similar age. What was their experience? Did they agree that we had become invisible? If so, what did that feel like? If not, why did they think we were being told that we've disappeared?

The interesting and varying responses I received, along with my growing indignation at the way in which it seemed that we were yet again being sidelined and dismissed for both being women and getting older, made me sure that here was a highly relevant and very personal research area. When I sounded out some of my correspondents on becoming co-researchers in an ongoing email 'conversation' about the emerging issues, there was a lot of enthusiasm which ended with seven women agreeing to be participants (see later section 'Choosing my travelling companions').

My reflections on the questions around the visibility or invisibility of older women evolved as I used *"writing to think"* (St. Pierre, 2005: 970), both in correspondence with my co-researchers and as I wrote and re-wrote sections of this work many times. As I listened and read and pondered, I became curious about the differing meanings of 'invisibility', both to those who experience it and those (sometimes one and the same) who use it as a label for all of us. It can seem both negative *and* positive, sometimes in the same paragraph.

Georgina, the 80 year old (fictional) woman in Frances Itani's *Remembering the Bones,* is recalling and re-telling her life, as she lies at the foot of a ravine, alone and badly injured after a car accident:

> *Women my age are invisible. When we reach our sixties, we're discounted, sidelined. Even before that … But it's our world, too. We live in it and we are many* (2008: 165).

It is indeed *our world, too* – and we have tales to tell that may well include loss of various kinds as we get older, but are about much more than that. Julia Kristeva speaks of the *"need to find a discourse that can answer the question: 'who are you?'* and the *"memory that underlies narrative"* (2001: 15, 17). As older women, there are things we know and remember which may interest and surprise; we may sometimes be boring or even wrong (though as Diana Athill (2009: 91) says: *"… being old doesn't necessarily make one wrong")* but we also have experience and knowledge, insight and humour.

This is, of course, a political and philosophical, as well as a personal, issue and there is some 'deconstructing' of old ideas and stories to be done (see Derrida, 1973) alongside exploring new possibilities.

> *Deconstruction is theory laughing at itself Deconstruction is power's banana skin* (Stronach, 2002: 302)

Karen Houle, feminist philosopher and activist, calls herself *"a joint-loyalist"* of 'deconstructionism' and 'feminist standpoint theory'. Both, she says, are *"coherent, long-sustained, and avowedly political responses"* to historical and theoretical conditions, adding that *"it is unusual to find these two perspectives in dialogue"* (2009: 172).

Writing *"as a feminist methodologist"* about 'deconstructing' her own earlier work, Patti Lather suggests using *"getting lost as a methodology"* (2007: 3), which very much appeals to me; not trying to come up with the answer; allowing for 'not knowing'. Feminist and poststructuralist philosophies are in part a critique of so-called scientific objectivity (see later section on 'Self-indulgence') but at least as importantly make clear the need to pay attention to an ethical and political awareness of our positions of power and privileges.

Questions arise for me around power and where it lies, alongside women's perceptions of being 'positioned' as invisible and powerless. Michel Foucault asks: *"Do we need a theory of power?"* (Faubion, 2001: 327) and seems to be suggesting that we need to try and get to a different understanding of how we are (or feel we are) 'positioned' by others (Davies & Harre, 1990; Drewery, 2005). Leela Dube tells us that, in order to do so, we must get away from *"the socialization of women with male models of how to perceive the world"* (Dube et al, 1986: xiv).

Polly Young-Eisendrath believes that women's *"desire for power and control has been transformed and hidden ..."*

> *For, in spite of feminism, female power – decisiveness, status, command, influence – cannot be expressed directly at home or in the workplace without arousing suspicion, confusion, fear, or dread. Both men and women still tend to experience female power as exotic at best and dangerous and despicable at worst"* (2000: 3).

Ruth Levitas (2011), in a seminar on *Heretical academic identity*, told us how her role as an older woman and a sociologist - who believes in grace and utopia as method - has been shaped in part by (mostly male) colleagues' perceptions. She talked about the *"conflict between our ascribed identity and our experienced reality"*. What, she asked, are the stories we are told about our identity from others (family, friends, colleagues, the media, etc.) and how do these affect us? What are the ways in which we may be – or allow ourselves to be – marginalised?

Now aged 70 and completely retired from paid work and the old ties (of various kinds) that entails, I put 'Writer and feminist' in those blank spaces that ask what my occupation is; this can invite interesting questions and feedback. Presenting some of my 'visible women' ideas at a recent academic conference, where many of the participants were less than half my age, I was heartened to have a lively and positive response to my use of this 'f' word. Some of the younger women talked of negative reactions to any mention of feminism or feeling diffident describing themselves as feminists. What was heartening was their interest in discussing these issues, which are still deeply relevant today (see http://www.thefword.org.uk/; Redfern and Aune, 2010; Cochrane, 2010).

Kat Banyard, the young founder of the campaign group UK Feminista, believes that *"there is a massive resurgence in feminism"* among young women (Davies, 2011: 15), and has been putting on annual feminist events since 2004, with an ever-increasing number of mainly young women now attending. She and others are adamant that there is a real appetite for addressing the issues of ongoing sexism, inequality, under-representation in government, etc. I am deeply heartened to learn that feminist organisations, 'suffragette schools' and other campaigning groups are being set up all over the country by young grassroots activists.

Although I'm sure this phenomenon of apparently becoming invisible is at least as much about ageism as sexism, I believe it is strongly linked with many of the feminist issues around misogyny and continuing gender inequality. Bidisha writes about *"A culture of contempt"*, giving many everyday examples of *"casual sexism"* and pointing out how difficult it can be to challenge this:

> *Misogyny is such a strong substance that women have absorbed and internalised it ... For men and women alike, casual misogyny is the climate and context of all their interactions. It is unconcealed and automatic* (2010: 19).

In an online article, commissioned for International Women's Month, Katie Toms talks about *"fake feminism"* and the *"lies such as 'we've never had it so good' and 'women are having it all' trotted out to placate women"*. She believes that the internet has become a space which *"far from being a haven for minorities ... is a world where bigotry is exaggerated, not diminished"*.

> *This misogyny has become so mainstream that women are increasingly perpetuating misogyny against themselves* (2010).

Sociologist Catherine Hakim has published a paper with the Thatcherite think tank, the Centre for Policy Studies: *Feminist*

Myths and Magic Medicine: the flawed thinking behind calls for further equality legislation. She sets about demolishing what she calls Twelve Feminist Myths and makes some astonishing claims, both about feminism and issues of equality. At the very start she declares: *"Equal opportunities policies have been successful ... transforming women's lives ... Women today have more choices than men, including real choices between a focus on family work and/or paid employment* (2011: 1). Ending with a section headed *La guerre est finie,* she states:

> *Equal opportunities policies have done their job. Overt and active sex discrimination has been outlawed almost everywhere* (2011: 42).

In contrast, Anna Bird, of the Fawcett Society, points out:

> *Forty years after the Equal Pay Act ... the persistent gap in pay between men and women is one of the starkest examples of inequality in the UK today* (Bawden and Rogers, 2011).

In what columnist Tanya Gold (2011), calls *"the most spiteful passage" of her paper,* Catherine Hakim says:

> *Women's aspiration to marry up, if they can, to a man who is better-educated and higher-earning, persists ... Women thereby continue to use marriage as an alternative or supplement to their employment careers. Financial dependence on a man has lost none of its attractions after the equal opportunities revolution* (2011: 24).

Michelle Bachelet, first executive director of UN Women, told those gathered to celebrate the March 2011 celebrations marking the 100th anniversary of International Women's Day:

> *The last century has seen an unprecedented expansion of women's legal rights and entitlements ... But despite this progress ... the hopes of equality expressed on that first International Women's Day are a long way from being realised* (Davies, 2011).

Ann Oakley, who has been writing and campaigning about feminist issues since the early 1970s, believes that *"there is still a big gap between what people say they believe and what they actually do in practice":*

> *We really thought there was going to be a transformation of the entire social and political fabric, because we had logic on our side.*

Why should women be treated differently to men? Why should they have fewer choices? (Cochrane, 2011b: 17)

It's time for feminists to stop being polite and smiley, says Suzanne Moore, in one of her invigorating rants about how fed up she is with women being told that the fight for equality has been won and to just shut up about it all. *"This makes me very angry indeed. Which I know may increase 'visible signs of ageing', but it's way too late now".* Sitting around politely hoping to be noticed isn't working:

> *Postfeminism – as personified by the Sex and the City generation – basically confused sexual liberation with shopping ... A woman over 50 get to be on TV! Whoopdiwhoop! It's a victory, sure, but is that all there is? ... How I miss those troublesome women like Andrea Dworkin and Shulamith Firestone. They may have been batty as hell but they had passion ... Feminism has been dumbed down into politeness and party-political promises for far too long* (2011: 33).

Hilary Mantel, in an interview after winning the Booker prize, talks about her mother who *"never sat an exam in her life ... but did her very best to make sure I got what she had missed, even though she wasn't perfectly sure what that was."* Appalled by those who have forgotten what her and her mother's generations encountered, she says:

> *Very annoyingly, you get women nowadays who are educated and have got on in their profession, saying, 'Oh, but I'm not a feminist' ... The only reason they can say that is that they're standing on the shoulders of their mothers, who fought these battles. I think for a woman to say 'I'm not a feminist' is [like] a lamb joining the slaughterer's guild. It's just empty-headed and stupid ... Women now take a great deal for granted, but of course the fact is that only a part of the feminist agenda as ever been worked through* (Edemariam, 2009).

In *The Future of Feminism,* a deeply thoughtful analysis of the challenges still to be faced, Sylvia Walby begins with a series of bold and heartening statements:

> *Feminism is not dead. This is not a postfeminist era. Feminism is still vibrant, despite declarations that it is over. Feminism is a success, although many gender inequalities remain. Feminism is taking powerful new forms, which make it unrecognisable to some* (2011: 1).

while acknowledging that *"Feminism is, however, less visible than before"* (2011: 2).

Although the main focus of this work is not overtly that of equality, as a feminist it is not an area that I could possibly ignore in my inquiries into our experiences of becoming older. There are important questions around status – including culture, race, class, gender, health and wealth - which I have borne in mind whilst writing and which have been specifically mentioned by some of my co-researchers. My major theme here is that there should be a choice; for older women to be seen and heard when we choose to be – not at the expense of other 'groups' but deserving of equal attention and respect. I don't want us to feel *discounted and sidelined*, neither hoping nor expecting to be noticed.

So ... what questions would we like to ask or be asked? What happens when/if we talk about it amongst ourselves? How do we contribute to our own experiences – positive and negative - of being older women? What stories do we have to tell, rather than have told for us? These are the 'bones' I and my co-researchers have been examining.

> *We need to look into women's lives ...*
> *and emphasise women's perceptions*
> *and subjective experiences.*
>   (Dube et al, 1986: xii)

1.2 My story – part one: the 'magic summer'

I need to see myself ... and I never have.
                              (Pilar, in *Take my eyes*, 2003)

As part of making sense of my need to set out on this exploration, I wanted to write myself into this text. Where to start? In my early handwritten notes:

> *... realise that I need to explore some definitions of visible and invisible. What do these words mean – to me – to the women I'll be researching with – to others? The importance of being visible to oneself – I think that has been my starting point for all this work, from my magic summer onwards. How do we do this? Or not do it? Because being visible to me is how I now maintain my sense of myself as mattering – at least most of the time – so as not to conform to the childhood rules of "DON'T".*
> (Personal journal, 7 September 2007)

Looking at these journal notes scattered like a 'spidergram' across the page, I notice the different coloured inks used (red, green, purple). I have used colour in writing in this way for a long time but realise (not for the first time) how very **VISIBLE** it makes what I'm telling myself.

Watching the film *Take my eyes* (2003) on television some time ago, I re-experienced old feelings of shame as Pilar is regularly humiliated by her husband while she continues to try and convince herself that he really loves her and will change. She finally leaves him for good, acknowledging that she must go because: *"I need to see myself ... and I never have."* It brought back memories that I would prefer to forget, but which are all too easily recalled.

> *Some memories appear to be more accessible than others.*
> (Crawford et al, 1992: 9)

My 'magic summer' and the months preceding and following remain as powerful, colourful, accessible images, partly at least because of the way they have become a tale that I have told and re-told myself many times. This story is part of who I now am and how I see myself.

My fiftieth year began badly – not so much to do with age as my having experienced a series of losses. Within a short time there had been four close family deaths – all of the same generation and in their 80s and thus not totally unexpected, although the first (my father) seemed to happen almost without warning, as though he had just decided not to live any longer. He was closely followed by my stepmother, with whom I always had a difficult relationship, and two aunts (one paternal, one maternal) who were important influences in my life. I had spent much of my 'spare time' for years visiting, supporting and sorting out various practical problems for one or other of them and their deaths were in some ways a relief, but also brought up the usual mix of grief, anger and unresolved difficulties, along with memories of the very early death of my mother.

The rather dysfunctional relationship with my then   partner finally ended painfully and stormily during this period of loss, my ex-husband was beginning his angry descent into alcohol-induced dementia, and my greatly loved son became depressed and unable to decide what he wanted to do with himself. Even though I felt like a bad mother (nothing new there), it was a relief when he decided to go travelling instead of to university and I had only myself to take care of. I presented my usual active, competent front to the world, whilst barely able to crawl around in a grey fog of hopelessness at home.

The director of the centre in Bath where I managed volunteer projects said to me one day: "Don't you think it's time you got a bit angry?" I was amazed that she'd noticed – but shortly afterwards, in a surge of energy brought on (at last) by what felt like welcome rage, gave in my notice, sold my house, paid off the mortgage and put most of my things in store. I bought a small, long-uninhabited house on the old ramparts of a Bastide town in the Dordogne, near French friends from the years of smallholding in the area with my son and ex-husband. On a beautiful, sunny June morning I set off in a small, blue Renault van with a sleeping bag, my bike, a portable typewriter and some books and clothes, heading south on a high after my months of depression.

Almost as soon as I arrived, my euphoria began to dissipate. *What on earth have I done? No income, a leaky, draughty, filthy, barely habitable house … actually, it's a bit like the first time living in France, except that now there's no partner or child. Ah, that's it – nobody is depending on me. I'm not responsible for anybody but myself – and I don't think I like it. Nobody needs me.*

At least the two-roomed house needed attention. After a few very hot days of frantic cleaning, I was on my knees scrubbing the floor with front and back doors wide open to let in any possible breath of air. One of my neighbours paused in the narrow street on her way past and – after the usual *"Bonjour, madame"* and *"Qu'est qu'il fait chaud!"* - asked (with a smile) what the hurry was.

"You told us you were here for a few months" she said. *"It's a lovely day. Can't the cleaning wait for a bit?"*

> And of course, it could …
> wait, that is …
> and as I stopped doing,
> I started slowing down …

In the spaces created by waiting, strange things started to happen. Time, quite remarkably, began to pass all by itself - without my having to do anything about it. I didn't have to 'fill' it or 'make the most' of it or, indeed, even know what time it was. I stopped looking at the clock or wearing a watch. I began to sleep better – eventually to sleep right through the night (something I have almost never done, before or since). I went to bed early - and woke early - often emerging in time to see the moon disappearing, flushed pink as it caught the first rays of the sun. Most mornings, before breakfast, I got on my bike and did a circuit of the hill road above the town, ending with an exhilarating downhill swoop, singing loudly all the way home. To cool down at the end of the hot afternoons, I swam in the slightly muddy *plan d'eau* – when the anglers had gone and the swallows were swooping and dipping. Afterwards, I would sit in my small patch of garden with a huge salad and a glass of wine, watching the sun go down behind the hills opposite.

One of my conscious intentions in giving myself this time out had been to start writing again – something which I had let slip out of my life almost without noticing. I told my friendly but curious neighbours that I was a writer – and I began to write, whatever came into my head, page after page of autobiographical stories, images, memories, dreams. Soon everybody in the small town seemed to know me as *'l'écrivain anglaise'*, which apparently excused my strange behaviour, particularly the lack of a telephone, television or radio . When not audibly battering my portable typewriter, I was no longer just sitting and looking, or wandering about the place - I had become a writer, 'thinking'.

I became a watcher, too, and could sit for hours in the shade of my back porch on the edge of the old ramparts, just looking … down into the valley and at the wooded slopes beyond, noticing the shifting colours and shapes, the surrounding bowl of hills against the sky as the light changed. In the evening I lay on the sloping, sun-warmed stone wall of the garden and watched the stars appear in an almost black sky. It felt magical - like being a child again but without anybody to tell me I should be doing something else.

To help fund my time there, I'd arranged to do some chamber-maiding for friends who ran a *chambres d'hôte*. Initially I was pleased to have something to do and people to see. As I started to slow down and ignore the clock, I became more and more reluctant to 'spend' time with anybody but myself. With so few other distractions, I began to learn something that seems very obvious now, but was then like a revelation – the things that I was thinking and doing were valid and had an existence *even though nobody else knew about them.* If I alone knew, that was enough. How amazing!

My fiftieth birthday came in September, towards the end of my magic summer. After some extremely hot, dry weather, there was a particularly violent Dordogne thunderstorm which woke me in the night. I went out to watch the display, as the sky flickered and shimmered, then was split apart with ferocious streaks of brilliant, almost blinding light. The distant rumble grew into violent crumping explosions, shaking the ground like a battle approaching. And then, at last, the rain. I was born (so I'm told) at around 2.00 a.m. and, standing just inside the cover of my back porch while the rain sheeted down and the storm passed slowly and dramatically overhead, I exulted in what felt like a special birthday gift – a display just for me.

The following day was all mine – apart from a meal with friends in the evening. Driving off early in the cool of the post-storm morning to Perigueux, elegant medieval city, I spent the day wandering the streets and shops and galleries of the old town. From a stall I bought myself a present, a pair of earrings, cascades of glittering, different coloured glass beads. After a spectacular ice-cream lunch (with sparklers and the female staff singing *'Bonne anniversaire'*), I sat and ate little cakes in the *patisserie*, feeling very visible yet somehow incognito, almost French and delighted with myself. It was the best birthday I've ever had. I loved being seen to be 50 and OK.

Is the story of my magic summer true? Well, I believe it is. It's how I remember and have retold it over the years.

> *… a thing can be true, but not true, but true nonetheless.*
> (Atwood, 2008: 4)

And then October came, the swifts and swallows left and it began to grow cooler – I could no longer swim in the *plan d'eau* or sit outside in the evenings. The rain that found its way between the haphazard roof tiles, and the infamous *courants d'air* that blew through the ill-fitting front and back doors, no longer felt so welcome. My 20-year-old son passed through, stayed a few days and told me of his plans to live with friends for a while - and it was good to be a mother again. I started looking at the clock (and the calendar) to remind me of the days and times the village shops would be open now summer was past and the nearby campsite closed. The *chambres d'hôte* was shut until the following year and I was running out of money.

With no clear idea of where to live or what to do, I was nevertheless determined not to lose the magically changed time and space this summer had enabled me to find. Eventually I returned to England in my blue Renault van in early November, still with sleeping bag, bicycle, typewriter and books.

I found myself heading for the coastal Dorset village where my maternal aunt had lived. She and her husband had, for part of my life, stood in for my absent parents and I discovered just before leaving France that she had unexpectedly left me some money in her will. Nobody else in our family had any to leave and I had never anticipated any windfalls – yet here one was, unexpected, unasked and very welcome. Standing by her and my uncle's graves in the quiet, leafy village cemetery, I thought of them both with love and said a tearful 'thank you'. And I decided to stay for a while, there on the edge of the land where I had lived for part of my childhood - to allow myself to 'take' more time, to walk by the sea, to think and write some more and discover what the autumn and winter would bring. And that is another story.

> *I amount to my own story. I am what I am.*
> (Itani, 2008: 281)

I walk at the edge of the land
next to the boiling sea

Images … memories …
layering of past and present

Drawn back
held here
still looking

1.3 In search of 'The Invisible Woman'

If only she would become visible …
then I could catch her
and impress upon her
the truth of the situation.

(Enright, 2008a: 5)

Searching through the literature, I did not initially discover much in the way of theory or academic texts about this mythical creature. But once started on the journey, I began to pick up references almost every day in newspapers, journals, on radio and television, in films and books, on the internet – almost all containing the words **'old(er)'** and **'invisible women'**. And as Suzanne Moore asks:

When we say 'older', what do we even mean any more? It probably used to be anyone over 60, but now it seems to be applied to women over 40 …(Saner, 2010: 18).

Emine Saner quotes journalist and presenter Anna Ford: *"How many [women] presenters do you know on television who are over the age of 60?"* and continues:

… glancing at our visual culture – television, films, billboards – it can seem that, with a few notable exceptions … older women have ceased to exist (Saner, 2010: 18).

TV and radio broadcaster Miriam O'Reilly took the BBC to an employment tribunal on allegations of age and sex discrimination, revealing tales of casual misogyny from both men and women, with older women presenters being told they needed to be *"careful about those wrinkles"* and asked if it might not be *"time for Botox"* (Cochrane, 2011a: 6). Professor and historian of the BBC, Jean Seaton says: *"Turn on the news and what you get is a young blonde and an older man. That's the format."*

Visual ageism is very frightening because people believe what they're seeing is reality. If you airbrush all pictures, you remove all wrinkles, and you make everybody look impossibly thin, then young women, middle-aged and ageing women all feel that they're failures (Cochrane, 2011a: 9).

This preference for the young (and often blonde) is not a new phenomenon, of course. In our local town hall there is a series of murals from the 1920s representing the long history of rope and net making locally. One of these depicts a beautiful young woman with long blonde plaits and a crown, dressed in an unlikely blue robe. A blog review of a book about the local industry refers to the many photographs it contains of older women 'outworkers' who had been braiding nets at home all their lives, adding:

> *You could argue that Fra Newbery made a mistake when he sought ... to represent the Spirit of Bridport as a beautiful flaxen-haired young woman, working with twine. Why not an older woman like Mrs Crabb?* (Hudston, 2011)

Sarah Churchwell writes about the contradictions in stories of older women being celebrated in our society at last: *"women [have been] assured that it is no longer the case that they become invisible once they reach middle age"*. Although it is true that some beautiful, well-known, older women are being featured in advertising campaigns, *"the fact is that all of these women look at least 20-30 years younger than they are – especially in photographs ... [they] are so airbrushed they're more like paintings"*:

> *How, if our images of older women look exactly like our images of younger women, does this represent progress?* (2010)

In France, where I lived for many years, there seems to be a huge gap between the cultures of television and advertising - where sexism and ageism are rampant and blatant - and cinema and theatre, which are regarded as art forms and where there have always been formidable older women actors and directors. According to an American production consultant living in Paris, French women film directors *"have contributed to changing the way we consider women, not women as girls but women as individuals"* (Gragg, in Poirier, 2011).

The actor Juliette Binoche believes that French women bloom once they get past 40. At the age of 46 she stated:

> *There's something that happens in the woman when they reach a certain age. You let go of certain things. You lose some illusions. Your choices become your own choices and less the consequence of your education or your fears or preconceptions. You've been broken so much that it becomes a sort of liberation. Who cares what I do any more?* (Brooks, 2010: 15).

While another well-known actor, Sheila Hancock, is quoted as saying in her autobiography *Just Me*: *"It is a proven fact that after 50 women do dissolve ... I neither expect nor hope to be noticed"* (Bakewell, 2008: 8). A 'proven fact'?

Michele Hanson, on the other hand, writes about the delights and freedoms of being in her sixties and says of a friend who complains about it:

> *She sees empty, I see full ... we're in a sort of retro-revolution ... So why gripe about invisibility? It means freedom ... This invisibility is just a win-win situation...* (2009: 16/17).

A group of older women artists who definitely do not intend to be invisible have, since late 2008, been putting on exhibitions in London called *WOW!! Wild Old Women.* They make a lot of statements in their publicity, including:

> *We have big ideas, we have been around for a while and we are outsider artists, so we do things exactly as we please. Ignore us at your peril.*

Addressing the issues of visibility, they say:

> *There is a myth that women slowly begin to disappear as they age. In their forties they lose definition, after fifty they are fading away, in their sixties they become totally ineffectual, and by the time they reach their seventies, they have achieved total invisibility. What an absurd, vicious and laughable rumour; what UTTER NONSENSE. We are loud, we are raucous and we are thrillingly, vividly visible.* (Wild Old Women, 2009)

In Canada and the US over the past couple of decades, groups *"in the tradition of wise women elders",* calling themselves Raging Grannies, have set out with a *"mission ... to promote global peace, justice and social and economic equality ... through ... song and humour".* Writing about their colourful presence at climate change demonstrations in Seattle, Mary O'Hara (2010) tells us:

> *In a culture obsessed with youth, where ageing is regarded as either invisible or a problem, the Raging Grannies fly in the face of any suggestions that they should quietly be drifting into dotage.*

I'm not sure about labelling ourselves 'grannies' (even if we are) – we're so many other things as well – but their argument is that, by satirising the stereotype of an old granny, they are subverting other people's tendency to use the term dismissively. As one of their members, former librarian and trade unionist Barbara Baxter-Berman, says:

> What we hope is that when young people see us out and about having our say, they will ask their own grannies what they think. Our generation has lived through a few things. We have things to say that matter (O'Hara, 2010).

Dorothy Rowe, a psychologist whose work I respect and admire, is a regular interviewee on BBC radio programmes about issues which include the problems of the ageing population in this country. Now in her seventies, she talks about the 'invisibility' of older people, often referring to *Time on our Side* (1994), written when she was in her sixties. In this book she writes with her usual clarity and humour of living with our fear of ageing and tells stories of incidents that illustrate her own experience of no longer being seen.

She describes the move from childhood (when she *"longed to become invisible"* to avoid parental criticism) to very visible young womanhood: *"Men looked, and wanted a response from me. Much as I wanted to be loved and admired I found the endless pressure from men wearying and irritating"*. As she grew older, however:

> It took me a while to realise that I was becoming invisible. Now I am completely invisible, except to a few wise folk who can actually see me (Rowe, 1994: 35).

She goes on to say that sometimes invisibility is useful: *"… for someone whose daily delight is observing people being invisible is just marvellous. What a lot I learn about people when they don't realise I'm watching and listening!"* (1994: 36); adding reflectively:

> I don't feel myself to be invisible. When I look in the mirror I see someone there. This is just another example of how we are always aware of two sets of perceptions – how we perceive ourselves and how we perceive other people's perceptions of us (1994: 37).

The negative connotations of 'invisibility' seem to be particularly painful for women *"whose self-worth rests primarily in appearance and sexual desirability"* and for whom *"passing fifty is like taking the veil … suddenly they feel invisible"* (Gail Sheehy, in Stensrude, 1995: 2).

Appearance and desirability are important to Nobel Literature Prize winner Doris Lessing, who has often spoken in interviews about the difficulty of being an older woman no longer getting male attention. The main characters in two of her novels - *The Summer Before the Dark* and *Love, again* - are women growing older who have been used to attention and feel themselves invisible when this ceases.

> *She had to know at last, that all her life she had been held upright by an invisible fluid*, the notice of other people. *But the fluid had drained away* (Lessing, 1983: 180).

In an interview for a book *On Women Turning 70,* Doris Lessing tells about her own experience:

> *The invisibility thing began to happen to me along about my fifties, when I suddenly became aware that men were no longer noticing me* (Caremark, 2001: 1).

Being intelligent, well-known, highly regarded and rewarded, and published all over the world, does not seem to compensate for no longer being 'noticed' by men. But, as with Dorothy Rowe, there are apparently some advantages to being invisible:

> *Then, when we get really old, we can be invisible to anyone – apart from people who know us, of course. I'm not necessarily saying this is a bad thing. It's quite interesting not to be noticed, because you can listen very attentively* (Lessing, in Caremark, 2001: 1).

In her online article, Janice Stensrude (1995: 1) cites an address by Carolyn Heilbrun as *"my introduction to the concept of 'the invisible woman', the failure of the ageing woman to so easily capture the attention of men".*

Germaine Greer claims that she isn't interested in being noticed by men. Although I often want to throw things at the radio or television when she is holding forth – at length and on almost any subject – she is consistently well-informed, intelligent, often self-deprecating and usually very funny. In her book about women, ageing and the menopause, *The Change* , she puts forward witty and cogent arguments as to why women should feel liberated by the arrival of the menopause rather than believing it to be the end of their useful life. It is a passionate and fascinating work:

> *The purpose of this book is to demonstrate that women are at least as interesting as men, and that ageing women are at least as interesting as younger women* (Greer, 1992: 35).

She tells of Mary Wollstonecraft's anger (in 1792) at a male writer who wondered what business women over forty had in the world – and asks:

> *What if we, the horde of women of fifty, cannot see what business we have in the world? Most of us are no longer sought as lovers, as wives, as mothers, or even as workers, unless there is a conspicuous dearth in our profession, and then only until we are sixty. We are supposed to mind our own business; if we do this we need to find a business of our own* (Greer, 1992: 24).

Reviewing Tracey Emin's retrospective exhibition on BBC Radio 4's Front Row, in her usual declamatory form, she told Mark Lawson (and us) that *"Tracey will be 50 in 2013, so she's menopausal now … she won't mind my saying that!"* And went on:

> *It's a tough time in a woman's life … we're told we've failed at this, failed at that and – guess what – we're not interested in you any more … What's different is her anger is coming back and coming from a deeper place, coming from the well of female frustration … we're in for a new sort of Tracey Emin, an older, angrier … more focused Emin. Which I long to see, because older women are so invisible in our culture, that if Tracey can just maintain this visibility, then go, girl, go!* (Greer, 2011)

She too, however, makes generalised statements about the importance of appearance:

> *Sooner or later the middle-aged woman becomes aware of a change in the attitude of other people towards her. She can no longer trade on her appearance, something which she has done unconsciously all her life* (Greer, 1992: 7).

… and complains that even *"in fiction, whether written by men or by women, middle-aged women are virtually invisible"* (1992: 22). As I can immediately go to my bookshelves and pull out a large number of books by and about middle-aged (and even older) women, I can only assume that there has been a revolution in publishing since 1992.

In *The Stranger in the Mirror,* Jane Shilling takes a reflective look at life as a middle-aged woman, talking about the gains as well as the losses and noting advantages such as *"the attractions of becoming Formidable"* (2011: 83). In her preface, she also adds to the stock of stories about us 'disappearing women' :

> *Throughout my adult life I had been accustomed to find my own experience as a woman reflected in the culture. Magazines and newspapers contained pictures of women more or less my age ... Programmes on the television and radio took as their raw material the lives of my contemporaries. In bookshops, the female experience appeared in myriad forms. Until the onset of middle age, when, all of a sudden, there was apparently no one like me at all. Like the children of Hamelin led away into the mountain cavern, we had all vanished.*

whilst adding: *"I exaggerate"* (2011: 2).

The issue of the apparent 'invisibility' of women historically is not just about age, although that is one of my main (and subjective) focuses here. Hilary Mantel, wondering why she had left the women out of the 1979 draft of her novel about the French Revolution, *A Place of Greater Safety* (eventually published 1992), asks:

> *How had I failed to notice that women hold up half the sky?... Even in the early 90s, much of the material we now have about revolutionary women was not generally available – or rather, it was there, but we weren't seeing it* (2008: 15).

Natasha Walter (2010) asks: *"Where are the women?"* and thinks women generally have *"gone missing"* from the public eye. Among her suggestions for remedying this lack of visibility is to revisit the old feminist arguments about the importance of addressing inequality and stop going along with what she calls *"the new sexism"* of men and women simply being *"different creatures"*:

> *We have to allow women to be as various, as good and as bad, as interesting and as dull, as experienced and as fresh, as the men beside them, rather than boxing them up into tired old stereotypes.*

What a relief that would be!

And one last gripe - why is it deemed such a compliment to be told that we look younger than we are, or that we don't look our age? It feels like yet another way of making ageing shameful and not fit to be seen. I'm with Nora Ephron in her riposte: *"I'm way past Age Shame, if I ever had it. I'm just happy to be here at all"* (2007: 201).

Maybe all this writing by women about 'the invisible woman' is just another way of being visible?

> *… maybe they just don't see the women,*
> *even when the women are right in front of them.*
>   (Pollitt, 2005: 3)

CHAPTER TWO

ON WRITING

Writing matters.
(Richardson, 1997: 86)

2.1 On writing – and not writing

Writing is learned from the inside out.
Writing is a discipline and, as with any discipline,
whether spiritual or physical, the doing is everything.
No one can do it for you.

(Enright, 2008b: 15)

I care about writing and how it's done; was always going to be **A Writer** when I grew up. I want to do it, I really do ... and yet ... so many things can get in the way of the finished 'piece', so many different ways of procrastinating, of not being quite ready to commit ideas to the page (or screen).

"There is a persistent confusion between writing and writing things down," says Hilary Mantel, *"a confusion between the workings of the writing mind and the weight of the paper scribbled over."*

> *'How many words do you do per day?'* *people ask, as if the product unwinds in a flowing, ceaseless stream of uncriticised, unrevised narrative ... the better you are, the more ambitious and exploratory, the more often you will go astray on the way to getting it even approximately halfway right* (2010: 15).

For me, there is the worry of *never* being able to get it right, maybe never finding that *"talk that sings"* (Bird, 2004: ix), the language that will really convey what I'm thinking and feeling ... not just *well enough*, of course, but so as to be the perfect conduit for my mental images, excitement, reflective silences. I want you, the reader, to care about what I'm saying – not in the same way I do, maybe, but care nevertheless. Quite a tall order.

Add to that the desire to be wonderfully creative ... different ... to produce something which will blow your proverbial socks off. Perhaps I just need to get on with it rather than trying to impress you.

> *Am I only visible*
> *if I get it right?*
> (Personal journal,
> 17 April 2008)

Maybe Anne Enright is right:

> *There is so much guff talked about creativity, and the more of this guff you talk, the more you are in danger of becoming blocked. 'Block' is like a panic attack – the minute you describe it, you have it: the word and the experience are the same* (2009: 13).

Will Self, one of the keynote speakers at a conference on *New Cultures of Ageing* (2011), said in response to a question: *"The job of a writer is to express the thinginess of things".* Which sounds about right to me.

There are so many inspirational, informative, funny and relevant thoughts about writing (gathered from my promiscuous reading across fiction, newspaper and internet articles and columns, academic journals, theoretical texts) that I could fill much of this work with them. I have various 'mentors' whose writing inspires and delights me, most of whom are referenced here. Almost all of them are women and one or two I've even met and worked with, which feels both exciting and a real privilege. It can be a curiously painful delight, sometimes, to read books or articles by these writing mentors – pleasure mixed with envy at their way with words and the power these can have to move, inform, challenge, uplift.

"The best writing", says Tessa Hadley (2010), *"breaks through the skin of the known world".* Now there's something to try and live up to.

Those enviable (in my world) beings, successful published writers, sometimes offer – or are perhaps persuaded to offer - what seems like conflicting advice when it comes to the 'how' of writing. There's the *"It's just a job like any other"* approach, where writers solemnly tell of going to their study/attic/garden shed at 9am every morning, writing x number of thousand words – and the importance of doing this, even if you think it's rubbish - and knocking off at 5pm. Others reject this approach as a waste of time and say they write only when the spirit moves them.

Hélène Cixous states (somewhat provocatively maybe): *"When I write I do nothing on purpose, except stop"* (2005: 191). In her *Writing Notebooks,* she tells us that *"I don't plan ever. The only thing I plan is not planning"* (2004: 122); then talks about the importance of writing by hand, what type of pen or pencil she prefers and how much she likes cheap A4 blank notepads.

There is often talk of the actual materials used – the arguments for and against pen/pencil and paper; whether computers help or hinder creativity; the occasional typewriter still gets a mention. Hilary Mantel thinks that writers (including herself) *"displace their anxiety on to the tools of the trade … The good news about the computer is its endless scope for procrastinative fussing. Is this a nice font? Shall I rename all my files?"* (2010: 15).

Perhaps the reason for much of this anxiety about writing is because, simply, *"Writing matters – theoretically and practically"* (Richardson, 1990: 9). In this monograph on *Writing Strategies*, Laurel Richardson tells us just how much she loves writing - and why – and why she believes it is such an important activity. In a later article she describes discovering *"writing as a method of inquiry"*:

> *I had been taught, as perhaps you were as well, not to write until I knew what I wanted to say … But I did not like writing that way. I felt constrained and bored. When I thought about those writing instructions, I realized that they cohered with mechanistic scientism and quantitative research … they undercut writing as a dynamic creative process"* (Richardson, 2005: 960).

Amy Tan, in her *book of musings,* describes in very similar ways what writing means to her:

> *Writing to me is an act of faith, a hope that I will discover what I mean by truth. But I don't know what that will be until I finish* (2003: 323).

Jane Gardam is described in an interview as *"utterly committed to the central importance of writing and occasionally mildly baffled by it"*, saying what a passion it is for her: *"I think I would have died if it* [her first book] *hadn't been published. I was desperate to get started – I was possessed"* (Clark, 2011: 11). She tells of her lifelong love of books and reading, discovering (aged 8) that the newly opened public library allowed her to take books home. Now in her 80s:

> *She knew that she wanted to write from an early age and is sure that part of that desire is inherited from her mother, who was a*

committed and vivid correspondent – 'off she'd go, like an 18th or 19th century woman, spilling out letters, letters, letters' (Clark, 2011: 10).

I discovered the absolute joy of reading early in life – losing myself in story, evoking powerful inner images and safe hiding places, a wonderful, secret pleasure which was even better than being read to. Writing quickly followed and has always been an important part of my life. When young, because of my love of writing stories (both invented and personal) and apparently doing it well, I assumed it was how I would earn my living, before discovering this was a great deal harder than imagined.

Letter writing, however, was still a normal, regular activity as I grew up. More than that, it was expected in the various households I was part of during the 1940s and 50s; it was how people kept in touch on all kinds of levels, from short, formal 'thank you' letters (whatever happened to them?) and information about some planned event, to multi-page minutiae of everyday goings on. There did not exist, of course, the innumerable ways of communicating that are now available and there were very different ideas around just how much personal communication was actually necessary. Many households did not have a telephone and those that did tended to use it sparingly and definitely not for 'chatting'.

As a young child, I mostly enjoyed writing (and receiving) letters – though I remember there was some procrastinating over the weekly 'duty' letters to grandparents and other family members. There seemed to be a rule about having to cover more than one side of a small page (A5-ish) and I have a few of these letters still, recovered from family paraphernalia. I see that my beginnings were always the same: *Dear ... I hope you are all right. I am ...* followed by a formula of trotting out something I'd done well in at school or elsewhere – often with illustrations, which took up a good amount of space – and ending with a joke or pithy saying such as *Night night, sleep tight, don't let the bugs bite. love Christine.*

I willingly wrote long (and much illustrated) letters to my two older brothers at boarding school – and waited impatiently for them to reply. Sometimes my letters were to family members (including my father) who lived far away in other countries, who I didn't see for years on end. It was a very important part of maintaining contact and a sense of continuity within relationships and, as an adult, I continued the family tradition of both travel and letter-writing.

There were later years, growing up and rebelling against all kinds of things (consciously or not), when I almost stopped writing altogether, apart from hidden, angst-ridden journaling or supposed fictional short stories which were minimally disguised autobiography. As Beryl Bainbridge is quoted in her obituary as saying: *"I have never really written fiction; what would be the point? What is more peculiar, more riveting, devious and horrific than real life? ... The only reason I wrote was to make sense of what went on in my past"* (Watts, 2010).

As a young adult, struggling to understand why I felt as I did and trying to decide what to do with myself - yet still with this desire to 'become' a writer - I lost confidence in my ability to write even for myself after too many rejection letters, or just silence, from publishers.

> *So why do I write? Because I once thought I couldn't, and now I know I can.* (Tan, 2003: 321)

Coming back to writing in various contexts (academic, professional and personal) in middle-age was affirming and exciting. When I discovered email in the 1990s, it seemed to be a good way of renewing my love of sending and receiving letters, despite the ever-present danger of overload. My decision to use email as the main way of communicating with my seven co-researchers emerged from an earlier successful experiment with narrative interviewing, where I used emails to have what I called a 'narrative conversation' (see James, 2007) with a fellow-student living in the US (see Bell, 2007).

It has been a wonderfully different experience of inquiry - and writing to and fro with my seven co-researchers for this work was an absolute joy. Far from procrastinating, I looked forward to writing my letters to them and looked forward even more to receiving their responses. It felt much harder when it came to the theory part – putting down my ideas and reasons for starting this journey in a way that would be 'acceptable' yet also different from the 'normal' dissertation. So I decided to treat it like writing a very, very long letter to my reader, whoever that might be.

2.2 My story – part two: the visible line

When someone dies, we exist for years on a thin line,
a wire stretched tight between remembering and forgetting.
When something touches that wire and makes it vibrate,
that's a ghost.

(Mantel, 2007: 4)

My mother, who died aged 40, has been often on my mind whilst researching and writing. I now live again in the small Dorset town where she died and is buried. Dora never got to be an 'older woman' (by my criteria) and, in conversations with her as I sit on the edge of her grave, I get vibrations along that 'wire stretched tight', of distant amusement at the whole notion of a group of women sending reflective letters to each other about how visible or invisible they feel. Yet despite that faint, ghostly smile – and feeling very young again as I experience it – I also get the sense of "Good for you!"

Beginning my journal for this exploration, I noted:

Thinking about myself – and the seven other women who've agreed to be part of this – it has occurred to me that we are not just maintaining /sustaining our own visibility when we tell our stories, but also carrying on this role ... on behalf of our mothers and grandmothers, aunts and other ancestors. My own stories involve them, sometimes directly ... or indirectly ... there would be no 'My Story' without them. (Personal journal, 13 August 2007)

I was six when Dora died at home in November 1947, after about 18 months of disappearances to hospital. Will, my father, gathered my two brothers and me together and told us not to cry because *"She's gone to be with Jesus"*. I don't know whether my memory of that bizarre scene is accurate, though my brothers (then aged 13 and nearly 10) have similar recollections. They bravely stood there, white faced and silent (I can see them now), while I sobbed defiantly and said: *"I don't want her to go to Jesus, I want her here!"* My father said nothing more (apart from a prayer or two) – and that was how it went on.

Her memory was silence. (Padel, 2010: 3)

It was as though we were somehow supposed to forget her, or at least not to remember the real person Dora had been but rather the perfect being she was becoming the few times she was spoken of. She was almost never mentioned in front of us and my brothers were very soon sent back to boarding school. I had not been allowed to go to the funeral and could keep pretending to myself for a while that she wasn't really dead at all, just back in hospital again. Will, when he was there, behaved as though everything was normal and I quickly learned not to talk about my mother or ask questions, which were clearly upsetting and never really answered. So I cried myself to sleep and frequently woke in the night after vivid dreams of her, which I could not talk about.

I was never told what she had died of and, even though I eventually worked out it must have been cancer, it remained something unspeakable within our family. It was not until I was 40, the age at which she died – beginning to allow myself to realise just how much I missed her – that I learned from my aunt some of the details of her breast cancer.

During Dora's long illness we had all gone to live with her older sister and family in their large house in Dorset, where my uncle practised as a GP. There were four cousins, the older three at boarding school like my brothers, and one three years younger than me. My kind Aunt Frieda did her best to parent us all, my uncle got on with taking care of all his patients, and my missionary father just kept disappearing 'on deputation' around the country, doing the evangelical work of The Lord. My mother had a mastectomy and whatever treatment was then available, and slowly faded from a tall, vibrant, striking, dark-haired woman with a beautiful alto voice to a gaunt, greying figure with jaundice.

When she became too weak and ill to sing or tell me stories and could no longer even get downstairs, I remember kneeling on the edge of her bed in the darkened room and painting her fingernails a dark crimson. And when even this became too much, I was still occasionally allowed to sit with her, playing with her lipstick and bits of jewellery, or dressing up in some of her clothes.

My father quickly gave away almost everything that had belonged to her after her death – and afterwards denied that she had ever worn make-up, painted her nails or smoked.   The few times she was mentioned, she became the perfect Christian wife, mother, sister, daughter, and my memories of her faded until I was no longer sure what I really did remember and felt unable to talk about her with anybody, including my brothers. I recently discovered that one of them still didn't know what she'd died of and had, like me, always been too inhibited by the family silence to ask.

Will returned to missionary work in China the year after Dora died, leaving my brothers and me in the care of various relatives. He came back after four years, ready to take up the role of father again and with a new (missionary) wife who was supposed to be a new mother as well – which didn't quite work out, but that is yet another story.

Why does visibility and being heard matter to me?
Who am I writing this for – apart from myself?
What do I hope it might mean to others? I need to revisit these questions again now, with the exciting offer of turning all this into a book.

Deciding to try my work out by 'presenting' at conferences and seminars over the past months has been a rewarding opportunity to both revisit my own questions and invite them from others. Is there a way to incorporate the feedback I've beengetting, to both my written and spoken presentations??It's been so positive – from different age groups, from men as well as women - encouraging me to believe there is real curiosity around the issues of 'visibility' - and real interest in my ideas of exploring the alternative stories to 'invisibility'.

Not counting, not mattering, as an individual – not apparently being seen or heard as a child ... the belief that duty/society/community is all that matters ...

It took me a long time to acknowledge that I carried positive as well as negative ideas from my upbringing ... justice and equality and care for others – wanting to make a difference –

basic ideals which have become vital underpinnings for the political and personal beliefs I have tried to develop and live by as an adult.
(Personal journal, 3 May 2011)

My family history (over the past few generations at least) seems overly full of a rather rigid sort of religiousness. Grandparents on both sides were from strict, not to say authoritarian, non-conformist backgrounds. My two grandfathers were flamboyant preachers, the sons of working class evangelical Baptist lay preachers, and they both married well-brought-up Presbyterian women from families with a bit of money (even if it *was* 'trade').

My main memories of Minnie, my maternal grandmother - who died a few years after her youngest daughter - are of a small, neatly dressed person with a handbag who wandered the house calling for Fred, my grandfather. I was told she had "*lost her mind*" – a terrible thing to imagine as a child who was beginning to discover her own. It seems that she was a clever, strict and rather distant mother, who adored her husband. Fred was tall, handsome and imposing, with a full head of white hair from the age of 30, a rich rhetorical style and ebullient personality. People spoke of him with awe, his women parishioners almost worshipped him – and I realised as a young adult that he was capable of being childish and a bit of a bully when he didn't get his own way; so he kept on getting it until he died aged 100.

My paternal grandfather's first (Dutch) wife died in Africa 'in the mission field'. John was from Ballymena, son of an evangelical Orangeman of Ulster, though my few memories are of a warm, loving, funny man before he disappeared into dementia. His second wife Jessie, a formidable woman, was in her 40s when she had her three children in China in the early 1900s. She lived into her 90s, crippled with arthritis and in a wheelchair for many years, but with a sharp mind and sense of humour. Will, my father, and his two younger siblings grew up in China and he (and his sister Jean) returned to continue the evangelical missionary tradition in the 1930s.

Dora and Will fell in love when my father was brought to England to finish his education and go to university, aged nearly 18. The two families were living near each other in South London and met at the local Baptist church, where Fred was pastor. My parents were apparently immediately smitten (what a word!) with each other. Dora was 16, nearly 17, the youngest of three and very determined – so Aunt Frieda told me when she finally broke all those years of silence and began to tell the stories I'd longed to hear.

The sisters, three years apart in age, were very different (physically and in other ways) and also very close; my mother (I was delighted to learn) was quietly stubborn and quite capable of going her own way. She not only persuaded her parents that she and Will should get engaged without delay, but also that she would go to university rather than follow Frieda into the local teacher training college. So with Will at Oxford reading 'Greats' before heading for theological college and then back to China, Dora finished school, studied in France, got a BA at Kings College and went to Brittany to teach English.

The missionary society who employed Will (and his parents before him) insisted that he returned to Northern China initially as a single man – just testing his resolve, I suppose. Dora was allowed to join him after about a year and sent to language school to learn Chinese – and they were finally able to get married after what had turned out to be a long engagement, with many separations. My two brothers were born in the 1930s, during a time of violent turmoil in China, including invasion by the Japanese – and I came along in 1941, after the start of the Second World War.

In 1944, as the bombing increased and the invaders moved closer, missionaries in the north were finally being evacuated. Will decided to stay but insisted that Dora and the three children went. I have a distinct memory, aged three, of standing on a windswept airfield, sobbing and refusing to let go of my father. My brothers tell me that, in the small RAF airplane which took us over the Himalayas to India, I went blue and lost consciousness, not from grief (at least I don't think so) but from lack of oxygen. This sounds wonderfully dramatic, but I don't remember it at all, although do have a memory of being stung very badly by a scorpion in Calcutta.

After a few months we got a very crowded boat to England and arrived in early 1945, with my mother initially not knowing if her husband was alive or dead because of the lack of reliable communication. The war in Europe was moving to an end, though not yet in the Far East, and it was a time of loss, deprivation, exhaustion and constant anxiety for almost everybody. From piecing together bits of information, it seems likely that Dora discovered a lump in her breast sometime during those months when she was waiting for news from Will and then for his return. She seems to have decided not to say anything to anybody until he eventually got to England himself more than a year after our arrival. I remember his return and the celebrations of being reunited – and I also remember an ambulance coming to the door and taking my mother away soon afterwards.

This part of my story has been painful to write and re-write, as difficult memories emerge and questions linger (with nobody who might know the answers now left to give them, even if they would or could). As a child I hated being taken to visit Dora's grave, never sure what I was supposed to be doing or feeling. There seemed no connection between the headstone calling her *'Beloved wife, mother and missionary'*, and the real person I was trying to remember. Since returning to live in this small town, I enjoy my visits to the peaceful cemetery, full of trees, birdsong and wild flowers. Sitting on the edge of her grave in fitful sunshine on the day of writing this paragraph, I spoke out loud the quotation at the start as I felt the vibration along that *"wire stretched tight between remembering and forgetting"*. I do not forget her, even though I hardly knew her, and do not intend her memory to be silence.

Minnie,
my grandmother

Dora
(aged 24)

Dora and me (aged 4)

2.3 Writing to be heard

I am a woman writing.
(Richardson, 1997: 4)

Laurel Richardson is my lode star and heroine of writing about academic writing. In the quotation above, she is musing on her role as a woman in a male academic world, learning to construct a way of writing differently, through *"contextualizing and personalizing ... re-visioning my life and work ..."* She notes that *"Joining the men's team, competing on their playing field ...* [does] *not enhance my work or my life"* (1997: 3,4).

> *I like my form of writing to 'tell', 'signal', 'display', 'be' what it claims to talk about, but I also believe texts should be accessible.*
> (Richardson, 1997: 5)

When reading academic and other texts, I have often wondered why it has remained accepted writing practice to refer to people by their last names only, using what seems like an old-style scientific, impersonal, masculine-oriented form of address; quite apart from anything else, this potentially keeps hidden the gender of the person concerned. As part of doing things differently and making my writing as accessible and personal as possible, I have chosen here to refer to people by what I believe are their full names (other than in the bracketed references to their work).

Karen Houle talks about the importance of inquiring into what is *strange* and making it *"familiar. Familiarized. The invizibilized, visibilized. Giving voice to the silenced"*.

> *In the idiom of continental thought: absence brought to presence. In this bringing in, and bringing out, the story goes, one may have (finally) democratized and diversified knowledge* (2009: 176).

Many years ago, on the first residential weekend of a training course in therapeutic supervision, one of the other women participants and I discovered (over a late night drink) that we had both once worked in journalism and had a passion for the written word from an early age.

I told her
after a drink (or two)
about writing
my autobiography
at the age of six
after the death of my mother.

She listened, seriously,
sipping her whisky,
looked at me and said
"Why do you write?"

Nobody had asked me that before!
The answer surprised me.
"To be heard", I said.

I have always turned to writing, especially when overwhelmed by feelings – grief, anger, love, joy. It seemed like a safe way of expressing the emotions that were apparently unacceptable to those around me. Nobody seemed to be listening but me. When I trained and practised as a counsellor and eventually a psychotherapist, becoming a professional listener, I discovered how to offer writing as well as talking as *"a powerful therapeutic technique"* (Wright, 2004: 12).

Diana Athill describes discovering her own ability to write as an older woman, after a lifetime of very successfully encouraging and editing other people's work. In *Somewhere Towards the End,* she tell us that her main purpose in writing books was to get rid of *"what was accumulating in the unconscious part of my mind, and the purpose of that accumulation, which I hadn't known I needed, was healing … I plunged straight into 'writing them out', as what seemed to me the natural and certain way of ridding my mind of distress"* (2009: 146,147). It seems that part of the 'healing' was through writing her experiences where others could read them as she plunges very honestly into 'writing out' her thoughts on the losses and gains of growing old.

Towards the end of her long life the writer, Jungian analyst and campaigner for women's suffrage, Florida Scott-Maxwell, produced a wonderfully vibrant collection of musings about ageing:

> *Age puzzles me. I thought it was a quiet time. My seventies were interesting and fairly serene, but my eighties are passionate. I grow more intense as I age. To my own surprise, I burst out with hot conviction ... I am so disturbed by the outer world and by human quality in general that I want to put things right, as though I still owed a debt to life. I must calm down. I am far too frail to indulge in moral fervour* (1979: 13, 14).

Margaret Drabble describes writing as *"an illness. A chronic, incurable illness. I caught it by default ... and I often wish I hadn't"* (Allardice, 2011: 13). She denies setting out to write explicitly 'feminist' books but has always had things to say about the lack of equality for women and her stories continue to chronicle the different stages of (mostly middle class) women's lives. Candida, the narrator's voice in *The Seven Sisters*, is in her sixties as she starts her diary during *"the third year of her sojourn"* in a third floor flat in a run-down part of West London. She is divorced, depressed and lonely – yet still wanting to be heard:

> *Nothing much happens to me now, nor ever will again. But that should not prevent me from trying to write about it. I cannot help but feel that there is something important about this nothingness. It should represent a lack of hope, and yet I think that, somewhere, hope may yet be with me. This nothingness is significant. If I immerse myself in it, perhaps it will turn itself into something else. Into something terrible, into something transformed* (Drabble, 2003: 3).

Jane Shilling, in the preface to her 'memoir of middle age', says: *"I wasn't convinced that defining middle age was a useful exercise ... I was more interested in describing than defining this passage of female experience"* (2011: 1, 2) . She continues:

> *Although the experience was (and is) harder and more painful than I thought; more full of confusion and loss, it is also more interesting than I had imagined. As it goes on, the process of ageing seems to me to be less about what is lost, and more about what remains* (2011: 3, 4).

Returning to this issue of the *"gains as well as losses"* involved in growing older, she says something that strongly resonates with me: *"All my life I had been apologetic ... But now I began to wonder if perhaps, even so late, I could learn how not to be apologetic ...*

whether there might still be time in which to please myself" (2011: 74).

In her Guardian column, Michele Hanson tells of being in her sixties where *"we're meant to be invisible and live in an empty nest with no one to look after. If only ... I wish I could stand and wonder. But ... I whizz about, keeping busy"* (2009: 16). She gives a very personal account of getting older, alongside a need to let others know what it's like. She has a particular take on the joys of being post-menopausal:

> *And another fabulous bonus – one can be free, free, free of sex ... you don't need to pretend, because no one's interested* (Hanson, 2009: 16).

Germaine Greer, in her fascinating study of women and the menopause, makes a similar point if in somewhat different language:

> *If the sexuality of older women were allowed to define itself, it is possible that we would discover that older women are not overwhelmed with desire ...* (1992: 7).

She points out that *"although the literature on menopause is vast, almost none of it has been written by women. Most of it has been written by men for the eyes of other men"* (Greer, 1992: 13). She was referring in the main to medical literature, and although some years have passed since she wrote this, the situation is only slowly beginning to improve. We need to be talking about our own experiences of getting older – and talking about them in places where they will be heard.

In her review of what she calls *"an emerging literature of the third age"*, Claire Armitstead describes a feminist analysis of how post-menopausal women are viewed: *"... the fear of menopause, and even some of its symptoms, are caused by a deep rooted misogyny which pervades western culture in general and the medical profession in particular"*. She writes of the need to address what she calls *"this sorry state of affairs"* as part of trying to understand why older women can experience themselves as invisible and unheard and points out that *"there is a direct link between invisibility and the poverty in which many old people find themselves, in a world geared to buying and selling"* (2009: 8).

Most of this 'emerging literature' about older women (both fact and fiction) is, of course, written by white, middle-class women and there is a danger of simply carrying on a patronising tradition of either writing about other people's experiences as though we understand them - or assuming that our own experiences are universal.

In a series of articles (later a book) that were *"a personal record of how I feel about being over seventy"*, Joan Bakewell (2007: ix) produced reflective pieces on personal, social and political issues. She was particularly touched by the number of people who responded to the experiences and memories she shared. *"I am made thoughtful about what it is to be old by some of the letters I receive"*, recognising the privileged life she lives, despite changes and losses: *"Recently a correspondent wrote about another kind of life than mine..."* (2007: 193). Her correspondents, too, wished to be heard.

When six women in their sixties calling themselves *The Hen Co-op* got together to write a book about their experiences, *Growing Old Disgracefully* (1993), it was because there seemed to be so little literature available *about* older women actually written *by* older women. *"What was missing were the voices of women like ourselves"*. What they had to offer was:

> ... to speak in our own voices about our own experiences and maybe some of you would find us speaking to your experiences as well. We recognise our privileges as white middle-class women and do not presume that our circumstances are representative of all women ... (Hen Co-op, 1993: 8,9).

The feedback from my seven co-researchers underlines both the importance and the demands of describing rather than trying to define our life experiences as women growing older. Keeping up a correspondence over many months, within an open-ended and lightly-structured agreement, was very powerful for all of us. Exploring the past and the issues around changing circumstances and perceptions in the present, and writing about them very openly, felt psychologically therapeutic for some, enlightening and enriching (and occasionally even excruciating) for others. We all learned from it – and it seems we all felt heard, by ourselves and by each other.

It's like a magnet,
because when you start writing,
it magnetizes the world.
                    (Cixous, 2004: 120)

2.4 Writing in visible language

Language is how social organization and power
are defined and contested
and the place where our sense of self,
our subjectivity, is constructed.
                                        (Richardson, 1997: 89)

The language in which we write seems to me as important as what we're writing about. Writing is – or can be – a powerful and exciting way of exploring and communicating ideas. Julia Kristeva speaks of writing as the *"foundation for thought"* (Oliver, 2002: 11).

Laurel Richardson calls it *"a way of 'knowing' – a method of discovery and analysis"* (2000: 923). In a two-part lyrical paper on *Writing as inquiry*, she and Elizabeth St. Pierre offer a brief, contextual history of writing and language. St. Pierre talks about *"nomadic inquiry"* and poses the question: *"What else might writing do except mean?"* then quotes Deleuze and Guatarri: *"writing has nothing to do with signifying. It has to do with surveying, mapping, even realms that are yet to come"* (St. Pierre, 2005: 969).

Along with Laurel Richardson's fluent, informative and readable style of writing, I particularly enjoy her insightful and challenging approach to the accepted mores of the academic world, with her emphasis on the importance of not boring your readers (1990, 1997, 2000, 2005). Much academic writing, however, appears to be in language accessible only to others in the same field. *"During my M.A."* says Eric Mykhalovskiy, *"I was struck by the extent to which academics spoke only to themselves"* (1997: 235).

At the start of writing my dissertation, I sent out a 'group letter' to my co-researchers, setting out my wish to communicate in ways that would be understandable to those not immersed in sociological texts (see 'Research as adventure' below):

> *… I have another of my queries. It's about the language I use in writing this dissertation - which, by the way, I'm finally getting into.*
>
> *As a bit of background (you can skip this bit if you want to go straight to the query at the end!) I've been feeling quite blocked*

about starting writing and had a very helpful tutorial with my supervisor last month, who did her usual wonderfully creative listening and suggesting. As a result I had one or two insights into / realisations about why and what I've been resisting.

To try and cut a long story a bit shorter - I've been telling myself I have to write 'chapters' (which is, of course, what people do for dissertations) whilst at the same time knowing I didn't want to do it that way. So I've now begun to write in what my supervisor calls my 'leaf gathering' mode - in other words, just writing down bits of stories, ideas, wonderings, theories etc. as they occur to me. I've already 'gathered' quite a lot this way and am really enjoying doing it.

My other main resistance is to academic language, which I find often incomprehensible, excluding and difficult to read. My hope is to write this dissertation in what I'd term 'visible' language - and I want to state that I'm doing this deliberately - making it accessible and understandable to me (as well as anybody else who chooses to read it).

I'd really like to know what your take on this is - how do you feel about the language that I use in this writing about us, as visible women? Do you agree or disagree with me? Either way, I'd welcome your views, ideas, comments.

With thanks, as always
Christine
(email letter 22.03.09)

... as for me, not being an academic in any sense of the word, I don't have a clue about what academic language is! So, I say write so that I can understand what you're writing! I'm really interested in reading what you make out of my episodic letters and those of the others, but if I can't figure out what it means, I'll be really disappointed. Do what you feel works, what your heart says is "real" and go with it girl! (Sara, 23.03.09)

I'm sure you know that I would really welcome it if you were to write in accessible non-academic language! That's probably because it's exactly the approach I would use. I don't think I could write 'academically' and when I worked very briefly as a local government policy analyst I could never write in the kind of report-writing style they wanted. I often feel that writing is like playing music - you write to the rhythms you feel yourself going along with. (Alison, 23.03.09)

Glad you have found a way to start your dissertation - must have been a very daunting task. I'm really happy for you to use whatever language you feel works but I think using 'visible' language will emphasise what you are writing about. (Val, 23.03.09)

Oh I completely tried to avoid academic language in my thesis, which might come back to bite me. I used footnotes to tie ideas to others which seemed to work pretty well. I completely vote for accessible, straight forward, clear, and world changing language! (Cindy, 23.03.09)

Thanks for your message and query. I really think this is a brilliant idea – it's about time academia got off it's pedestal in relation to the tight 'boundaries' that are supposed to indicate this is heady stuff! Imagine being able to read academic stuff in understandable visible language - it sounds too wonderful. Go for it gal, you've always gone for doing things differently, and you do it WELL. I love it. (Jane, 25.03.09)

You must use any language you feel appropriate as this is your work. In my opinion and as the work is about visibility, a real and accessible, visible language is very appropriate. Also, because I'm dying to read the said work I'd like to understand it. (Lynn, 13.04.09)

I don't know if I will ever be able to just let words and thoughts flow anymore without censure but I did want to say to you that 'your writing' in place of 'dissertation' captures the essence - you only ever do your writing, without self conscious adornments or jargonese, and I so look forward to reading the final version. (Marie, 15.04.09)

I was warmed by their feisty responses and moved (as always) by how much they engaged with this 'visibility' issue at so many levels. As I said to them:

> *It's been very good for my writing heart to have such a resounding YES to what I plan to do … I feel very supported in my writing by all this affirmation of my determination to do it My Way - and excited by the way in which you all seem eager to read whatever comes out at the end of it.Quite a challenge!*
> *My continuing thanks to you all,*
> *Christine*
> (excerpt from email 16.04.09)

> *The first task for contemporary feminist narratologists is to expose both the workings of the master script in women's narratives and women's subversions of it so that we can better learn how nonunitary subjectivity can be represented.*
>
> (Bloom, 1998: 66)

2.5 Writing into the gaps

I do not want to see what is shown.
I want to see what is secret.
What is hidden among the visible.
                              (Cixous, 2005: 184)

When thoroughly bogged down in writing my MSc thesis (Bell, 1995), searching for the language to convey the excitement I felt about my inquiry into change and right brain, creative thinking, I stumbled across the philosophical writings of two men, one from the 1930s (Lev Vygotsky) and the other the 1960s (Michael Polanyi). Despite my prejudices about male theoreticians – and the fact that the language and ideas can seem out-dated and difficult to read - I found their work, around how we think and then tell our thoughts, interesting and relevant.

Vygotsky wrote about 'inner speech' and how difficult it can be to turn thoughts and ideas into communicable language: *"inner speech is ... a dynamic, shifting, unstable thing, fluttering between word and thought"* (1986: 249). He seemed to be describing my struggles with processing what I wanted to say.

I took heart from Michael Polanyi: *"I shall reconsider human knowledge by starting from the fact that we can know more than we can tell"* (1967: 4), feeling eligible to join what he calls *"a society of explorers"* (1967: 83). I don't know what my reaction would have been if I had encountered him when he was writing this in the 1960s. As a young woman then, I was running away as fast as possible from the kind of philosophical and moral thinking I grew up with, and not at all sure what I was running towards. *"The anticipation of discovery, like discovery itself, may turn out to be a delusion"* (1967: 25).

Launching myself into the exploratory journey for this current work, browsing the literal and virtual libraries now available - with much help and guidance along the way - I have excitedly devoured the writings of some of the current giants of philosophical thinking (see 'Research as adventure' below). I have, at last, begun to get a better sense of the truly enormous undertaking by those feminist and poststructuralist thinkers and writers who have led the way in subverting the 'master narrative'; allowing for gaps and for not knowing, searching for another language to describe the journeys they are on. Although I have felt encouraged in attempting to tell stories rather than make statements about what I am experiencing and learning, it has, much of the time, felt like writing into an unknown space – not at all sure what, if anything, I am discovering that may be of interest to others.

In a seminar at Bristol University in 2008, Jean Clandinin talked about the book she jointly edited on *Narrative Inquiry* (Clandinin & Connelly, 2000) and of beginning to think about knowledge differently. Learning how to tell the stories of what we know in a different way – of *"embodied rhythmical knowledge alongside 'known' knowledge"* - and the importance of wondering about what happens in the spaces in between, *"the borderlines and cracks between stories",* Jean Clandinin wondered what all this might mean to us as researchers. She ended by telling us about *"trying on the hat of being poststructuralist"* and *"maybe deciding to take it off"* – and of her reluctance to *"nail down"* any theoretical position, preferring to put something together *"just for now"* (Clandinin, 2008).

I think that will do very nicely for me, for now.

CHAPTER THREE

ON NOT DOING RESEARCH

You don't need to know everything.
There is no everything. The stories
themselves make the meaning.
(Winterson, 2004: 134)

3.1 Research as adventure

This nomadic writing journey ...
has been both gruelling and exhilarating ...
This story has no beginning and no end ...
(St. Pierre, 2000: 276)

'Research' can be a problematic as well as a useful word, from my perspective. I feel the need to put at least mental inverted commas around it, in order to disentangle my current understanding from the old science-based approaches that I grew up with and rejected. On starting to re-write this section, it made my heart sink to look again at the definition in *The Concise Oxford Dictionary:*

> **research - 1 a** *the systematic investigation into and study of materials, sources, etc., in order to establish facts and reach new conclusions. **b** (usu. in pl.) an endeavour to discover new or collate old facts etc. by the scientific study of a subject or by a course of critical investigation* (1991: 1022).

Sociological research, which I had once imagined to be a bit more 'fluffy', or at least more humane, seemed instead to involve a mysterious and patriarchal process carried out by experts who knew (but didn't necessarily tell what they knew or how they knew it), on 'subjects' who were studied and questioned in various ways (but were not allowed or encouraged to study or ask questions back).

It was a relief to find respected academics such as Norman Denzin, in his chapter on the ethics and politics of interpretation, apparently having similar thoughts and quoting negative descriptions from the point of view of the researched:

> *... the term 'research' is inextricably linked to European imperialism and colonialism. The word itself, 'research', is probably one of the dirtiest words in the indigenous world's vocabulary* (Smith, in Denzin, 2005: 993).

It seems that some scientists are also challenging old thinking about research producing 'truth' and 'facts'. At an annual web-based exercise which invites scientists, philosophers and artists to give their views on a current question, the topic in 2011 was 'What scientific concept would improve everybody's cognitive toolkit?'.

Physicist Carlo Rovelli *"emphasised the uselessness of certainty ... the idea of something being 'scientifically proven' was practically an oxymoron ... A good scientist is never 'certain'. Certainty is not only something of no use, but is in fact damaging".* The director of the Massachusetts Institute of Ethnology's Centre of Bits and Atoms, Neil Gershenfeld, *"wants everyone to know that 'truth' is just a model ... The most common misunderstanding about science is that scientists seek and find truth"* (Jha, 2011).

"Reason without emotion is nothing", says clinician Michael Mosley, in his informative and thought-provoking television series (The Brain: a secret history, 2011).

My unplanned foray into the doctoral world at Bristol University began after taking part in Jane Speedy's narrative workshops at a therapy conference or two in the early 2000s. Her enthusiastic recruiting for the 'narrative and life story research' doctorate she was in the process of setting up, along with her challenging some of my prejudices about the academic world and my eligibility to be part of it, combined to effectively lure me in. She was (and is) a creative advocate for the power of story to actually make a difference, personally and politically:

> *I want to question an assumption that policy makers, albeit more inclined towards outcomes than process, are not also influenced by 'stories'* (Speedy, 2004: 44).

This use of story to bring about positive, radical change included the exciting notion of 'writing as methodology'. Writing as a way of thinking, as a method of discovery, fitted so well with my (mostly non-academic) experience over the years that I found it difficult to believe that it was somehow legitimate as a serious form of research. Not only that, but there were fascinating things being said about the potential for expanding our understanding of the world and 'society', not just through studying other people, but by something as seemingly self-indulgent as thinking and writing about ourselves. This was an approach that I (along with many others) had been using to good effect for years within my psychotherapeutic and other work with individuals and groups, and here it was being validated as an academic practice. Yet more of my assumptions being knocked on the head.

By using our own memories and lives in written narratives, we can begin to locate these biographical experiences in larger historical contexts, making sense differently, perhaps, both of ourselves and of the wider world. I hear an echo of my own life experience and beliefs in Laurel Richardson's :

> *I am discovering that my concerns for social justice across race, class, religion, gender and ethnicity derive from these early childhood experiences. These have solidified my next writing questions. How can I make my writing matter? How can I write to help speed into this world a democratic project of social justice?*
> (Richardson, 2005: 967)

"Writing is not an innocent practice", says Norman Denzin in an earlier article proposing that qualitative writing should be assessed *"in terms of its ability to advance the promise of radical democratic … justice"* (2000: 256).

This particular writing venture has, inevitably, involved reading a large number of academic texts which were new to me, containing fascinating and sometimes quite revolutionary ideas about changing the ways in which reflective thinking and reflexive research is carried forward. I have often, somewhat resentfully, struggled to understand the terminology and language used - which can seem exclusive and impenetrable for those not part of the scholastic world (see 'Writing in visible language' above). I have nevertheless felt the old familiar thrill of reading something that takes me into different spaces:

> *What am I doing when I lock myself with it in a tête-à-tête from which I cannot wrench myself? I get up ten times. I return to the book. I am summoned, bewitched, held back by the mysterious forces of Reading. I can hear its siren's murmur* (Cixous, 2011: xi).

Patti Lather seems to be inviting us to enjoy feeling dislocated and unsure of ourselves through exploring the idea of *"getting lost as a methodology"* (2007: 3). She proposes 'troubling' accepted theory in order to *"produce different knowledge and produce knowledge differently"* (2007:13).

> *In a certain way, there is perhaps no voyage worthy of the name*
> *except one that takes place there where, in all senses of the word,*
> *one loses oneself, one runs such a risk, without even taking or*
> *assuming this risk: not even of losing oneself but of getting lost.*
> (Deridda, in Lather, 2007: 11)

The philosopher Julia Kristeva was instrumental in the move away from *"structuralism ... as accepted knowledge ... our task was to take this acquired knowledge and immediately do something else"* (Kristeva, in McAfee, 2004: 6). She was born (the same year as me) in Bulgaria, leaving in her early 20s to study in 1960s Paris, where *"intellectually and politically ... revolution was in the air"* (McAfee, 2004: 6). Becoming part of an extraordinarily dynamic circle of intellectuals - including Derrida, Foucault, Lévi-Strauss, Lacan, Barthes - *"in an extremely male-dominated environment"* (Moi, 1986: 3), she was *"one of the people who helped to formulate a type of post-structuralism"*, explaining that:

> *... mere structure was not sufficient to understand the world of meaning in literature and other human behaviours. Two more elements were necessary: history and the speaking subject* (Kristeva, in McAfee, 2004: 6,7).

These are, of course, two essential elements of my inquiry into this phenomenon of the perceived visibility/invisibility of older women; firstly the story of what has gone before, both personal and in the outer world, and just as importantly, the actual voices of us, the women.

Julia Kristeva talks of the way language changes when it is spoken by what she calls the *"living, breathing, speaking being"* (Kristeva, in McAfee, 2004: 6). I get a sense of the excitement generated by her innovative and exploratory thinking in her massive doctoral thesis in 1974, *Revolution in Poetic Language*, where she suggested that it is possible to transform the structure of literary representation:

> *...a revolution in poetic language is analogous to a political revolution* (Kristeva, in Oliver, 2002: 24).

In an interview in 2007, her work was described as *"a theory of language that foregrounded the disruptive elements – the playful, lyrical, rhythmic, emotional aspects (the 'semiotic') – which are always, she believes, in dialogue with the rational business of denoting meaning (the 'symbolic')"* (Miller, 2007: 11).

In her work on feminist methodology and narrative interpretation, Leslie Bloom engages with *"theories of the speaking subject whose individuality and self-awareness or subjectivity is multiple, conflicted, complex, fragmented, and in constant flux".* These theories, she says, are slowly displacing *"the master narratives of unified individuality"* (1998: 2); in other words, we're all a lot more complicated than some early sociological/anthropological researchers would have us believe.

"Our project has been to bring theory into collision with everyday life", say Bronwyn Davies and Susanne Gannon (2006: 4), playing around with alternative approaches to social science in their innovative, multi-authored book on doing collective biography, a *"post-structuralist writing practice"* (172). They draw on the memory work of feminist Frigga Haug and her colleagues in Germany in the 1980s (Haug et al, 1999), who set out to disrupt existing theory through exploring the actual experiences of women.

> By taking oneself and one's own ongoing experiences as the data ... the gap between memories and the interpretive analytic work of research is closed (Davies & Gannon, 2006: 3).

In what they call *"a conversation about the struggles of collaborative writing"* (114) the two editors pay lengthy tribute to Hélène Cixous, who uses intricate and evocative poetic language to develop her own ideas and to tell of her struggles with writing about what happens within as well as outside herself (see 'The Wilful Extremist' below):

> When I feel that I'm totally defeated by the task, by something which is too big for me ... noting it is as if I were at least drawing the line where I have been checkmated - there at least, and there, I can't go further. And usually it helps me take a rest, and start again (Cixous, 2004: 121).

Although Hélène Cixous is sometimes grouped together with other female original thinkers and writers in France of her generation, I agree with Mireille Calle-Gruber:

> *I am surprised that people generally name Cixous – Irigaray – Kristeva together, amalgamating works between which I see mostly differences. Particularly: literary difference. Irigaray and Kristeva are theoreticians, they do not produce writer's work* (Calle-Gruber, in Cixous & Calle-Gruber, 1997: 7).

While there is nothing the matter with theoreticians (at least in theory), the talk that makes my heart and brain sing (see Bird, 2004) is that which tells the stories of *how* people hold their knowledge.

In the quote at the start of this section, Elizabeth St. Pierre sums up her experience of interviewing a group of older, white southern women in the rural American community where she grew up. She was surprised to find herself still attached to the place itself, after 20 years away. Her work moved from being a study of 'others' to an exploration of how women's lives (including her own) and sense of themselves are shaped – especially as they get older - by *"the limits and possibilities"* of what's available to them. She learned to stay with and enjoy the *"nomadic journey"* to *"places I have been unable to imagine"* (2000: 258) rather than expecting/hoping to reach conclusions.

The study was started because, as she too grew older, she had become curious about what these women *"who taught me how to be a woman … have done and continue to do every day that makes them who they are …*

> *My research is not motivated by the desire to produce knowledge for knowledge's sake. I urgently need to hear what these women tell me about thinking and doing; in fact, during our interviews two years ago, I often sat on the edge of my chair waiting for their responses to my questions"* (St. Pierre, 2000: 259).

I like this urgency of needing to hear responses, which became so much part of my own experience as I wrote letters to my seven 'visible women' and waited (sometimes impatiently) for replies. Keeping the very many different strands of correspondence on the go over a period of a year and more was demanding, exciting and totally fascinating. As I told Jane, my dissertation supervisor, *"I'm in love with my research"*. So much so that I needed to come off the edge of my chair and bring the letter-writing part of the adventure to an end, if I was ever going to get on with any other kind of writing.

3.2 The wilful extremist

The person we have been is now an 'I was',
the character from our past.   She follows us,
but at a distance.
(Cixous, in Cixous & Calle-Gruber, 1997: 138)

According to the blurb on the back of Hélène Cixous's book *Stigmata* (2005), she was described by the London *Times* as a *"wilful extremist"*. Her work is apparently (and not surprisingly) often misunderstood; it is potentially difficult and I have heard it described as impenetrable. Unlike my (slightly resentful) struggles with some of the academic texts described earlier, however, I can feel myself opening up and responding to her words in an emotional and physical way; not trying to understand exactly what she means but simply allowing images to emerge, following the thoughts and feelings they engender.

From her preface to *Stigmata*:

> *The texts collected and stitched together sewn and resewn in this volume share the trace of a wound. They were caused by a blow, they are the transfiguration of a spilling of blood, be it real or translated into a haemorrhage of the soul* (Cixous, 2005: xi).

I experience her shaping language in the way that Louise Bourgeois created her art (see 'Doing, undoing and re-doing' below), with metaphor and symbol to tell and re-tell her memories, to explore past wounds and present experience. Her words are like exotic antennae, 'feeling' her way into whatever she is exploring, circling around it, sometimes probing deeply, sometimes gently brushing across the surface and withdrawing to see what might happen.

> *A kind of work takes place in this space that we do not know, that precedes writing, and that must be a sort of enormous region or territory where a memory has been collected, a memory composed of all sorts of signifying elements that have been kept or noted – or of events that time has transformed into signifiers, pearls and corals of the 'language' of the soul ...* (Cixous, in Cixous & Calle-Gruber, 1997: 29).

The work of Hélène Cixous has been one of my inspirations during this process of inquiry. I have enjoyed entering and 'getting lost' in the depths and complexity of her ideas and stories around the self and the other, literary theory, philosophy, post-colonialism, her personal history, relationships, politics, power, feminism, family, place – and the pain and pleasure of writing - weaving poetic narratives as she goes.

When I begin to write,
it always starts from something unexplained,
mysterious and concrete ...
It begins to search in me.
And this question should be philosophical;
but for me, right away it takes the poetic path.
That is to say
that it goes through scenes, moments, illustrations
lived by myself or by others,
and like all that belongs to the current of life,
it crosses very many zones of our histories.
I seize these moments still trembling,
moist, creased, disfigured, stammering.
                    (Cixous, in Cixous & Calle-Gruber, 1997: 43)

I have often declared my admiration for Hélène Cixous,
for the person and for the work:
immense, powerful, so multiple but unique ....
I have even written ...
that Hélène Cixous is in my eyes, today,
the greatest writer in the French language.
                    (Derrida, in Cixous, 2005: ix)

3.3 Self-indulgence – or just another way of reflecting?

In thinking about self-indulgence, I was particularly drawn to feminist postmodern critiques that called for more self-reflexive social science ... These analyses supported my view that the abstract, disembodied voice of traditional academic discourse was a fiction ...

(Mykhalovskiy, 1997: 232)

In my proposal for the thesis on which this work is based, my criteria included: *"allowing subjectivity and self-indulgence – i.e. giving weight to my own and other women's individual experiences through telling our stories".* 'Self-indulgent' is the term sometimes used in the academic world to dismiss biographical narrative writing.

It's as if reflecting on your own experience - or making yourself visible when exploring other people's - in some ways invalidates any hope of your work being taken seriously. My initial indignant reaction to the dismissive voices is to ask:

Why not use different terms, such as self-knowing, self-respectful, self-sacrificing, or self-luminous?
(Sparkes, 2002: 210)

What could be more self-indulgent (and worse, boring) than academics so often writing – apparently – only for each other? This point has already been made very effectively (and interestingly) elsewhere (Bochner, 2000; Mykhalovskiy, 1997; Richardson, 1997).

In fact, I believe it is much more demanding – and dare I say it, even more rigorous – *not* to hide behind the anonymity of the academic researcher. In putting myself and my own story clearly in view, alongside those of my co-researchers, I am unable to become the *"disembodied voice"* that analyses, interprets and draws conclusions about the lives and experiences of others. I am not, of course, alone in believing this (see many of the feminist and poststructuralist voices already referenced). Zigzagging my way around the doctoral track for six years or so, sometimes finding it hard to get started and often feeling ill-equipped for the task, I was greatly supported by my supervisor and other tutors at Bristol in my quest to find creative ways of 'breaking the rules' in academic writing (Bond, 2002; Reed 2006; Speedy, 2005a,b).

In *The Tacit Dimension,* Michael Polanyi's wonderfully laconic opening sentence is: *"Some of you may know that I turned to philosophy as an afterthought to my career as a scientist"* (1967: 3).

How about that? Becoming a philosopher *as an afterthought* ...

His reasons for turning to philosophy included realising that scientific claims to reach valid conclusions based only on objective facts were not absolutely true. And what was even more astonishing for a scientist at that time, he had come to believe that there was no such thing as an 'objective fact'. What he calls the *"leap to discovery"* in research of any kind comes about through the choices we make about what to believe, what interpretation to put on what we are inquiring into; *" … to some degree, we shape all knowledge in the way we know it"* (Polanyi, 1967: 77).

I am interested in, and fascinated by, the way our own stories and histories are constructed through the multitude of subjective (and no doubt self-indulgent) ways in which we all experience, remember and then 'know' and shape our knowledge. How do we then decide to share this with others? What do we leave out – and why? Which stories do we tell to which audience – and why?

In her study of how a group of incarcerated women maintained (or did not) their sense of themselves, M. Carolyn Clark says *"I found my theoretical ground in the literature on subjectivity … How we think about ourselves is shaped by culture, ideology and language, therefore our subjectivity is not straightforward"*. And she gives one of the best and simplest definitions I've seen of 'non-unitary subjectivity':

> The self is non-unitary in the sense that there is no single, core self that exists separate and unaffected by its sociological context. Instead we experience multiple selves (2001: 14, 15).

In *Transpositions*, Rosi Braidotti talks about *"nomadic subjectivity"* and explores *"the possibility of a system of ethical values that, far from requiring a steady and unified vision of the subject, rests on a non-unitary, nomadic or rhizomatic view".*

> *Non-unitary subjectivity here means a nomadic, dispersed, fragmented vision, which is nonetheless functional, coherent and accountable, mostly because it is embedded and embodied (2006: 4, 5).*

Referring to feminist critics of objectivity, she tell us that *"feminist poststructuralists go even further into this critique than other schools of feminist thought".*

> *Ethical accountability is closely related to the political awareness of one's positions and privileges. Poststructuralist ethics is consequently concerned with human affectivity and passions as the motor of subjectivity ... Alterity, otherness and difference are crucial terms of reference in poststructuralist ethics* (Braidotti, 2006: 13).

I believe my questions (above) about subjectivity and selectiveness could be usefully applied to 'truths' and 'facts' of any kind, however apparently non-personal. Claiming subjectivity – rather than pretending to be objective - could be seen as an essential to good, ethical research. It is simply making visible what is actually going on. And if writing about or referring to oneself can become self-indulgent, in that it's too self-absorbed or badly written (which, of course, happens), then it must be seen as part of the writerly task not to let this happen - to remember Laurel Richardson's strictures that *"writing matters"* (1997: 87) and we must not be boring if we want to be read.

I have read a great many autobiographical books and auto-ethnographic texts over the last few years, partly as academic research (and obligation) but mostly for pleasure and/or information. My bibliography could have been a great deal longer if I'd decided to reference them all – but that might have seemed too self-indulgent even for me. I have occasionally been bored or critical, or even embarrassed by what I experience as bad writing, but have perhaps learned something from those less positive experiences about the 'how' and 'why' of shining the research light, in order to better illuminate the stories my co-researchers and I would like you to see.

One of the books I was surprised to enjoy was Diana Athill's memoir, *Somewhere Towards the End*. Writing in her ninetieth year, she recognises the privileged position she was born into, rejecting what she calls the *"tribal complacency"* of her family which was *"based on wicked nonsense"* (2009: 179). The most interesting part of it for me was not the sexual and other revelations so many reviewers referred to, but the way she uses the stories about herself to describe how she 'became' a writer *in order* to tell the stories; letting her readers know what it's like for *her* becoming an older woman, as she experiences changing relationships with friends and family, sexual partners, work, home, religion, reading habits, gardening, clothing …every part of her life.

> *I believed, and still believe, that there is no point in describing experience unless one tries to get it as near to being what it really was as you can make it, but that belief does come into conflict with a central teaching in my upbringing: Do Not Think Yourself Important* (Athill, 2009: 148).

That conflict with upbringing is one I know well – and by writing myself into this text I am consciously and deliberately Thinking Myself Important. In doing so I recognise my privileged position as a white, middle-class woman in being able to do this, knowing that my own and my co-researchers' experiences and stories are just that … our stories. I hope that, at the very least, they will make an interesting read and, more than that, they will make you think.

> *Many women's personal narratives unfold*
> *within the framework of an apparent acceptance*
> *of social norms and expectations*
> *but nevertheless describe strategies and activities*
> *that challenge these same norms.*
>   (Personal Narratives Group, 1989: 7)

3.4 My story – part three: adventure as research

I saw the world as some sort of exchange scheme
for my ideals, but the world deserves better than this.
(Mantel, 2004: 12)

If my father's plans for me had gone as they were supposed to, I would have been immersed in preparation for bettering the world in some way, preferably academically and at Oxford, his old 'alma mater'. It was for this, he told me, that he had insisted I stick with Latin all through my schooling. Instead, in November 1961, a couple of months past my twentieth birthday – having failed to make much of a mark at anything, let alone becoming A Writer (part of *my* plan) - I was a degree-less 'ten pound pom' on an ancient and overcrowded P&O liner slowly steaming towards Australia. Reasons for going included:

I'll be half a world away from most of my family and their expectations

   I can get that far away for £10!

         I want to do something different – all on my own

Following my birth in China and eventual arrival in England (via India) aged three, I had become quite an experienced long-distance traveller between continents. At 15 I had sailed to Trinidad with my father (who was delighted to be back in the 'mission field' again), stepmother and four-year-old half-brother on a French liner. Delayed and violently tossed about by a hurricane on the way, we were all confined to our cabins for days – the only time I've ever been seriously afraid at sea. I returned much more peacefully on my own two years later on a banana boat, calling at most of the other Caribbean islands on the way and honing my secretly-acquired, non-approved skills of drinking (rum and coke) and dancing (to steel bands).

Until deciding to emigrate, there had been little or no say in where or why I was travelling. This time it was my choice and, the more the 'grown ups' suggested it wasn't a good idea, the more determined I was to go. It was only as the boat began its stately turn away from Tilbury docks that my determination began to wobble slightly, as I stood amongst the crowd at the rails and wept, waving to my two much-loved older brothers on the quay.

Going to the other side of the world then was still a real adventure. It took five weeks or more to get to the west coast of Australia by sea and the £10 deal (more then than I earned in a week) committed immigrants to spending at least two years in that country. Telephone contact was expensive, had to be booked in advanced and was often virtually inaudible. Long-distance air travel was out of the reach of most people and many emigrating from Europe went not knowing if they would see their home country again. I was aware of all this – it was one of the reasons for going as far away as possible; what I didn't know, of course, was how it would actually feel.

Once the weeping stopped – somewhere around the time we were steaming out of the Thames Estuary into the English Channel – I began to look around and feel surprisingly all right. There were a lot of young people about, most of them apparently on their own, too, looking very lost and quite a few also very seasick. At least I'd experienced this sort of 'leaving' before – and had never been seasick.

The tiny, airless, below-the-waterline cabin, with three bunk beds, six drawers and six clothes-hooks on the walls for its six inhabitants, was a bit of a shock; previous sea voyages had never been luxurious but this was definitely 'steerage'. It was rowdy, cramped and increasingly hot below decks and there were occasional flare-ups and fights amongst the male emigrants (mostly white) and some of the lower rank crew (mostly non-white).

The other five young women in the cabin were all away from home for the first time and both sea and homesick. They were all office workers, like me, but had all still been living with their parents - whereas since leaving school at 18 I had been in a shared flat in London. Though still very shy and lacking in confidence, I felt suddenly quite knowledgeable and experienced, having spent much of my life moving around between different households, places and countries.

For the first day or so the six of us stuck together, not knowing anybody else. The enforced closeness of the cabin quickly produced disputes, however, rather than friendships - squabbles over someone using more than one clothes-hook or making a lot of noise at night, somebody being seasick and regularly not making it to the communal washrooms. I discovered how much my familiarity with shipboard routines worked in my favour, as I found other, quieter places to sleep - in the lounges, on the floor of the library, even in the dining room, as long as you were up and away before the cleaning staff came round. I knew in advance about the boredom and the claustrophobic atmosphere, the importance of having time to myself and of getting some exercise, even if it was only walking round and round the decks.

Life on a long-distance liner happened within an enclosed, isolated environment, with very little to do for weeks on end except wait for the next port of call. There were well over 1,000 passengers and, as we bucketed our way through the Bay of Biscay and into the relative calm of the Mediterranean, the particular hierarchies of relationships and groupings that happen on board ship began to emerge and develop.

What really surprises me now, recalling and reliving the story of that voyage, is how well I seemed to have managed to maintain my (often shaky) inner equilibrium during this literal and metaphorical transition from one side of the world to the other. Without knowing it then, I recognised enough about the various clusters forming and re-forming (amoeba-like) around different leaders – 'enough' at least to know that I didn't want to become part of any of them …

Good looking and popular

Clever and arrogant

Intellectual and distant

None of these and don't care

Desperate to be allowed to join

Fuck off - I wanna be alone

Having learned as a child to keep quiet and be watchful when not sure, I joined in without joining and retreated as things got drunken and edgy … and noticed a few others doing something similar. About a week into the voyage, as the boat neared the Suez Canal, we 'others' had become a sort of non-group; walking or swimming together in twos and threes during the long, boring days; spaced around the public areas reading on our own; meeting after dinner and drifting out on deck to talk or look at the moon, when most people were rowdily in the bar.

I thought being part of this non-group was wonderful, like being in a novel. Our ages ranged from me (20) to Nancy, probably in her late thirties and a refugee from first class, where she found the company boring. She seemed impossibly sophisticated and glamorous, with an expensive wardrobe and exotic taste in cocktails; yet she decided to 'mother' me, letting me use her first class cabin during the day to catch up on sleep and have a shower in peace, offering me make-up tips and taming my wildly curly hair.

There were seven of us, as I remember it:*

Nancy: rich, charming, clever and often drunk, on a recuperative round-trip 'holiday' after the death of her brother and husband in a car accident.

Murray: hunky, handsome, blonde, Australian outback ranch-worker and writer, just had his first novel published and returning home after 'doing' Europe.

Nat: (known as Hiram), thin, darkly funny, intense, with black horn-rim glasses, Jewish-American just out of Harvard and going to an academic post in Sydney.

Lisa: strikingly pretty, with an Indian mother, very articulate and lively, a teacher emigrating for more money and better weather.

Jill: swimming champion, muscly, sporty and fun, who had spent her childhood in Western Australia and was returning to teach P.E. in a country town.

Toby: good-looking, gentle and quiet, a sort of low-key English playboy without any money, on board because he couldn't quite decide what to do with himself.

*[Only the names have been changed]

I was astonished to have been noticed at all, let alone have my opinions solicited and listened to by these clever and interesting people. I felt terribly grown-up and almost relevant. It all happened 50 years ago, yet my memories of that voyage still seem very clear as I recall them – whether they are 'true' or not. Re-telling the story for the first time in many years, I wonder if this apparent clarity of memory is to do with it being the first time I had really felt separate enough as a person in my own right, supported by being recognised in some way by those who had been complete strangers and who I got to know through being 'seen' and acknowledged.

Within that artificial environment, as a young woman on an adventure of my own choosing, it would have been easy to get lost in all kinds of negative ways. It was possibly a more than usually chaotic voyage, in an old liner on its last long-distance journey, with delays due to engineering problems and at one point an outbreak of dysentery due to contamination in the drinking water. As we passed through the Suez Canal – with some emigrants already deciding they'd made a mistake and disembarking at Port Said – it began to get unbearably hot below decks; there was a lot of tension and frequent rows and I only visited the multi-occupancy cabin for a change of clothes. In addition to my other sleeping places, we were allowed to use basic army camping 'cots' set out in rows on the open decks late at night, though these decks were hosed down very early in the morning, whether people were sleeping there or not.

Once into the Indian Ocean, with no land in sight for day after day and only the endlessly rolling sea, there was a change in the atmosphere; not calm, exactly – maybe a mixture of exhaustion and inertia from the heat and the endless round of doing nothing. I was even more grateful for the safety and the stimulation of the non-group, as we drifted around together – and separately – sharing stories, silences, meals, books, music and jokes. I stopped feeling so unsophisticated and naïve around Nancy, accepting her offerings and listening to her pain as she drank and told the story of the car accident that had killed her husband and brother.

I spent hours talking with kind, handsome Murray – who I strangely didn't fancy at all, he seemed far too much like a big brother. He was engaged to somebody "back home" he wasn't sure he loved any more after his time away in Europe, and all he really wanted was to publish another book. We talked about his writing - and mine, in which I had lost confidence during the battle to do things my way, leaving school, not going to university, becoming independent. Our conversations – and his interest - helped me remember how much writing meant to me still and I took it up again with renewed enthusiasm. After a year or so, I even earned my living from it when, in the Australian spirit of 'give her a go', I was offered the chance to research and write articles for an educational publishing company (and spend blissful hours reading through restricted archives in libraries).

Thinking about this part of my story, memories from my time in Australia emerged and jostled for attention and I wasn't sure how much (or how little) would seem relevant. As I started to write, the chaotic outward journey and the 'non-group' became my focus, I realised that those weeks on board – which at times had seemed both endless and pointless – were an important part of my entry into a new life; *the transition was, in itself, transformational.*

The journey for me ended, symbolically, on New Year's Day 1962 and I disembarked in Fremantle excitedly, if a little sadly. I would miss 'the group' (and we never met again) but the next bit of the adventure had arrived and I was more or less ready for it.

> *People are called to their wilderness*
> *in order to alter themselves*
> *and miscall it 'finding themselves'.*
>   (Stronach, 2002: 294)

3.5 Stories as witness

One of the most persistent but elusive ways
that people make sense of themselves
is to show themselves to themselves through multiple forms.
(Myerhoff, 1986: 261)

"I am studying my own kind", says Barbara Myerhoff in the touching documentary film (*Number Our Days*, 1977) about her research with a group of marginalised, elderly immigrant Jews living in poverty in Venice, California. It is an affecting film, made even more so by her expectation of becoming *"a little old Jewish lady"*; yet we know that she died (aged nearly 50) of breast cancer a few years after completing the study.

She was interested in – and shocked by - these people's *"severe invisibility and the consequent disturbing psychological and social consequences of being unnoticed"*. They eventually *"made themselves be seen"* through what she calls *"a definitional ceremony"* (Myerhoff, 1986: 262, 263):

> *Definitional ceremonies deal with the problems of invisibility and marginality; they are strategies that provide opportunities for being seen in one's own terms, garnering witness to one's worth, vitality and being* (1986: 267).

The problem of invisibility seems to arise for any of us when we experience ourselves, our lives and stories not being acknowledged and 'witnessed' in some way. Whilst I am not in any way equating my work with Barbara Myerhoff's, she has fascinating things to say which seem relevant for this exploration, about how perceived invisibility is *"not irreversible"* if we have enough *"ingenuity, imagination and boldness ... flying in the face of external reality* (1986: 263) to gather witnesses to our stories and existence.

> *By denying their invisibility, isolation, and impotence,*
> *they made themselves be seen, and in being seen*
> *they came into being in their own terms,*
> *as authors of themselves.*
> (Myerhoff, 1986: 263)

3.6 Telling stories

Stories long to be used rather than analysed,
to be told and retold
rather than theorised and settled.

(Bochner, 1997: 431)

Returning to the dictionary definition of 'research' at the start of this chapter, I wonder what might change if we could allow that, rather than trying to discover, establish or collate 'facts', research is actually about the uncovering of multiple stories through asking questions? And perhaps even more challenging, if we could accept that these stories may not lead to conclusions, but simply to more stories? In her small book about *The Gift of Story*, Jungian analyst and storyteller Clarissa Pinkola Estés says:

> *Among my people, questions are often answered with stories. The first story almost always evokes another, which summons another, until the answer to the question has become several stories long. A sequence of tales is thought to offer broader and deeper insight than a single story alone* (1994: 1).

Storytelling in many forms has always been an important part of my life and I have found many different way of enjoying and exploring this over the years – listening, watching, reading, imagining, telling, writing. When practising as a psychotherapist, one of the things I became good at, and also found the most demanding, was listening – really listening - to people's stories about their lives, and why they were in therapy. Being properly listened to (when it happened) was the most helpful part of my own therapy. I didn't want clever analysis of my neuroses or interpretations of my dreams, I wanted the time and space to tell my own stories in my own way; to hear myself telling them and to believe they were being heard and treated seriously by this other person, as though I mattered.

With some clients it was a long, slow process of inviting and allowing space for stories to emerge; with others, the stories just poured out and I needed to slow things down in order for me (and the other person) to really hear them and explore the tales within tales. Becoming a really good, deep listener also involved becoming a carrier of stories, remembering them – especially when clients 'forgot' them - sometimes telling them back and inviting their re-telling. I offered writing, drawing, using objects of various kinds as alternative ways of telling or representing the stories that needed to be told. It seemed that this was the most therapeutic gift I had to offer – my ability to enable and hold the stories in such a way that they could flow backwards and forwards between us, being told and re-told, experienced differently in a way that might at least help make another sense of things or even make the unbearable less so.

In his book about how therapists can learn from their 'patients', the psychoanalyst Patrick Casement says:

> There are many different ways of remembering. In everyday life, memory is usually thought of as conscious recall. When unconscious memory is operating another kind of remembering is sometimes encountered – vivid details of past experience is being re-lived in the present. This repetition of the past is by no means confined to good times remembered, as in nostalgia (1985: 2).

One of my clients, a highly intelligent, successful and articulate man, was very skilled in avoiding any real contact. My usual ways of slowing people down seemed to have little effect and I often felt overwhelmed as he vividly described his apparently dysfunctional life. His phrases, however, would stick in my mind and were included in the notes made after sessions; I sometimes reminded him of them, inviting reflection on what he was telling me, now and previously. He would immediately deny any memory of having said these things and query whether, indeed, he had. With his agreement I started making brief verbatim notes during our meetings, then transcribed his words into the form of a poem and sent one to him after every session. This transformed the therapeutic relationship between us.

He was deeply touched that I was interested enough to write down his actual words and then bother to construct poems: *"I couldn't believe you would take time to think about me between sessions"*. Taking time to think during sessions became possible, as silence was allowed into the room. A space had been created within which he could reflect on the stories given back to him and bear to think about the questions waiting to be asked.

Silence – and leaving space for reflection – is an vitally important part of telling and listening to stories of all kinds (inner and outer) and the learning and insights they can offer. In her meditative journal extracts on ageing, Florida Scott-Maxwell says:

> *Silence receives too little appreciation, silence being a higher, rarer thing than sound. Silence implies inner riches, and a savouring of impressions ... Silence is beyond many of us, and hardly taken into account as one of life's favours. It can be sacred. Its implications are unstatable* (1979: 148).

In many people's lives silence and space, even if desired, are hard to find – and are far too often actively avoided. But I believe that, without seeking quiet and even solitude, it is very difficult to get to the questions we need to ask of ourselves and others. This is something that good storytellers know and practice, for themselves and for their listeners.

Clarissa Pinkola Estés believes in the importance of *"intentional solitude"* and says that, *"in addition to gaining information about whatever we wish to see into, the taking of solitude can be used to assess how we ourselves are doing in any sphere we choose"* (1992: 295). One of the archetypal tales re-told in *Women Who Run with the Wolves* is that of the Seal Woman, torn between her human family on land and longing for her home under the sea – to find her sealskin and return to being herself again (1992: 258-262). Women can lose the sense of *"feeling ... wholly in our skins"* in all kinds of ways, including:

> *becoming too involved with ego, by being too exacting, perfectionistic, or unnecessarily martyred, or driven by a blind ambition, or by being dissatisfied ... and not saying or doing anything about it, or by pretending that we are an unending source for others, or by not doing all we can to help ourselves* (1992: 266).

Through answering questions with stories, which often led to more questions, my seven women co-researchers and I shared our experiences of our different ways of 'being in our skins' at the ages we now are, living the lives we now live. This way of exploring took us into some deep places - where we had come from; where we might be going; gains and losses along the way; things learned and things still left to learn. Stories were told with honesty, humour, pain; with excitement and a sense of adventure, with sadness and an acknowledgment of griefs.

All that one might need, all that we might ever need,
is still whispering from the bones of story.

(Estés, 1992: 17)

3.7 A narrative conversation

Interviewing ... is essentially a conversation ...
(Oakley, 1981: 32)

My intention, as I firmly told my seven women correspondents at the start, was *not* to interview them, but to have what I called "*a sort of ongoing email conversation*". I would ask occasional questions and hope to initiate an ongoing, two-way narrative dialogue with each of them – and possibly have a bit of group chat as well. I would be using my own experience and story as well as theirs in this exploration, and very specifically invited questions and comments back from them on any aspect of our dialogue.

Bearing in mind Ann Oakley's wonderfully scathing feminist text on the absurdity of the *"correct interviewing behaviour"* of not allowing *"properly socialised respondents"* to engage in *"asking questions back"* (1981: 35), I must have chosen my co-researchers well. They have all done what they felt like doing, including not always answering my questions and often resolutely *not* asking questions back or making comments.

The interview has become a means of contemporary storytelling ...
(Fontana & Frey, 2005: 699)

Their approaches were all different, but as a generalisation, most of the 'visible women' seemed interested in taking the opportunity to do some personal reflection on and general storytelling about their lives. Two of them chose to write about themselves more objectively, within a clear political and social framework. From my perspective – and they have all told me they share this view – we were having via email something that resembled a genuine dialogue, rather than the sort of 'pseudo-conversation' that continues to maintain the old power imbalances between interviewer and interviewee (Atkinson & Silverman, 1997; Fontana & Frey, 2005; Kvale, 1996 ... and others).

... any researcher with a strong commitment to conversations as collaborative research endeavours can fairly swiftly learn how to position themselves alongside people as de-centred and influential co-researchers (Speedy, 2007: 132).

Whilst believing that our correspondence does not bear much resemblance to old patterns of sociological interviewing, I am aware that there are, of course, power imbalances implicit in the fact that the 'conversations' were initiated by me and the focus was ultimately the work for my dissertation (and now this book), shaped and written by me. In their article, *'Doing Rapport' and the Ethics of 'Faking Friendship'*, Jean Duncombe and Julie Jessop examine the ethics of some qualitative methodologies, starting with a quote about the perceived irony that the *"feminist, ethnographic method* [of interviewing] *exposes subjects to far greater danger and exploitation than do more positivist, abstract, and 'masculinist' methods"* (Stacey, in Duncombe & Jessop, 2004: 107).

They argue that there is a danger of misusing a professionally acquired ability to 'do rapport' in order to gain the trust of those being interviewed, in ways that could be unethical. Interviewers might be tempted to do *"the kinds of 'emotion work' that women, in particular, perform in their relationships by simulating empathy to make others feel good"* (2004: 107). Their unease emerged during recent sociological research projects, when *"in order to persuade some of our women interviewees to talk freely, we needed consciously to exercise our interviewing skills in 'doing rapport'* with – or rather to – them."

> *Uncomfortably, we came to realize that even feminist interviewing could sometimes be viewed as a kind of* job, *where, at the heart of our outwardly friendly interviews, lay the instrumental purpose of persuading interviewees to provide us with data for our research, and also (hopefully) for our future careers* (2004: 107).

They are focusing on the more traditional forms of face-to-face interviewing and specifically mention 'techniques' that can clearly become manipulative (dress, language, emotional warmth, tone of voice, eye contact, etc.). While these particular methods do not apply in the same way to my form of 'interviewing by correspondence', there are, of course, all kinds of ways of misusing power and manipulating others (awarely or not) and these are important ethical considerations that I have kept clearly in view.

Leslie Bloom has some interesting things to say about both 'interviews' and 'conversations' being what she calls *"natural speech events"* (1998: 40) and disagrees with Ann Oakley's (1981) premise that interviewing women is a contradiction in terms. She believes that *"if the goal ... is to collect narratives, then ... [it] is an interview"* (1998: 41). One of my initial goals was certainly to elicit stories, in order to construct the narratives; but I think what we were doing amongst and between ourselves took us beyond 'collecting' to something more like collaborative writing (Davies & Gannon, 2006) and the *"interpretive community"* which Jerome Bruner says can emerge in time from *"the sharing of common stories"* (2002: 25).

The initial agreement with my co-researchers was based on an informal email, telephone or face-to-face invitation from me, when I laid out my wares in a sort of 'car boot sale' style. It was very much open to individual interpretation of what they would or would not want to be doing, how this would be happening and for how long; most were happy for the process be open-ended, while one definitely wanted to be able to set a time limit. I followed this up with some slightly more formal scene-setting and practical information, such as my working title (which became the final title of this work), with some explanation of what I hoped to be doing and what was being asked of them. It was also agreed between us that the research 'conversation' would be by letter (preferably email) and not face-to-face. Two of the women live in the USA and although I did, in fact, meet up with all seven over the period of our working together, those meetings were social and not recorded as part of the research.

It was made very clear that any of them could withdraw at any time, for whatever reason, and that each individually could edit what would appear from their correspondence in the final text. I sent occasional request and information emails, both individually and eventually to the 'group', asking for necessary permissions (around such things as names and other identifying personal details) and letting them know how things were progressing. None of the seven women knew each other and, with everybody's agreement - after over a year of my corresponding with them individually - there was a brief period of email exchanges between all the women in the 'group'. These were mostly responses to ideas or questions put out by me, but there were occasional other individual initiatives or pieces of shared news which provoked replies. Whilst I and some others very much enjoyed this part of the collective experience, three of the women made it clear that they wanted this group contact to be limited – because of time, emotional energy and other commitments.

> *Telling others about oneself is ... no simple matter. It depends on what* we *think* they *think we ought to be like* ... (Bruner, 2002: 66).

Being *"in love with my research"* (see 'Research as adventure' above) made it difficult to bring the conversation to a close with the six who had not already chosen to do so. I was still fascinated by the story gathering, the unasked and unanswered questions, the things I might now never know about these women who had told me so much about themselves. My decision that the correspondence nevertheless needed to end made it clear again, of course, that this wasn't just an ordinary 'conversation' and that my needs came first, however careful I might be about respecting theirs.

So I wrote to them all, with thanks and appreciation for what they had given me – and we said a sort of goodbye, even though our contact actually continued. Each of them said, in their different ways, that our narrative conversations deepened and enriched the relationship we already had, so that we 'know' each other (and ourselves) differently.

> *Writing stories and personal narratives*
> *have increasingly become the structures*
> *through which I make sense of my world.*
>   (Richardson, 2005: 966)

CHAPTER FOUR

WOMEN ON A JOURNEY

From Penelope to the present,
women have waited …
If we grow weary of waiting,
we can go on a journey.
(Morris, 1996: xxii)

4.1 Doing, undoing and redoing

I have been to hell and back.
And let me tell you, it was wonderful.
                                    (Bourgeois, 2007)

This brief 'postcard from the edge', with its tale of a hellish yet wonderful metaphorical journey, is beautifully – incongruously? - embroidered in blue silk on a small, blue and white checked, cambric handkerchief. Part of the extraordinary and often disturbing art of Louise Bourgeois, who *"never makes work to please"* (Morris, 2007: 11), it encapsulates the story that its author told, untold and retold endlessly throughout her remarkable working life. She told us that her work was forever mining her painful childhood memories: *"I am eternally repeating the quest"* (Imagine, 2007); and then (apparently playfully) produced another stitched message in a book of cloth napkins: *"I had a flashback of something that never existed"* (Bourgeois, 2007).

After studying at the Sorbonne and the École des Beaux-Art, she left Paris in her twenties, travelling to New York with her American art historian husband and living there until her death in 2010 aged 98. She had three sons, one of them adopted in France, and continued working creatively to the very end of her life. She produced an immense collection of drawings, paintings, texts on paper and fabric, sculptures in various materials (hard and soft) and of wildly differing sizes, installations and rooms or 'cells'.

She did not come to public attention until she was in her seventies, creating her art in relative obscurity, neither seeking fame nor attracting much attention: *"I worked in peace for forty years. The production of my work has nothing to do with the selling of it"* (Ekman, 1994: 16). This gave her freedom to develop as she chose, without reference to artistic fashion or market trends. Much of her work has still not been seen publicly.

> *Recognition of Louise Bourgeois's work could only come with the emergence of a new sensibility typical of the 'post-modern generation' that advocated a return to subjectivity, to a form of expressionism, to an eclecticism perceived as liberating in the face of strict formalist norms ... Bourgeois's special status also stems from her feminist stance ... (Bernadac, 1996: 7).*

Despite this and other references to her feminism, Louise Bourgeois herself would say typically provocative things such as: *"I'm a woman, so I don't need to be a feminist"*. Adding: *"I was lucky enough to be brought up by my mother, who was a feminist, and to have married my husband, who was a feminist, and I have brought up boys who are feminists"*. At another time, perhaps in another mood, she said: *"My feminism expresses itself in an intense interest in what women do"* (Morris, 2007: 131).

Much of her work was based on what seemed like an obsessive, yet analytic, revisiting of her childhood, her dreams, fears and anxieties:

> *It's that anxiety is then transformed into something specific, as specific as a drawing. Then you have access to it, you can deal with it, because it has gone from unconscious to the conscious, which is fear. So my work is really based on the elimination of fears* (Morris, 2007: 42).

She told us: *"I am a prisoner of my memories and my aim is to get rid of them"*, and at the same time: *"I need my memories – they are my documents"* (Bourgeois, 2007). She seems to have been on a continuous journey of exploration of her past, much of it driven by an intense, passionate anger. Her early story – constantly retold through her work over the years – was of family traumas and loss within the parent-child relationship; memories, dreams and fantasies are made visible, given meaning and shape (see Bernadac, 1996; Morris, 2000, 2007). A painted text that refers to her vivid, red 'Insomnia Drawings' says starkly:

> *The landscapes of the night have invaded the day* (Bourgeois, 2007).

She wrote diaries and expansive notes for years, using language in as intense and passionate a way as she produced her other art, yet said: *"I am suspicious of words. They do not interest me, they do not satisfy me"* (Morris, 2007: 294). Nevertheless, she produced words which, along with all her other work, evoke space and territory, inviting often tortuous journeys from one place to another.

"Art is notoriously hard to talk about", says Clifford Geertz, so we tend to respond to it by trying to *"describe, analyze, compare, judge, classify"* (1983: 94, 95). It is difficult to avoid these ways of

trying to understand and articulate the inexplicable, yet I hope to stay away from doing any of those things, apart from a brief subjective description of a personal journey through, on and around a monumental artwork.

In an interview Louise Bourgeois said: *"Art is the experiencing – or rather the re-experiencing – of a trauma"* (Bernadac, 1996: 8). I first became fascinated by both the woman and her work after my unnerving encounter with her installation of three huge, steel 'mother' towers – I Do, I Undo, I Redo – and an immense spider called Maman, at the opening of Tate Modern in London (Bourgeois, 2000). Six years later I produced a 'life story' piece about it (Bell, 2006), the writing of which was in some ways as troubling as my original experience.

My tale of being alone in the huge turbine hall early one morning - exploring the towers, with their disturbing hidden objects and distorting mirrors, vertiginous open spiral staircases and claustrophobic enclosed spaces - was told from the three coincident perspectives of Parent, Adult and Child (Berne, 1968; Steiner, 1990). It was an extraordinarily powerful internal and external journey. When presented as a paper at a couple of conferences, it evoked strong reactions in those present and I am intrigued by the impact of art such as this, and the 'liminal spaces' (Turner, 1982) which are offered towards experiencing and exploring emotions.

In the feature-length documentary, *The Spider, the Mistress and the Tangerine* (2008), talking about the immense size and weight of some of her work, Louise Bourgeois says: *"The emotions are too much for me to bear. So I have to put them into sculpture"*. I went to the first, roughly edited showing of this film as part of her major retrospective at Tate Modern in 2007-8. According to the directors, they started filming in 1993 and it took five years for her to agree to appear in person at all. She came across as rude, difficult, funny and uncompromisingly challenging, as well as continuing to be as creatively full of ideas at the end of her long life as she had always been.

Louise Bourgeois told us that there is something peculiarly and essentially female about her work. She often used strong visual images of needles and spiders – saying they were benign and

reminiscent of her patient mother sewing and restoring tapestries –
to spin and weave stories with words and shapes and spaces. She
has been an important reference point in my own emotional and
writing journey over the past few years and seemed to embody the
"memory that underlies narrative" (Kristeva, 2001: 17).

The articles and obituaries after her death all repeated many of the
stories about her life which she had so skilfully woven and
perpetuated. I like to imagine her continuing to enjoy the stories and
confusion she created, if she could be bothered to notice it at all.

> *Art is a way of recognizing oneself,*
> *which is why it will always be modern.*
>   (Bourgeois, in Morris, 2007: 246)

4.2 The Unexplorer

There was a road ran past our house
Too lovely to explore.
I asked my mother once – she said
That if you followed where it led
It brought you to the milkman's door.
(That's why I have not travelled more.)
                    (Edna St. Vincent Millay, 1922)

The 'unexplorer' was written by someone who travelled far from home, both literally and metaphorically – and who rebelled against 'the rules' throughout her life. Along the way, she:

❖ was the first woman to win the Pulitzer prize for poetry
❖ became a political activist and supporter of women's rights (particularly sexual freedom and independence)
❖ was arrested protesting against the American death penalty
❖ wrote anti-war poems and plays (then propaganda verse during World War II), as well as lyric ballads and sonnets
❖ had numerous lovers of both sexes
❖ was probably addicted to drink and drugs
❖ was found dead, alone, at the foot of the stairs, aged 58, a year after the death of her husband,

Quite a journey for an unexplorer.

4.3 A Vindication

*We might be tempted ... to see something unique to women
... prevented from isolating themselves in the obsessive
fortresses of pure thought, where men compete so
successfully, and are anchored instead in the reality of their
bodies and in relationships with others.*

(Kristeva, 2001: 3, 4)

Mary Wollstonecraft was 32 years old in 1791 when she wrote *A Vindication of the Rights of Woman,* which was published the following year. Unmarried and without social standing at a time when this mattered particularly for women, she had no formal education or money, yet possessed an intelligent and forceful personality and had already published other works. Claire Tomalin, in her fascinating biography, describes *A Vindication* as *"a book without any logical structure: it is more in the nature of an extravaganza. What it lacks in method it makes up for in élan* (1974: 105).

Despite the fact that she wrote it in about six weeks and apparently *"made no attempt to study the history of the subject or do any special reading or research"* (1974: 105), it is nevertheless a remarkable and important radical feminist text that comes from the heart. It states the simple truth that women are thinking, feeling human beings and should be treated equally as such. She was a passionate, argumentative and energetic woman, who believed in justice and social equality and threw herself completely into whatever she did, whether it was proselytising, writing books and pamphlets, joining the Revolutionaries in Paris or falling in love (usually somewhat unfortunately).

In her twenties she had set up a school with her two younger sisters, when teaching required no qualifications and *"had become the traditional last resort of the penniless"* (1974: 30). Living in Newington, an area that had attracted dissident intellectuals and reformers, she met and was made welcome by some of the well-known Dissenters of the day, where she was exposed to optimistically philosophical ways of thinking that would strongly influence her.

> *Mary wanted to believe that individual willpower and energy could better the state of the world, and that human nature was improving ... It seemed to her far preferable to hope that men might grow less vicious as the circumstances of their lives grew gentler, rather than accept that women were given an appearance of virtue only by the crack of the whip* (1974: 35).

Mary was impressed and inspired by Dissenting women writers who were *"not afraid to tackle a variety of subjects"* (1974: 35), including politics and education as well as poetry.

The Dissenters, who were discriminated against as a class and barred from universities and other institutions, had set up their own academies, which were turning out intellectual revolutionaries *"trained to approach all subjects with a critical rather than a reverent eye"* (1974: 43). Through her association with their ideas, Mary began to learn to think critically about society and to make comparisons with the ways in which women as a group were generally excluded from education and civil rights, *"something for an embryonic feminist to brood on"* (1974: 43).

She got to know some of the most brilliant and non-conformist thinkers in London, including the young William Blake, who came from an even less privileged background and who illustrated the second edition of her *Original Stories,* a children's book about the extremes of suffering of many poor families. She became fascinated by what was happening in France, and developed a *"fervour for the principles of the Revolution ... unmixed with any doubts"* (1974: 93).Her pamphlet, *A Vindication of the Rights of Man,* was dashed off in answer to Edmund Burke's attack on the Dissenters for their support for the French revolutionaries.

The following year she produced her best-known work - *"thirty years' rage distilled in six weeks' hard labour"* (1974: 110), which almost immediately became a best seller. *A Vindication of the Rights of Woman* made her famous and she began to attract fervent disciples for her feminist ideas, men as well as women. She also infuriated many and in one of his letters Horace Walpole called her *"a hyena in petticoats"* (1974: 110). If she knew about it, I hope she might have been able to enjoy such a powerful image.

Mary died in 1797 from septicaemia, aged only 38, not long after finally getting married and less than a month after the birth of her second daughter (another Mary who became famous). The years following the publication of *A Vindication*, including her time in revolutionary France, were exciting, sometimes dangerous, almost always turbulent and emotionally fraught. She continued to fall in love with men who did not love her, gave birth to her first daughter, and twice attempted suicide. Then, in her usual determined way, she began to get her writings published again, seeming to recover herself and be ready to appear once more in the intellectual circles of London. She was at the start of a potentially more settled, stable and secure part of her life when she died. It is fascinating to wonder how her tempestuous and rebellious nature might have responded to that.

In her epilogue, Claire Tomalin tells us that *"not a house Mary lived in in London is still standing, and not a street or college is named for her"*. But she goes on:

> *She was tough ... her ideas were enduring ... She was ... an anti-heroine to be reckoned with. She got herself an education as best she could, she wooed her own men, and was sometimes selfish and insensitive, sometimes comical. She endured ridicule and beat it down by sheer force of personality; she faced extreme unhappiness with the outrage of one determined to impose her will on fate; and, while the world busied itself with great concerns, she spoke up, quite loudly, for what had been until then a largely silent section of the human race* (1974: 257).

4.4 My story – part four: some curious gifts

The fossil record is always there,
whether or not you discover it.
The brittle ghosts of the past.
Memory is not like the surface of the water –
either troubled or still. Memory is layered.

(Winterson, 2004: 149)

During the process of choosing my travelling companions for this journey, I finally read a book that had sat unopened on shelves in the many different places I've lived since 1985, the year Penguin republished Pat Barr's *A Curious Life for a Lady: the story of Isabella Bird, Traveller Extraordinary.*

The book was a (surprising) 44th birthday gift from my soon-to-be ex-husband, from whom I had been separated for some time and who had often forgotten my birthday during the years we lived together. He was a skilful wordsmith, an extrovert with a seductive voice and a destructive drinking habit, who had made his living as a journalist in Fleet Street, where we met in the 1960s when it was still the vibrant hub – and 'watering hole' - for most of the major national newspapers. Scottish, charismatic and a generation older than me, he had two children from a previous marriage. After the birth of our son, he thought I should be happy staying at home in a nice house in Surrey – though he was seldom there - and no longer approved of my strange need to find new challenges and my own kind of space. Although I realised after a while that we did not actually share many beliefs in common, we did have a lovely son and stayed together through some very difficult times, ending up getting married and running a smallholding in south-west France, 'living off the land' for six years. All of which certainly met my need for new challenges.

I resolutely chose not to read the unexpected birthday present for over twenty years, but (untypically) also chose not to take it to the charity shop or book exchange. Ten years after my ex-husband's death, I finally made the acquaintance of the remarkable Isabella Bird, intrepid lady traveller, who *"quietly and serenely side-stepped the conventions of her time"* in a way that was *"quite astonishing"* (Barr, 1985: 14). From being a sickly and dutiful clergyman's daughter, living with her sister and doing good works in Edinburgh, she became a decidedly visible woman in an age of stifling Victorian gentility, travelling – often alone – for months or even years to areas around the world far from the known globetrotting routes.

She wrote successful travel books about her adventures, based on letters home to her sister, Henrietta – *"long, discursive, personal, discerning epistles"* – which she would edit on her return to Edinburgh, removing most of the personal detail and adding *"chunks of historical and political information and then publish them ..."* (1985: 20). Her book about Japan received particularly favourable (and serious) reviews and she wrote to John Murray, her publisher, *"I am specially pleased that the reviewers have not made any puerile remarks on the feminine authorship of the book or awarded praise or blame on that score"* (1985: 188).

She did not start travelling seriously until she was 40 (in 1872), although she had already been on relatively conventional journeys in Europe and America as part of her search for physical and mental health. Her chronic spinal disease led (not surprisingly) to insomnia and depression, as she lay on her sofa in genteel Edinburgh, planning charitable schemes for the poor, studying metaphysical poetry and writing articles on hymnology and moral duty. She found travel enlivening and stimulating: *"I am often",* she wrote to Henrietta, *"in tempestuous spirits"* (1985: 22). Remarkably, she became physically and mentally able to cope with, and indeed seek out, extremes of discomfort, weather, terrain, remoteness, as well as enjoying living within very different environments and cultures, from the Rocky Mountains to the Sandwich Islands, through Japan, Malaya, Kashmir, Tibet, Persia, Kurdistan, Korea and China.

> *That reckless lady with 'the up-to-anything and free-legged air' ... who went breezing about remote parts ... for thirty years* (Barr, 1985: 13).

I cannot know what my ex-husband intended by his curious birthday gift, but am sure he would have read the book carefully, and wonder now whether it was some sort of (possibly unconscious) acknowledgement of the struggle I had maintained during our difficult years together to continue to hold and voice my own opinions and be seen as a separate, independent person? I like to think it might have been so, and to remember how, early on in our relationship, we were able to enjoy (usually over a drink or two) talking about – and often disagreeing on – politics, philosophical ideas, poetry, books and writing, travel, other languages and cultures.

After we returned from France - and following our separation, initiated by me – it became even harder to find ways of communicating that were not confrontational, reinforcing our differences and the emotional distance between us. He was past retirement age by then and eventually went back to Scotland, where he had not lived since a young man, and we saw very little of each other over the years that followed, only communicating at all when it concerned our son.

Looking back at the 'fossil record' of those times, when I often felt like a failure, inadequate and guilty, I can nevertheless find the outlines and traces of many of the elements that have come to sustain me since then. First, and most importantly, was becoming the single mother of an intelligent and inquiring 10-year-old boy, which seemed far less demanding than trying to find ways of reconciling very different approaches to parenthood; my son and I were now able to enjoy each other's company – most of the time, at least – without many of the old background tensions.

Living in rural Somerset, I had found work as a medical practice manager, within a socially-minded group of GPs who were willing to 'give me a go' (as all those years before in Australia) at something I'd never done before. With their advice and encouragement I began counselling training, the start of my journey into a very unfamiliar world. At the same time – and undoubtedly part of my usual 'displacement activity' - I became very involved and active with CND (the Campaign for Nuclear Disarmament). In the early 1980s there was a huge resurgence in the anti-nuclear movement, due partly to the bellicose Cold War rhetoric of Margaret Thatcher and the new administration of Ronald Reagan, along with the threat of deploying Cruise and Pershing missiles in this country and elsewhere.

Among the things my ex-husband and I had never agreed on were my political beliefs and he was strongly opposed to my involvement in the peace movement. After our separation, I was delighted to get a job working from home for a year as a part-time regional organiser for CND - which also meant I could be around more often for my son. The work included helping to set up, support and offer training to local groups (which were emerging everywhere), as well as organising public demonstrations and other events. Along with other regional organisers around the country, I was offered training in group work, public speaking and other relevant skills, all useful additions to my somewhat erratic c.v.

After the year's funding was up, I went back to practice managing and then running projects in the voluntary sector to earn my living, but continued my active involvement with the peace movement. There was regular talk by politicians and the military in the 1980s of possible nuclear war – much of it sounding quite mad, with the apparent need for yet more weapons in a world already armed to destruction. It was a dangerous time – which had its own excitement, of course. Protests increased outside nuclear and other military sites, including and especially the permanent camps at the gates of Greenham Common, which were women only. We all went on non-violent-direct-action training and I, along with many others, was arrested.

And here was another curious gift; for the first time in my adult life, my father - retired from the mission field but still preaching The Word in small Baptist chapels on the Welsh border – approved of what I was doing. Not only that, he was actually proud of me, apparently (so I was told by others). As a pacifist, my father supported the non-violent protests, including being arrested if necessary, and would occasionally come to stay and look after my son when I went on demonstrations. His approval … finally … if not of me, then at least for something I was doing.

On reflection, that longed-for approval – limited as it was - enabled my beginning to recognise other gifts, not always appreciated but nevertheless integral parts of my being. I am, indeed, in many ways very obviously my father's daughter – both positively and negatively: evangelical about things I believe in; prepared to stand up and speak about my beliefs, even (maybe especially) when they're not popular; passionate about injustice; impatient for change; determined and often single-minded in the way I pursue things – and sometimes apparently oblivious to the effect this has on others.

In my 70th year I have received another curious, unexpected and wonderful gift, one I didn't know I wanted – that of becoming a grandmother. The surprising joy of this small being, my granddaughter, coming into our lives - the delight of the love that has flooded me, and which I see in her parents - reminds me of how it was when my son was born. How precious it is, this gift of loving.

> *... while one is consciously afraid of not being loved,*
> *the real, though usually unconscious fear is that of loving ...*
> *Love is an activity.*
>
> (Fromm, 1985: 105)

4.5 Choosing my travelling companions

Women, I have come to feel, move through the world differently from men … for many women, the inner landscape is as important as the outer, the beholder as significant as the beheld. The landscape is shaped by the consciousness of the person who crosses it. There is a dialogue between what is happening within and without.

(Morris,1996: xviii)

Looking back over the landscape we have been crossing together, I remember the deliciously slow and 'self-indulgent' process of choosing the women who became my travelling companions. Bearing in mind Arthur Bochner's thoughts on criteria being *"ultimately and inextricably tied to our values and our subjectivities"* (2000: 266), I wrote myself some helpful hints which – interestingly – I cannot find anywhere among my heaps of notes and journalings.

It went something like this:

- *over 50 (at least)*
- *range of experiences and preferably backgrounds*
- *have known and lived through 'difficulties'*
- *an ability to reflect on and write about these things*
- *different enough from me, in how they think and tell*
- *(to make it interesting and challenging for us)*

and I remember it seemed important to choose women who I knew well enough to be sure they would be 'good respondents'. Leslie Bloom, in her section on 'feminist methodology', has some ideas on this:

Being a 'good respondent' is as problematic a role as being a 'good listener'. To be a good respondent, it is necessary to be able to talk, to narrate experiences and feelings, and to reflect on these (1998: 21).

I also wanted to be one of my own respondents, to actively take part in this journey and find travelling companions who would be happy to experiment with collaborative research (Davies & Gannon, 2006), where I was using and sharing my own experience alongside theirs.

I talked and emailed with about a dozen women who fitted my personal criteria and (I hoped) might be interested in exploring ideas around visibility/invisibility – women known over the years through work, educational programmes, campaigning activities and other contacts. I was surprised and delighted that they were all, without exception, fascinated by the idea, though some decided early on that a long-term correspondence would be too big a commitment.

Eventually, I ended up with a 'long list' of eight who were interested and seemed to have the time. After a productive time with large sheets of paper and different coloured pens in my hut up the garden, mapping out some ideas and potential timescales, I contacted each of the eight asking whether they could commit to an open-ended, ongoing email correspondence on their experiences of being 'older women' (whatever that might mean to them).

I had expected at least some of them to say No. They all said Yes – though one had to withdraw early on, because of a series of life events which became too immediately demanding. So there I was in the autumn of 2007, with seven women ready to go … ALISON, CINDY, JANE, LYNN, MARIE, SARA and VAL.

> … *starting from the lives of women is critical*
> *because it allows women to define themselves …*
> *and validate their own experiences.*
> (Bloom, 1998: 145)

CHAPTER FIVE

FRAGMENTS

Keep looking,
even when you don't know
what you are looking for.
(Pina, 2011)

5.1 My story – part five: Feeling my way in

*How different it can be made to appear if the storyteller
starts at an unexpected place on the web
and feels [her] way in along the thread
nobody else would have chosen.*

(Dunmore, 1995: 173)

Coming to the end of the first half of the doctoral journey in 2007, with one more assignment to go, my head told me to take the option of what was called a 'supervised individual study', rather than an eighth taught module. This would allow me, I reasoned, to do a theoretical 'pilot' for my dissertation. It didn't, of course, quite work out like that, and I seemed unable to get started at all. I felt completely stuck – my heart had not joined my head and I couldn't seem to write – didn't want to write – none of it seemed worthwhile - and I probably couldn't really do it anyway – who did I think I was to be doing a doctoral dissertation, anyway, etc.

Jane Speedy, my supervisor, responded with her usual offer of a listening ear and a tutorial. Three days after the 60th anniversary of my mother's death, feeling tired and despondent, I wept into my coffee and began to unload some of what was getting in the way of writing. November, for me, has always been a depressing month when endings are around, close and heavy, and it can feel even harder than usual to believe that anything I do has much meaning. I felt pathetic and incoherent as I tried to describe my difficulties, which led to telling about the very recent suicide of somebody I'd been supporting professionally, which had affected me deeply. Jane listened carefully and said: *"I wish I'd brought a tape recorder. You've just fluently told Helen's story – not an 'um' or an 'er' to be heard. That could be the basis of your assignment, if you want to do it".*

She talked about 'messy texts' (see Marcus, 1994; Denzin, 1997) and reminded me of the many different ways of 'framing reality' that I had experimented with in my writing over the past few years – and suggested it might be possible to transform a difficult and painful experience into something creative through telling the story in different ways. My journal record of this meeting concluded with her saying, with a smile, as we got ready to leave: *" … and of course, you could always decide to do an un-assignment!"*

An un-assignment - what a thought! I could feel things beginning to unstick - and on the two hour drive home, images started to create themselves in my head. I really liked the idea of 'messy texts', but wanted more than written material to make visible my feelings of fragmentation. I began to imagine something big - a sort of art project, maybe. Multiple ways of telling and showing how it is for me to be here now, as an older woman, experiencing loss in a world that sometimes seems not to value many of the things that I have learned to find important.

The title emerged at the start (something that often happens with me): *Messy Texts and Visible Fragments* (Bell, 2008). What is it about titles? I don't believe it's my attempt to 'nail something down', but it certainly seems to be an important part of getting going with the process of writing. I can spend a lot of thinking and imagining time - mostly enjoyable, often playful - on finding the one that sounds, feels, looks right to me.

My partner was away, so I had a week with the house to myself - and the day after my session with Jane I went to the local art shop and sorted out 12 different coloured sheets of good quality A3 paper. Back home, I got out all my coloured pens and felt tips, my partner's acrylic paints and a variety of brushes – and got to work. The pile of things on the table grew as I added glue, along with interesting remnants of material from my sewing box, ends of knitting wool, bits of ribbon and cord, leaves from the garden, personal photographs, articles, cartoons and other images from magazines and newspapers. And all the while music – occasionally soothing Schubert or Mozart, mostly Ella Fitzgerald, Billie Holiday, Sarah Vaughan, Nina Simone, as I sang along with their powerful laments about betrayal, loss and death.

Fragments

> It's hard to write
> in anything but
>   fragments
> in November

> There's always too much
> death
> around

>   and I am six again
>   and do not
>   understand

Most of my 'messy texts' were in poetic form, handwritten in different colours. Printed extracts from letters and quotations from literature and theory were cut out and stuck on randomly to the large sheets, along with scraps of cloth, painted images, leaves, ribbon. There were many photographs, together with poems from years before or those more recently forming in my head.

Helen's story

> just the bare bones
> of her life and death

> a sometimes visible woman

> who was
> quiet
> funny
> clever
> depressed
> angry
> passionate
> stubborn

> who worked too hard
> at everything

> who never felt
> that she was
> good enough

and silently
killed herself
when nobody
was looking

I made collages of photos and brief extracts from email correspondence with Cindy and Sara, who had both already agreed to be participants in my dissertation. They responded enthusiastically to the emailed images of their pages:

Sara: *"I loved the pictures of your 'un-assignment' work; very impressed!"*

Cindy: *"Wow – I'm sitting here dumb struck – with seeing my words being reflected back in this way. It's incredible! Like having someone sing a song that you wrote or watching someone being moved by a poem. Just amazing!"*

My old, black silk shirt, folded in half, was carefully sewn on to one of the pages, using soft red wool. On the right breast pocket I fixed a photograph of my mother and myself (aged three) and on the left a painted red heart. On the back of the sheet was a poem, written sitting on the side of her grave, on the 60th anniversary of her death. An old pillowslip became an additional page, to make visible something I seldom speak of – my insomnia and disturbing dreams. In felt tip pen, I etched out a poem written many years before, *Sleeplessness*, and surrounded it with nightmarish shapes in vivid yellow, blue and red acrylic paint.

It took me nearly a month to complete, finishing by stitching all the pages together and making a decorated, hand-sewn cover. It had by then become such an emotionally personal project that it was difficult to let it go. I drove to Bristol to submit it in person just before the Christmas break – it felt far too fragile (and large) to entrust to the post at that time of year. I was assured that they would take good care of it and was later pleased to be told it had caused *"quite a stir"* in the department, with positive feedback about it being beautiful. In the New Year I was even able to comply with the request for *"a few more words"* by following my supervisor's suggestion of *"doing a Laurel Richardson"* and producing a 'writing story' (Richardson, 2005) of how it had come about.

Producing my un-assignment took, of course, far longer than writing an assignment; but the process of revealing my fragmented self on those pages was emotionally cathartic and deeply satisfying, and became the foundation for my dissertation and this current work.

> *She has been looking at the external city;*
> *but the internal city is more important,*
> *the one that you construct inside your head.*
> *That is where the edifice of possibility grows ...*
>   (Mantel, 2004: 243)

5.2 Some thoughts on 'messy texts'

Messy texts are many sited, intertextual, always open ended, and resistant to theoretical holism but always committed to cultural criticism ... the text becomes a place where multiple interpretive experiences occur ... Ethnopoetics and narratives of the self are messy texts: they always return to the writerly self – a self that spills over into the world being inscribed. This is a writerly self with a particular hubris that is neither insolent nor arrogant. The poetic self is simply willing to put itself on the line and to take risks. These risks are predicated on a simple proposition: this writer's personal experiences are worth sharing with others (Norman Denzin, 2005: 224-5).

One way to confront the dangerous illusions ... that texts may foster is through the creation of new texts that break boundaries ... that transgress the boundaries of conventional social science; and that seek to create a social science about human life rather than on *subjects ... Experiments with how to do this have produced 'messy texts' ... texts that seek ... to break the rules in the service of showing, even partially, how real human beings cope with both the eternal verities of human existence and the daily irritations and tragedies of living that existence ...*

As much as they are social scientists, inquirers also become storytellers, poets, and playwrights, experimenting with personal narratives ... (Egon Guba and Yvonna Lincoln, 2005: 211).

Mindfulness, as present-moment awareness, becomes a way of positioning oneself in relation to experience without the hindrances of pre-existing thoughts, opinions, assumptions and values. This positioning of mindfulness is critical in addressing some of the ethical dilemmas and struggled involved in lifewriting, particularly in regards to contradicting truths, memories and stories ... (Marilyn Metta, 2010: 219).

5.3 Women Who Run with the Wolves

*Women's 'heal everything, fix everything' compulsion
is a major entrapment,
constructed by the requirements placed upon us
by our own cultures,
mainly pressures to prove
that we are not just standing around
taking up space and enjoying ourselves,
but that we have redeemable value –
in some parts of the world, it is fair to say,
to prove that we have value
and therefore should be allowed to live.*

(Clarissa Pinkola Estés, 1992: 283)

5.4 The power of longing

Like other exiles, her longing grew a narrative of its own.
Her desire told itself as a memory. Her past was a place
that none of us could visit without her.
(Winterson, 2001: 143)

In his book about the relationship between myth and landscape (literal and metaphorical) and our need for vision and story – whether we know it or not - mythologist and storyteller Martin Shaw proposes that *"one way to carry the Forest to the Village is through longing ... Longing not as frittering away our lives, but the impulse towards a deeper reality than just our daily chatter"*. He suggests that *"we have replaced longing with a kind of trance state, engineered by clumsy media spells"* (2011: xxvi). A trance state where we are endlessly disappointed with the material things we've learned to want and continue to strive for in this society, yet which don't fill us up as we hope they will – don't feed our hearts, souls, minds.

The old stories are full of tales of wealth and plenty which does not bring happiness, of seemingly unending, impossible quests and tasks whilst awaiting/longing for some kind of catalyst, often a wise being in some form, to achieve the desired goal – which is seldom the one aimed for at the start. In the world of myth and poetry – and in any world, perhaps – it seems we have to lose our way more than once, fall apart in whatever way, before we are able to reach the next stage of being or understanding ... fragmentation before transformation.

At this stage of life I have become more aware, in my ongoing encounters with storytelling, of the importance of 'elders' in the story world. In a group on Dartmoor over a series of weekends this past year, Martin Shaw has been inviting us on an exploration of some of the great myths and stories. As a shamanic teacher who has done his own work very thoroughly, Martin told us of 'finding' the absent women in these stories and giving them their due place and prominence in his interpretations. *"The hero stories have their roots in pre-literate mother cultures ... they were not wheeled out to support a patriarchal order* (Shaw, 2011: 123).These mythic women have sometimes been well hidden, referred to in passing or even removed altogether when ancient, dark, oral tales were finally written down and converted into 'fairy stories', with women's roles often becoming peripheral and decorative - princesses or deserving, poverty-stricken maidens.

As we journeyed – sometimes literally through the challenging and beautiful landscape of Dartmoor - I recognised my longing to 'belong' in the company of the wise old women, the potently visible and terrifying witches, the wily crones, those who point the way (often deliberately the wrong one), offer words of advice or abuse, induce fragmentation and invite transformation in its many forms. Baba Yaga, she of many incarnations, has been called the Old Wild Hag/Mother/Goddess and can appear in the guise of a cunning and terrifying ugly old witch or wise Mother of Days and Nights, keeper of the sky and earth beings. Clarissa Pinkola Estés tells us that *"Baba Yaga is fearsome, for she is the power of annihilation and the power of the life force at the same time"* (1994: 92).

As the oldest person in the group by some years, I mused (out loud) about the interesting experience of growing older and potentially a bit wiser - and wondered what might qualify me or anyone else to be an elder, as it is certainly not just about reaching a certain age. I still don't have an answer, of course, but our discussions helped give me a deeper understanding of my own longing, through hearing about the importance for the younger people in the group of there being 'elders' around, including (maybe especially) Baba Yaga, warts and all. Older people hold experiences that can be interesting, relevant, challenging and containing, especially when we share them in a way that is about offering, rather than simply 'telling'. Something happens, too, when we are both listened to and listeners, open to questioning.

> *The job of the elder is to be nuttier, more curious, occasionally fierce and more connected to the eccentricities of wildness than the youth ever dreamed. More than anything, the elder has seen some rough pattern to their life and knows how to express it through a story. This carries tremendous hope with it* (Shaw, 2011: 11).

I have already, in this work, paid tribute to a number of women elders who have *"seen some rough pattern to their life"* and have the ability to tell us about it in their own very particular fashion. Another extraordinary teller of stories was described as a *"ferocious and smiling feminist"* in one obituary: *Pina Bausch, she who made dance speak* (Steinmetz, 2009). She died of cancer (aged 68) during the filming of *Pina* (2011), which started as a collaboration between this visionary modern dance choreographer and the director, Wim Wenders; it ended as a tribute to her extraordinary legacy of work. Her artform was sometimes poetic, always immensely physical, often bleak, savage and shocking in its impact on audiences.

A lyrical and talented dancer, Pina Bausch created her first work, *Fragment,* in the 1960s and followed this with other short, disconnected pieces, saying she was looking for her own language: *"I didn't want to imitate anybody"* (Jennings, 2009). She offered us demanding and troubling images - sometimes of rage, sacrifice, destruction - extraordinarily beautiful movement and stories full of loss and longing. The film shows both the extreme physicality of the dance alongside poignant interviews with her bereaved troupe of dancers, one of whom quoted Pina, asking: *"What are we longing for? Where does all this yearning come from?"*

Dance, dance, otherwise we are lost.
(Pina, 2011)

5.5 Frightening old women

There are positive aspects of being a frightening old woman.

Though the old woman is both feared and reviled,
she need not take the intolerance of others to heart,
for women over fifty already form
one of the largest groups
in the population structure of the western world.

As long as they like themselves,
they will not be an oppressed minority.
In order to like themselves,
they must reject trivialisation by others
of who and what they are.

A grown woman should not have to masquerade as a girl
in order to remain in the land of the living.

(Germaine Greer, 1992: 2)

5.6 A Few Figs from Thistles

First Fig

My candle burns at both ends;
It will not last the night;
But ah, my foes, and oh, my friends –
It gives a lovely light!

Second Fig

Safe upon the solid rock the ugly houses stand:
Come and see my shining palace built upon the sand!

(Edna St. Vincent Millay, 1922)

CHAPTER SIX

FINDING A VOICE

In the endless babble of narrative,
in spite of the daily noise,
the story waits to be heard.
(Winterson, 2004: 135)

6.1 Poetry and 'poetics'

… history in its most conventional sense …
can also be a poem.
                                        (Brady, 2005: 992)

The poet Rita Dove says that poetry is *"the art of making the interior life of one individual available to others"* (Dove, in Brady, 2000: 951). When seeking to convey aspects of the interior lives of others rather than ourselves, I believe that presenting their words in poetic form can help to make their stories immediate in a way that is different from a more straightforward 'transcription'. Miller Mair talks about *"a poetics of experience"* and suggests *"the importance of a poetic understanding of our experiencing, of our world: poetic rather than prosaic"* (1989: 63). The form in which words are presented - how we hear the rhythm of the words themselves, how we see the shape on the page - seems to be an essential part of how we engage (or don't) with poetry in a way that is very different from prose.

Ivan Brady describes poetics as *"a topic usually associated with the systematic study of literature, but … it extends to anthropology in several ways"* (2000: 949). Doing something that could be called anthropology makes me feel slightly nervous, as well as a bit of a fraud. It sounds a bit too scientific and distanced from my idea of 'gathering stories' about my group of women and myself. But there is something exciting and strangely pleasing about discovering that there is apparently a form of writing and inquiry called 'anthropological poetics'.

Lamenting *"the generally sad state of anthropological discourse today – that is often 'painful to read', enormously self-serving …"* (2000: 957), Ivan Brady stresses the importance of paying attention to *how* we write and the language we use. We can *"raise the illumination of our human commonalities to an art form without losing the ability to inform more traditional social science concerns … the collective work of scientists and poets is in the broadest sense complementary"* (2000: 964).

Monica Prendergast (2009) has helpfully produced a list of what poetic inquiry entails: *29 Ways of Looking at Poetry as Qualitative Research*, rather like a narrative poem.

No. XIX
Poetic inquiry is a way of knowing through poetic language and devices; metaphor, lyric, rhythm, imagery, emotion, attention, wide-awakeness, opening to the world, self-revelation.

No. XXI
Poetic inquiry is called by a multiplicity of names in social science but is always interested in expressing human experience, whether that of Self or Other or both.

No. XV says it is *"most commonly seen as poetic transcription and representation of participant data".* Which is what I have chosen to do in presenting the stories of the seven visible women that follow in the second part of this work, told in their own words, extracted and 'sieved' by me from the letters we exchanged.

Laurel Richardson, one of those in whose giant footsteps I have been treading for much of this work, writes lyrically about what she calls *"the poetic representation of lives"* (1997: 139). Some twenty years ago, an academic at Ohio University and a feisty sociologist, she created a narrative poem - *Louisa May's story of her life* - from an in-depth interview. She *"used only Louisa May's words, syntax and grammar"* (135) to produce *"a poem masquerading as a transcript and a transcript masquerading as a poem"* (139). And she said:

Transforming a transcript into a poem has transformed my life (135).

Among the transformations was the relationship to her own work, where she found her analytic social scientist self being *"replaced somewhat by a gentler, more consciously revealing, more accepting poet-sociologist"* (135). Creating that first narrative poem also *"revealed to me a story of my life"* (136), as she understood that the questions she had been asking of others were the ones she needed to ask herself; and she became *"more cautious, more contemplative, about what 'doing research' means"* (152).

The story of her innovative work with Louisa May, the impact on Laurel Richardson herself and how she shared this with colleagues and other audiences (sometimes quite hostile), is fascinating. She elegantly led the way in making (almost) acceptable a more feminist, revolutionary, subjective form of both 'doing research' and representing it:

> *... poetic representation reveals the process of self-construction, the reflexive basis of self-knowledge, the inconsistencies and contradictions of a life spoken of as a meaningful whole ... (1997: 143).*

My wish, in using poetic representation to tell the stories of 'my' women in their own words, is to adequately convey the openness and generosity with which they shared their ideas, memories, experiences during our evolving 'conversations' during my lengthy correspondence with each of them. What I hope emerges as well is their sense of pleasure (and occasionally pressure) at being invited to reflect on themselves and their lives; this was commented on in individual letters as well as in the final group communications when they shared their experiences of taking part in this work.

Ivan Brady (2005) talks about paying attention to myth and storytelling as a way of helping us understand the importance of how words are grouped when we come to 'decipher' what others are saying – cadence does not just apply to oral telling of stories. I spent weeks immersed in reading and re-reading the letters from (and to) each of the seven women, gradually highlighting the passages that particularly struck me, the words that "sung in my ear". From each re-reading I emerged with what felt like new insights or another way of hearing what was being said. My own responses by letter sometimes seemed to have missed the point – or at least *a* point – and at times I felt incompetent at best and crass at worst. However, I reminded myself how little it had actually seemed to matter when this had happened as a therapist – that as long as I was reliably present and a truly 'good enough' listener, the story still got told.

> *We have always wanted to know. Who has the key?*
> *Never mind. There seems to be more than one door*
> *and some of them aren't locked. See you inside.*
>   (Brady, 2000: 964)

6.2 Sisters in poetry

How you talked! And how I listened,
spellbound, humbled, daughterly,
to your tall tales, your wise words …
(*Premonitions* - Carol Ann Duffy, 2009: 2)

After more than 300 years of men … on the 1st May 2009 we finally got a woman poet laureate.

She feels like one of us.
She's in her 50s and openly gay.
She's wonderfully visible and has a sense of humour.
She donates her laureate's annual stipend to the Poetry Society
but she wanted the 'butt of sack' that goes with the post up front –
and her 600 bottles of sherry dry.

At her 'anointment' Carol Ann Duffy said that she felt privileged to be *"part of a generation of poets who … regard poetry as the place in the language where everything that can be praised is praised, and where what needs to be called into question is so"*.

It is a great day for women writers … It highlights the way that women writers have changed the landscape of literature in this country… (Duffy, in Higgins, 2009: 3).

Carol Ann Duffy was one of the two judges (with A L Kennedy) for the Bridport Prize for fiction and poetry in November 2011. She also gave a schools' reading and an evening with musician John Sampson, who (she told us) was *"given to me by the Queen – she apparently didn't need him any more"*. At the awards presentation in my home town, she said: *"*[Poetry] *does make a real difference. We are in very difficult times and poetry is important and needs supporting, needs reading, needs listening to …"* (Duffy, 2011).

Poetry, above all, is a series of intense moments …
I'm not dealing with facts
I'm dealing with emotion.

(Duffy, 2010)

6.3 Letters and 'letterness'

My mother on her death bed (three years ago
now) stops, raises her finger. There's a box at home
with all your letters in it do you want it?
she asks (hard blue stare) – astonished I fumble, didn't
know she kept them –

(Carson, 2010: 2.1)

There is something special about writing and receiving personal letters, in whatever form they are written. I have already told about my childhood experiences of letter-writing within the family and the importance this played in all our lives; and it was an emotional and surprising discovery, after the death of my father, to find that my letters over the years were kept, whatever that might have meant.

When we write a personal letter, there is usually the anticipation and expectation of a response, as in other ways of communicating, yet the time dimension is on a different level. On receiving one, depending on who it's from, what it contains, we may want to respond immediately ... or we can wait ... reflect ... perhaps feel some 'ought to' pressure to reply ... or not think about responding at all until we choose to. Writing letters is, potentially, a much more reflexive process than many other forms of communication, with both sender and receiver able to decide on such things as frequency, length and level of engagement. It seemed to me an ideal way of conducting an ongoing 'conversation' with the women who had agreed to take part in this inquiry into ourselves.

As declared in my earlier section 'On writing', I decided to use the internet to correspond with my seven co-researchers following a successful experiment with narrative interviewing by email with Cindy, a fellow doctoral student (and participant in this work) who lives in California. Among other advantages, it meant that I could freely invite people who lived at a distance, including other countries and continents. There is a growing literature about this use of email (for example James & Busher, 2006; James, 2007) with some interesting things to say about the positives as well as the dilemmas, from the perspective of both researcher and researched.

Despite the dilemmas ... around the authenticity of participants'
voices and how that was affected by power and control in the
interview process ... the article recognizes the contribution that
web-based approaches can make to research by allowing
researchers to hold asynchronous conversations with participants,
especially when they are distant from the researcher, and to
generating reflective, descriptive data (James & Busher, 2006: 403).

My co-researchers all agreed that being invited to participate via email was a strong inducement to taking part, as it meant they could do it in their own time and at their own pace. Even the one person who had determinedly resisted using email to that point, told me – equally determinedly – that this would finally encourage her to 'have a go'.

I very much enjoyed the 'own time and pace' aspects of these email conversations – it felt like a luxuriously spacious way to engage in this particular voyage of discovery, rather like being invited to use Nancy's first class cabin en route to Australia all those years ago. From my perspective, as the 'gatherer' of stories, there was the relief of not having to transcribe endless hours of recorded interviews. My last experience of transcribing some years ago – playing and replaying tapes into the night, trying to decipher what had been said and not sure whether I'd really heard correctly, followed by weeks of writing the interviews up – ended with my swearing never to do it again.

It has been interesting to look at websites and articles exploring the ideas of *epistolary research* as a way of 'representing lives' (for example Jolly & Stanley, 2005; Stanley, 2009). At a conference on *Life Writing*, I was fascinated to hear about *'letterness'* for the first time from Liz Stanley, talking of her commitment to the *Olive Schreiner Letters Project*: *"I want the Schreiner letters to be read worldwide before I die"* and the importance of letters *"as a way of thinking about the historical past"* (Stanley, 2010).

In *Re-Theorising Letters and 'Letterness'*, Sarah Poustie (2010) says:

For writers and readers of letters, the 'truth' of writing lies in the
relationship perceived to exist between them ... reciprocity in the
usual sense of the word is not necessarily a defining characteristic

> *of a letter or a correspondence; and letterness does not rely on a*
> *literal or figurative distance between writer and reader.*

Most enjoyable has been reading collections of letters between people, whether real or fictional, where we can get a sense of developing and changing relationships as the exchanges progress. There are many examples of the literary device of using letters (and emails) to tell a story from differing perspectives. Michael Steinman, in *The Element of Lavishness: Letters of Sylvia Townsend Warner and William Maxwell 1938-1978* (2001), simply presents us with the correspondence between two writers living on different continents, who apparently met only twice, but who wrote frequent and eloquent letters.

The professional relationship between them developed over the forty years of corresponding, from respectful formality (Miss Warner, the distinguished writer and poet, and Mr. Maxwell, the *New Yorker* fiction editor), to *"a real, unshakable love"* (Steinman, 2001: xv) between Sylvia and William. The detailed and perceptive ways in which they wrote about their work, their thoughts about social and political happenings and, gradually, their personal and everyday lives, has an extraordinary intimacy about it which seems to be *because* they did not see each other in the ordinary way of things.

> *Never mislay a pleasure. I might die in the night, so I will write to*
> *William now* (Sylvia Townsend Warner to William Maxwell, in
> Steinman, 2001: preface).

In her biography of Sylvia, Claire Harman says of her many long-distance friendships, founded on letter-writing:

> *She loved, and needed, the uncluttered intellectual intimacy which*
> *depended on distance and separateness and which such*
> *correspondence allowed. 'A correspondence kept up over a length*
> *of years with never a meeting is a bridge which with every letter*
> *seems more elastically reliable'* ... (1991: 309).

That description of an 'elastically reliable bridge' is a delightful one, which beautifully describes my experience of exchanging letters with each of my seven women correspondents.

There are such riches in the stories I'm receiving ... Stories without endings, even though some [women] have wrapped them up and presented them very neatly. As I unpack them – again and again as I read and re-read them, respond to them – they reveal more, open up more. And not just about 'them'. In responding, I am discovering more of my own story ...
(Personal journal, 18 August 2008)

Chapter Six

6.4 My story – part six:
The Russian Doll Theory of Visibility

My Russian Doll theory grew from journal musings, as the correspondence with individual women developed and I began having more intense internal conversations with myself, as well as external discussions with others, about the nature of visibility and invisibility - and what it seems to mean for each of us.

> *Reading Hilary Mantel's piece in the Guardian Review last Saturday about failing to notice that women hold up half the sky when she was writing her first version of her novel about the French Revolution. About her realisation that she needed to put the women in there – make them visible – even though her research hadn't shown anything about the women – she learned to invent – because of the lack of written information ...*
>
> *"... or rather, it was there, but we weren't seeing it."*

> *As I write more letters to my visible women – both in response to them and also about myself – I can almost feel the whole idea expanding – tentacles exploring – what I meant, or thought I meant, when I started and what it's now turning into.*

> *So the meanings of 'visible' and 'invisible' keep changing, almost morphing into each other in an unexpected opening up of the potential sense of freedom in being able to be visible to oneself through becoming (sometimes) invisible to others.*

> *The potential power of allowing oneself not to have to be 'out there' / seen – unless choosing to be*

> *I'm also very aware of the choices I'm making in what to respond to in other women's letters – and what to say about my response / why I've responded – and then what to reveal/tell about myself. I really want to put myself in there,*

alongside the others – even when not invited. Yet also know that I can't tell every story I might want to tell for reasons of space, appropriateness, relevance, etc.

So I'm self-editing all the time, sometimes writing lengthy pieces and then cutting them – sometimes just sitting in front of the computer screen and letting the images and stories flow through me – and eventually choosing what and how much to write.

What is emerging – sometimes blinking – into the 'light' of being seen and then maybe being shown to others is a real choice of how I am beginning to learn to be differently visible.

It doesn't feel like that challenging, in-your-face, 'look at me' sort of visibility that I was trying out all those years ago on the MSc. Even though I know I'm trying out new ways of writing along with wanting to challenge the norms of research in academia. But it's not primarily about 'look at me' – or 'aren't I clever?' – even though I'm sure that's in there.

It's more 'WOW!!' This is really exciting and interesting and makes me want to explore further and deeper and wider – really test the limits – but quietly.
(Personal journal, 27 May 2008)

One of the images that came up after writing the above was of a set of wooden Russian dolls I played with during my childhood – one doll within another, within another, within another ... I couldn't recall where this was, or who they belonged to, though remembered they were called Babushkas. The following journal entry was made the next day:

Chapter Six

The Russian Doll Theory of Visibility

There's the Big One out front that everyone sees first –
they may know there are others inside
but they don't know

- *how many*
- *what they look like*
- *etc ...*

So I used to go out there into the world
as the big Mama Doll ...
smiling ... confident ... knowing what's what ...
and all the others could stay
safely tucked away
out of sight
unless safe enough
to emerge ...

(Personal journal, 28 May 2008)

I tried out the theory on some of my co-researchers and two of them responded by sending me their own sets of Russian Dolls as inspirations. One group of seven (see over), lent by Lynn and since returned, stood on the table in my 'hut' in the garden, where I often wrote in good weather. Another smaller group of five, from Jane, is still on the windowsill in the room where I'm currently writing, with the rain lashing against the window.

6.5 First letter to visible women

(This is an amalgamated version of my first letter in 2007 to each of the seven visible woman.)

Dear ...

I'm sending these [email attachments] *like letters because it helps to keep me (and you) in informal chat rather than academic paper mode – at least I hope it does. What I'm hoping for is a sort of ongoing email 'conversation' with you and the other women involved about aspects of what it's like to be you, now.*

My provisional dissertation title is VISIBLE WOMEN: STORIES OF AGE, GENDER AND IN/VISIBILITY. Very basically, I'm interested in exploring the experiences of older women (we're all in our 50s and 60s) and how visible or invisible we feel in the world – why this is – how different it may be in different environments – what's going on with people close to us – how is any of this different from how things were in the past. In other words, I want you to tell me stories about 'stuff'!

Seven women have agreed to take part, with different backgrounds but all having led what I would describe as 'interesting' lives. So far I've started email dialogues with ... others. I'm using my own experience in my research, so will be including my own side of the dialogue and inviting questions back from you as part of what we're doing.

I'll start the whole thing off with very open questions, which you can answer (or not) in whatever way you choose. If other, more pertinent questions occur to you, then answer those instead – or if mine just lead to more questions (such as 'why ask me that?') then that's fine as well! Also feel free to send things like poems, drawings, photos or whatever else seems relevant to you.

So here are my starters:

a) In the context of becoming/being an 'older woman' (whatever that means to you – and I'd be interested in that as well) what does being 'visible' or 'invisible' mean to you? Have you thought about this before? Does it matter to you?

b) What's it like being you now, at the age you now are, living the life you now lead? Who, what and where are the people, things and places that are important to you – and why?

c) Are there major differences between your current life and the way you feel about it (and yourself) and the life you led previously? e.g. [examples for each woman from my current knowledge of their lives, such as having changed employment, retired, experienced illness, moved, etc.] *If so, what are the stories you would like to tell about these differences?*

I know that these are such open questions that you could probably write a book or two in answer, but (if you're happy to answer them) pick the main things/thoughts/images that come up for you and tell me about them. Your answers can be as long or as short as you want – and we can just see how it goes. Please ask back any questions (including personal ones) that you want to.

The timescale is very open, but I'm intending to spend this year having these 'conversations' in one way or another, whilst continuing my reading and other research. So please don't feel pressurised into starting before you're ready. Also - and as already discussed - you are, of course, free to withdraw at any time.

Many thanks for agreeing to do this. I look forward to what comes next and to hearing from you when you've had time to think about it all.

Christine

6.6 Time and memory

The idea that memory is linear is nonsense.
What we have in our heads
is a collection of frames.

As to time itself – can it be linear
when all these snatches of other presents
exist at once in your mind?

A very elusive and tricky concept, time.

... you realise that
while you're divided from your youth by decades,
you can close your eyes and summon it at will.

(Penelope Lively, 2009: 10)

CHAPTER SEVEN

VISIBLE LIVES

When I was a child ... no one supposed
that women over 50 were invisible.
On the contrary, they blacked out the sky.
(Mantel, 2009: 9)

7.1 The stories

Through narrative, we construct, reconstruct,
in some ways reinvent yesterday and tomorrow.
Memory and imagination fuse in the process.
                                        (Bruner, 2002: 93)

What follows is the correspondence between each of the individual women and myself. The essence of their letters - stories, memories, ideas, queries - is presented in poetic form, using their own words. These are interspersed with extracts from my responses, which include my questions to them (sometimes answered, often not) and my own stories and thoughts, often triggered by theirs.

I have begun each woman's section with a brief autobiographical poem, drawn from a page or two written at my request at the end of our correspondence. I suggested they wrote whatever they would like to say about themselves for an unknown 'public' readership, after having taken part in this inquiry.

One of the elements of personal narrative, re-discovered for myself whilst writing all these letters over a period of 18 months or so, is the delightful elusiveness of memory and 'reality' - just how much our stories change as we tell and re-tell them, depending on the audience, what else is happening in the world (both internally and externally), and so on ... And all the versions are true.

Each time I told the story, the details were different.
She didn't seem to mind what was fact and what was not.
The truth is, I made up almost everything
because it was story itself that interested her until, finally,
she'd heard every variation I was capable of inventing.
                                        (Itani, 2008: 136)

7.2 Lynn

*Being noticed
in our household
could be dangerous*

(Lynn's autobiographical letter dated 15.04.09 at the end of our correspondence)

Aged 65 in June
plump
pink and purple hair

Married for 36 years
    second marriage
    first lasted 6 years

One son - married

One of four children
two of whom are stiffs
    Very family minded

Began life in a small town in Essex
    that place is the home of my soul
the woods and fields
were a marvellous playground

    My father was a binge alcoholic
I'm not sure what to say really

I've been counselling since I was about 4
and began training when I was 34
    I was a terrible rescuer
After lots of training
in several theories
I became less of a rescuer
and less intense of course

There came a time
when I would think
'Oh for God's sake!!'
about a client's problem
and the time had come to give up
    I've done a bit of clown training

I love
the theatre and cinema – reading - playing bridge
the countryside – London – travel - staying at home
friends - family - animals
good food - nice wine
    and the odd adventure

Is that enough?
I don't mind
particularly
what is in my blurb

(Lynn, email 23.01.08)

Subject: visible/invisible

WOW! I bet you never thought the day would come! This makes me visible doesn't it?

As I'm the master of visible/invisible I need to find new ways of hiding and being seen.

This was Lynn's first ever email, sent after we had talked on the phone and face-to-face and she had agreed to be a co-researcher – and I had sent her my first 'visible' letter on 09.01.08 (by ordinary mail, as she did not then have an email address). I told her letters could be written in any medium she chose, but she was determined to 'have a go'.

(Christine, email 23.01.08)

> *Subject: visible/invisibleWOW indeed! And I'm very impressed to be your first ever email correspondent. I shall be interested to see if / how you manage to disappear into the wallpaper on email.*

Lynn sent five letters between that first internet contact and when we ended this correspondence in April 2009. Four were sent as emails and were about a page long; letter number three came as five handwritten pages, produced whilst she was in Canada and full of news and thoughts - which were a delight to receive on her return.

She is the woman I know best out of the seven, as we did our psychotherapy training together years ago and have been colleagues and become friends since then. We talked about the need for 'boundaries' for this visible women work and it has been an interesting addition to our relationship, including making elements of each of us and our histories more visible to the other.

(First letter from Lynn, 07.02.08)

Unseen/seen

At the age of sixty three
similar things are as important
to me
as at age two
> *but with different emphasis*

Family/friends/quality/laughter/purpose
(not necessarily in that order)

The main difference is
I am not fighting to please
EVERYONE ALL OF THE TIME

It took up most of my time
for years

As a 'mistake'
and the youngest of four
I was overwhelmed by the need
for acceptance
and to be seen
as worthy of life

I had no power
no voice and no opinion
within my family
and quickly learned how
to circumvent anything
that frightened or worried me

My parents
took any opportunity to row
and I would be used
as their tennis ball
I had to please them
didn't dare make a fuss

I learned
that it would blow up
and become very unpleasant indeed

So I sat perfectly still
staring into the fire

I knew if I sat still
and let the conversation change
no-one taking any notice of me
I could slither away

I felt my family wouldn't change
therefore I will
The freedom of giving myself a choice
rather than other people
making choices for me

It is usually
my family of origin
that causes me problems
about being grown up
which is normal I guess

The most wondrous thing for me
is to have the choice
    and know I'm worthy of life
on my own terms

(Christine, 11.03.08)

I really liked your heading of 'unseen/seen' and will come back to that later – at least I think I will, though never quite know where these letters are going to take me!

Tell me some more about being overwhelmed ...
    and what it's like not fighting to please
    EVERYONE ALL OF THE TIME.

That bit about sitting perfectly still and staring into the fire so as to be 'unseen' is incredibly powerful. Each time you tell this story I feel a bit shivery. If you were a 'client' I would be wondering about all kinds of things.
    How does it sound to you now?
    How has it changed over the years?

Being their tennis ball ...
    What did they do?
    Could you avoid it by disappearing?

I know you've worked hard to disentangle yourself from 'pleasing everybody'.
    How did you get to the freedom / choice?
    How are you different with your family now?

My family – especially my father – kept on being unavailable. I have tried to keep enough of an emotional distance as a sort of 'buffer' – and made resolutions not to get hooked into 'If only …' but it often didn't work and I still kept wanting what I couldn't have.

Because in the past I chose partners who behaved like my family (even when I believed the opposite) there goes on being the challenge of not quietly 'disappearing' and hoping everything will sort itself out.

With David now I regularly practice 'being seen' – and he (unlike anybody else I've been with) goes on engaging even when he finds what I do quite challenging! So neither of us disappear, now I come to think of it.

Your last point …
> *What does being 'worthy of life' mean to you?*
> *And what are your own terms?*

I'm looking forward to having email conversations with you as well as the other ones we have. It's different when it's written down – for me, at least.

(Lynn, 02.05.08)

Acceptance

Your constipated collection from me
carries on …

The acceptance I yearned for
as a child
what I saw around me
in family and friends

A respect perhaps
tenderness
acceptance that I had
    a right to exist

Rarely from my Father
My Mother loved me
I knew that
but also that I was
a nuisance

An example
I had fallen
cut my leg
and was crying
I was told not to make that stupid noise
'for God's sake
don't let the blood stain the sock'
        'Oh, you are a pest!'
        should have been my middle name!!

Being told I was a mistake
made utter sense

To avoid nastiness and confrontation
        I learned to keep quiet
not mention it
 (whatever 'it' was)
        Another way of not being seen

Shared a room
with Jenn
ten years older

Must have been difficult
and she would often scream
and threaten me
        probably quite rightly

I didn't mind
I knew she loved me
Told me later
what a lovely baby I'd been
how sweet

Aged ten I met Jenn's future husband
and bathed in the glow
of being seen as
 'pretty – intelligent – fun - good mannered'
Roy stood up for me

He appeared to enjoy
being with me
        I shone in his company
I was in awe of him
The difficulty was
I couldn't disappear very well
with him

Everyone behaved differently
with him in the house
No rows
Yippee!!

        *Some of this I had all but forgotten
        and was quite painful ... gulp*

There is more that I'm editing

(Christine, 28.05.08)

Very interesting and moving to hear about what's emerging whilst you struggle with this 'visible women' business. What powerful childhood images and memories have been stirred up. You said you're a bit older in letter no. 2 – if we keep this up long enough, maybe we'll be into our future selves!

Here come lots of questions – answer whatever you feel like answering:

What's it been like as an adult to receive tenderness?
Did you recognise it? And if so, how?
And what about acceptance?
When / where did you begin to experience that?

For me as a child it was not so much about being a pest as not the right shape to fit the hole 'they' had put my name on. I imagine / hope it wasn't like that when my mother was alive – can't remember – but once she'd died it seemed as though my main role in life was to somehow take her place, live up to how she had been (perfect, of course) and to make her proud of me, up there in heaven. All totally impossible of course – a perfect way to keep me from feeling visible as myself and try to shape me into something I could never be.

I became adept at lying, pretending to be things I wasn't – and developed a complicated inner self, kept well out of sight of almost everybody.
Did you do any of this?

It sounds as though there were very different stories being told to you about you.
How did you know Jenn loved you? When did the screaming stop?
What were the ways Roy stood up for you – and who with?
What made it difficult to disappear with Roy? Was it being noticed?

I realise I'm intrigued by this 'being noticed' thing. You often don't seem to want to be noticed particularly, or even care whether you are or not. In groups you seem very unassuming and non-attention-seeking – you quietly watch other people 'performing' (including me, sometimes), not doing the 'Me, me, what about me!!' like most of us. And then (in the clowning training, for instance) you can suddenly become exceedingly visible (in my eyes) – assertive, funny, insisting on your rights in a way I couldn't do. Fascinating!

Does this sound right to you?
What does it mean to you?

I've just come up with my 'Russian Doll theory of visibility' ... saying it's possible to be apparently visible but actually mostly invisible at the same time. I think it's my version of T.A. theory with vodka and dancing and lots of singing.

(Lynn's handwritten letter from Canada, August 2008)

Next exciting instalment

Feels very strange
to be writing this in Oakville
looking up a cousin
I haven't seen for fifty years

More of this later
        Back to (some of) your questions ...

Jenn showed tenderness at times
A touch or secret glance
then I would become clingy
and silently implore
        '*more - more - more*'
And this could irritate her

Aged six
I fell off a roundabout onto concrete
and thought
'I'm in trouble
My face is bleeding onto my dress

I've spoiled things
by drawing attention to myself'

My Uncle *ran* towards me
and lifted me up gently
and cleaned the blood away
    He called me 'poor girl'
    which took my breath away
My Mother
didn't look happy

    Different stories I was told ...

My Mother said I was a mistake
but told me that when I was born
she immediately loved me

My Father was irritated
by my presence in a room
but bought me large presents

As a child and young adult
I took responsibility
for being *forced* upon them
    In my mind I was an intrusion
but loved somewhat as well

    But ... I was determined that I would exist

It was difficult to disappear
with Roy
because he sought me out
to play games or talk
He took my side
and saved my face
    I was visible to him

Being noticed in our household
could be dangerous
My parents' unhappy marriage
and alcohol

meant the fall-out area was huge

Within a group now
it feels enough to be acknowledged
to begin with
that I exist
I am happy not to be particularly noticed
        unless doing my own performing!

Clowning is permission to perform
and scream out
 'look at me – me – me!!'
        It's interesting
        that I need the permission, isn't it?

The odd bit of being assertive
is an adventure
It does feel *very* visible
but OK for a short time
I think it means a form of freedom

Here in Oakville
I'm just across Lake Ontario
from Syracuse
where you were visiting a cousin recently
Snap!

Meeting up with cousin June
and family
has echoes of visible/invisible
        She looks so like my Mother
        I was transfixed

June is tactile – warm – interested – funny
She is worshipped carefully
within the family
There are clear rules
and schedules are very important
        I of course immediately reverted
        to old habits

In many ways
June is like Jenn
Quiet - firm - pleasant and welcoming
Then relaxes and becomes funny
and far more talkative

I'm still working all this through
I know you are particularly good
at reading new families and homes
I hope you can make sense of it all

(Christine, 21.10.08)

It's been ages since that lovely hand-written letter. But our 'visible women' communicating has continued in other ways – including the group emails – and the set of seven Russian dolls you lent last time we met are helping me on the desk.

Writing about tenderness, you said that when Jenn showed this you wanted *'more – more – more'* and then she became irritated.
    What happens now when you're shown tenderness?
    And what happens if somebody wants more than you want to give?

Your 'different stories' sound deeply confusing. It seems that, as children, most of us somehow make enough sense of it all to survive (more or less) and not completely disappear.
    How did you reconcile the 'different stories' told?

Tell me more about the 'adventure' and 'freedom' of being assertive.
    Who is giving you the permission to perform now?
    What's OK about being very visible when you become assertive?

Your stories about June and the family are fascinating. June sounds like an interesting combination of warmth and control and it seems as though you did a lot better than reverting to 'old habits' – remaining fully visible and adult despite the strange rules!

Do you know how you managed to do that?

I really like your group email about being 'good at playing', and receiving and answering other women's emails as 'like a wonderful sharing game'. I'm delighted that you and some of the others are enjoying it and would love to know ...

what it is that you're enjoying?
and why it feels like playing?

Talking of playing, I went to see 'Mamma Mia!' at Bridport's Electric Palace last night ... full of women of all ages ... great atmosphere ... Cosmo cocktails at the bar ... reminded me of us two in San Francisco a few years back!

After getting all seven women's permission, I started a series of emails in early September 2008 (see 'The Visible Group' below) inviting a group response to the experience of letter-writing and co-researching. Lynn initially joined in very enthusiastically and then didn't respond to group and individual emails and I was unable to contact her by phone.

(Christine, email 28.10.08)

Subject: are you there?

Hope you're OK and have been getting my 'naming the visible women' emails. You seem to have gone strangely silent – though I'm sure not invisible. Anyway, everybody has now agreed they're happy for me to use their names, so hope you feel the same – but do let me know either way.

We eventually spoke on the phone and Lynn apologised for what she called her 'rudeness' and told me she had been *"trying out hiding behind the wallpaper"* on email, to see if it worked. We talked about what the *hiding* meant to each of us and Lynn said it was more of the *"being good at playing"* from her point of view; she wanted to see what would happen.

I had to acknowledge all kinds of difficult feelings, from being worried when I didn't hear from her, then getting a bit upset, to eventually annoyed and affronted that my serious work was not being treated with proper respect … and (at last) to feeling that what she was doing was not only relevant and interesting but also funny, and one of my reasons for asking Lynn to take part in the first place.

(Lynn, 25.11.08)

Some answers to questions

I have been rather ignoring you haven't I?

I do believe
I've been behind the wallpaper
just to prove to myself
that I can still do it
    How ridiculous is that?

But I didn't mean to ignore you
    I humbly grovel at my stupidness

You asked me several questions
which I have thought about
in great depth
but only come up with a couple of answers

The stories of my birth
were very forthcoming
from Mum and my sisters and brother
rather like a proper debrief

but over a few years
with each person's perspective
of that day

The short version is
that the labour started early
my heart began to fail
then 6lbs 12oz of red face and black hair
was born at 7.50am on a Monday morning
          They all felt differently about my arrival

The question of tenderness ...
it seems to be easy or natural
for me to feel this
I remember as a tiny child
feeling tender towards all creatures
except some humans
          If someone presses me
          I tend towards silence

My ability to haggle
has always been there
I put it down to being the youngest
and trying to get my way sometimes
It was worth a try even if it didn't work
          We were not allowed to sulk

I assume I made the best of it if I didn't win
That word win says it all really!!
Now it feels like a mini-adventure for me
          Am I still trying to get my own way?
If I am
I hope I am gracious about it at least

(Christine, email 26.11.08)

Thanks very much for this and I didn't really think you were being
rude – not for long, anyway - though did begin to wonder what was
happening ... and if I'd upset you ...

ANYWAY, glad to hear it was just you having a different go at being behind the wallpaper ... And it sounds like it was quite a successful disappearing act, so well done!

I shall come back to the other contents of your letter in my next one.

(Christine, 13.01.09)

I wanted to come back to your 'disappearing behind the wallpaper' and my not knowing why ... or what to do ...Should I persist in making contact? It brought back childhood memories of friends who suddenly stopped talking to me and I didn't know why and had no idea how to handle it.

So what you say about proving you can still disappear both makes lots of sense and is also a huge relief! But – being me – I'm now really interested in knowing a bit more about ...
Why did you decide to do it?
What was it like for you?

Your heart beginning to fail at birth is a very dramatic beginning – for you and everybody else. No wonder there are many different stories of that time.
What's your story about it?
What was it like to be given the 'debrief' by your family?

You do normally seem very tender and gentle, which is why it's a surprise when you're not. One of the delights of beginning to get to know you [during our psychotherapy training] was to realise that you were actually very feisty – except when you did your disappearing act. I was fascinated by the way that J [our tutor] seemed to misread you in overdoing her positive feedback – as though she wanted something from you and had

somehow missed whole, very important bits of you. That looked like being 'pressed' to me.
Is that right? Does it happen still?

Good question – about trying to get your own way.
How does it work between you and B [husband]?

You seem exceedingly gracious when you've 'won'!

Is this more quietly visible stuff?

For me, it's about having my point of view heard and knowing that it counts – even if I don't 'win'. I didn't have enough of that when growing up – it used to make me feel as good as invisible and certainly that I didn't matter.

I'm struggling at the moment with needing to start on the 'serious' bit of writing this dissertation, which feels very difficult. I'm still so much enjoying writing and communicating with 'my' women that I just want to keep on doing this.

When I saw Lynn in February 2009, she told me a story about her new laptop computer. She was refusing to use it because every time she opened it up, it said B [husband's name] on the log-in screen and she didn't feel it was anything to do with her. She would not be using it or sending emails until this was changed – and so far this was apparently proving difficult to do.

I sent out one or two more group emails in the early part of the year, including letting them all know that I was beginning to write the introductory parts of my dissertation and would be bringing our correspondence to a close. I 'chased up' Lynn in April for a possible final letter.

(Christine, email 13.04.09)

Subject: visible woman letters

This is sort of 'formal' notification that, as I'm now really getting into my writing, I'm beginning to bring the exchange of letters to an end. It would be really nice to have one more from you – if you can manage it! And thank you so much for your wonderfully creative and heartfelt contributions so far. I've loved getting them and responding to them.

My other request is – when you have time – could you let me have any brief, background autobiographical information that you would be happy to see as part of your story in these writings. Although I already know lots about you ... I'd like to know what you're happy to have made 'public'. Possible areas would be: age, current living arrangements, what you do now and what you used to do (work, play, etc.), anything relevant you want to say about marriage(s), sons, relationships, family history, roots etc. Hope this looks do-able. Let me know if it's not clear enough.

(Lynn's final letter, 15.04.09)

Here goes again ...

I'm so sorry I didn't answer your letter of January
I forgot all about it

Back to your questions ...

Because I'm more immediate
in dealing with problems
or other expectations now
I rarely use the wallpaper method

 It was an experiment
but I felt I was behaving rudely
and hoped you would understand
Thank you for that xxxxxxxx

I am ever curious about my own
and others' stories
The 'birth debrief'
helped me make sense of how or why
certain people acted the way they did
        Dad called me 'You'

People often only see my façade
You never have of course

As a child
visiting adults would often say
'Isn't she sweet?'
wondering why Jenn
made snorting and sneering noises!!!
She and I would laugh together
because we knew that
        most of the time I'm not 'sweet'

I try not to hurt others
but my sarcasm/disbelief/humour/cynicism
is very much to the fore
most of the time

Quietly visible ...
there are few material things
I actually want
(perhaps I've been very lucky)
so when I DO want something
it's more important
to get my own way

To be heard
is another matter
Sometimes I don't care
if the other person is not important to me
But I do have my say – however quietly
if the other person matters
I need them to hear me
I need them to know

I hope that's enough of an answer
I have to go and lie down
in a darkened room now!!

7.3 Val

I feel in control of my life
and able to do what I like when I like

(Val's autobiographical letter dated 16.04.09 at the end of our correspondence)

Age 66 - will be 67 in November
don't mind getting older
        just pleased to still be here!

I had a happy childhood
        an only child
which has helped me
to be independent
and like my own company

My parents were a loving couple
they loved and supported me
so I was very lucky

My first job was brilliant
at the Central Reference Library
helping people find
the information they wanted
        I already loved books
so it was heaven
to be surrounded by them!

        I married too young
It was the expected thing to do
When I realised it was a mistake
after six months
I didn't have the nerve
to become 'a scarlet woman'
and get divorced
Religious parents would have been horrified!

Trying to make it work
        I spent years compromising
Found out about
my husband's affairs
just before my second son was born
and didn't have the nerve
to leave with two small children

Gave up outside work
when my first child was born
but did an external History degree
When the boys were at school
I started part time
at a local radio station
and gained some independence

Eventually I moved out
sharing child care with my husband
and met someone else
        who helped me regain myself
and we lived together for five years

Was employed in campaigning organisations
for some years
and continue to regularly give my time voluntarily
My paid work has been mostly in libraries
which I still do part-time
and really enjoy

Living very happily
with my current partner
for 21 years
It works well
despite or because of
a 20 year age difference

        We're both independent-minded
like travelling
and been all over the world together
Since officially retiring
I've been able to indulge

in studying Egyptology
   a real passion of mine

My grandparents and parents
died of cancer
when not much older
than I am now

My younger son
died after an epileptic fit
two years ago
so the only family member
I have now
is my older son
   We have a very good relationship

I've survived
two car crashes
two hip replacements
and a house fire

   I plan to make the most
   of whatever life I have left

Val and I have known each other since the early 1980s, when we were both very involved in campaigning activities and job-shared for a year working for one organisation. Since then, we have often not seen each other for long periods, but have always stayed in touch.

One of the maintaining interests and strengths of our relationship (and a reason for asking her to be a co-researcher) has been our different approaches to, and ways of dealing with, practical, organisational and emotional issues. We exchanged five letters over eight months. In November 2007, after agreeing to be one of my correspondents and having received my initial letter, she emailed:

(Val, 15.11.07)

Thank you for sending me your first questions – deceptively simple but will require some thinking about!

Her next email, with her first letter (of four pages) attached, soon followed.

(first letter from Val, 27.11.07)

Being 'an older woman'

I feel older – and don't feel older!
A lot depends on the definition of 'older'
Don't feel any different
most of the time
from when I was younger

   Think I'm part of a fortunate generation
with so many improvements
in nutrition – health care – education
and labour-saving devices
we are not getting as worn out
as previous 'older' people

Don't lie about my age
or conceal it
       but it seems irrelevant
because it isn't affecting how I live my life

Assume you want my personal view
about being 'visible' or 'invisible'
rather than a discussion
of the wider picture
of 'invisible women' in the western world ...
unequal pay – glass ceiling – abused women
lack of female politicians etc.

Would be interested in knowing
what you think being an invisible older woman means
I might be one without realising it!

I'm not given to analyzing myself
Never thought
about being 'visible'
or 'invisible'
in relation to myself

Don't get the feeling
that I'm being ignored
or patronised
or my opinion discounted
It's my opinion that is important to me
I don't need
a lot of positive feedback
in order to function

Perhaps being an only child
has made me self reliant and independent
I like to be in control
and make all my own decisions
based on my evaluation
rather than other people's advice

Happy to be anonymous
when I choose
which is why I like living in a city
Can opt into
whatever level of interaction I want

At this point in my life
I can only say
I don't feel invisible in any way
working only the hours I want
with enough money to do what I want
my brain still functioning
enough good friends
a satisfying social life

and a strong relationship
with T [partner] and L [older son]

Realise I'm in a fortunate position
Financial independence
helps prevent women of any age
from feeling powerless and invisible
Hope I don't end up
like one in five female pensioners
living below the poverty line

Asked friends of a similar age
if they felt invisible
their first reaction was 'yes'
but when we talked about it
    they were missing
    the admiring male glances
They say
the emphasis in the media
on youth and beauty
makes them feel inferior

I think
paying for unnecessary medical procedures
in order to delay the ageing process
is a form of brain washing
we should try to resist!

    Perhaps it's a question of self-esteem?

I feel in control of my life
and able to do what I like
when I like
    I'm really lucky to be in this position
We lead such privileged lives
in the western world

I'm really enjoying the freedom now
there is time to slow down
and appreciate things more
    I always have a new project

I have no problem saying 'no'
to things I don't want to do

Being older means
coming to terms with the prospect of dying
I don't find the idea of death distressing
but so many of my family died
relatively young
without doing most of the things
they really wanted to

So I made a list of things to do
before I died
> *I've done them all*
> *and have a sense of completion*

Now fascinated and curious
about where mankind came from
and where it is heading
More chance to use my brain
than when younger and so busy with 'life'

The Egyptology course
just completed
was pure delight
because I had the time
to become completely engrossed

I read the newspapers
watch documentaries
read fascinating books on endless new topics
and explore the world

No longer feel
I have to be contributing to society
to feel useful and visible
> *because this is 'My Time'*

I think my next career move
will be to become a practising Hedonist!

I've worked all my life
brought up a family
and can now be selfish and indulge myself
without feeling guilty
as long as I'm not a burden to anyone else

I feel really fortunate
to still be alive and healthy

(Val, email 27.11.07)

... I found it really difficult to write a coherent account of what I feel about myself! I'm used to accepting that I function and I don't analyze why, so I hope what I have written is along the lines you wanted. If not please let me know and I'll try again!

Also I know you said responses could be as short or as long as I liked – what is your definition of short/long?

(Christine, email 28.11.07)

This ... is exactly what I want – and very thought-ful. Not that I'd have expected anything else from you ...

What a good question about my definition of short/long! Not sure that I've given it a lot of thought, but now that I do, short would be anything from a one word answer to a sentence or two – and I'd count what you have done as long (and very reflective).

(Christine, 17.12.07)

I really enjoyed your responses to my 'deceptively simple questions' ... and your questions back ... the start of what I hope will feel like a two-way 'conversation' rather than an interview.

We are certainly fortunate to be part of a generation of women who have benefited from many improvements ... but conversely, as you say, there are the medical 'procedures' which younger as well as older women are putting themselves through.

> *Why has it become so important to look younger than the age we are?*
> *And why should we be expected to be flattered to be told this?*

If at some stage I thought I had a definition of what being an 'invisible older woman' is, I no longer do. The more I read and think, the less clear I become! Which is why I'm wanting to explore women's actual experiences rather than just what gets reported about it. Women give examples of being ignored in shops or apparently being overlooked in other ways – but on asking further, it seems more a general feeling of not getting the sort of attention they would like, especially from men – and mourning their loss of beauty/good looks whatever ... I'm amazed that some women miss being shouted/whistled at by the classic builder-on-the-scaffolding type male.

For me, visibility and invisibility is about much more than literally 'being seen' ... it includes our right to be here, be heard, seen, respected in all kinds of ways. Also, very importantly, the right to *not* be visible when we choose it, not to be given unwanted attention.

I agree that self-esteem seems an important part of being visible, although in my work I have found that some loud, apparently very visible people have quite low self-esteem.

I admire the way in which you seem to quietly choose your own level of visibility and (as you say) not need much positive feedback from people.
Where does this confidence come from?

Being in control now and able to say 'no' sound very important to who and how you are. You've had many reasons to feel bruised or hard-done-by over the years, yet you never seem to.
How does this link to your sense of visibility now?

How amazing – to make a list of things to do before dying – and then do them all!
What was on your list?
What's that 'sense of completion' like for you?

(Val, 31.12.07)

What kind of attention would women like?
What were they used to getting
that they don't get now?

Feminists used to complain
about being regarded as sex objects
now they are older
they seem to be complaining
about not being regarded as sex objects!

I've never been ignored in shops
but don't think it is age or gender specific
Is it about status?
Not having an important role in life?
Feeling lost without a 'job title'?

Do women feel used and unappreciated?
Empty nest syndrome?
Lack of fertility after the menopause?

Part of the 'Sandwich generation'
struggling to cope with caring for parents
and/or grandchildren?

Makes me feel relieved
that my parents are no longer alive
I miss them and found their deaths traumatic
but wouldn't want to be responsible for them now

>   *I have a horror*
>   *of ending up with dementia*
like my grandmother
who didn't know any of us or where she was

Plan to keep my brain active
with things I enjoy
but have given L [son]
permission to shoot me
if I start losing it!

Seems to me that
>   *low self-esteem plays a large part*
>   *in people's perceptions of their visibility*
It doesn't matter how much others tell you
that you are respected - valued
if you don't feel it yourself

TV and newspapers
have hours and pages to fill
and discussing why older women feel invisible
assumes that they are in the first place
Big business has created a market
for selling beauty products
>   *playing on older women's fear of ageing*

You've set me thinking
about why older women might feel visible or invisible
Since you asked me to do this
I've noticed numerous articles and programmes
which I might have ignored in the past
>   *and the topic is fascinating*

I know you want personal experiences
so will try and relate it
to my life!

Not sure it's my vanity
stopping me identifying as 'old'
I think the goal posts have moved
I'll take care of my body
and make myself look attractive
because that pleases me
not because I'm trying
to pass as young

In the past
reaching 40 was an achievement
and age and its appearance was prized
Older people used to be respected by society
Who would now choose to look old?

I don't think an old person
male or female
can be a thing of beauty
though they can be attractive and interesting

At whatever age
the majority of women seem dissatisfied
with some aspect of their appearance
Older women seem to believe
that looking old puts them at risk of being invisible
in a youth and appearance obsessed society

There is a lot of negative stereotyping
and older women are much more likely than men
to be poor and considered invisible

Perhaps it's the attitudes of a lot of males
in society that is the problem?

I regained my independent spirit
after my divorce
My husband did a very thorough job

of ridiculing and demoralising me
It took some time to become assertive again
 to realise I was entitled to my opinions
 right or wrong

I spent all the money
from my share of the house
on travel
to places and cultures
I wanted to experience
and don't regret a penny of it

 Having a sense of control
is very important to me – and to everyone
just small choices
can improve well being

My parents both died of cancer
without fulfilling
their hopes and plans
to travel
 I had an insatiable travel lust
 when I wrote the list!

Having ticked off the list
gives me a sense of completion
I won't lie on my death bed
full of regrets
for things I haven't done

My aim has always been to do things
that interest stimulate and satisfy me
 and I feel I've done that

In this second (nine-page) letter, Val reflected on - and put forward ideas, arguments, statistics and questions about - a whole range of issues around ageing, gender, poverty, status, self-esteem, appearance, the consumer society, politics, the 'Baby Boomer generation'. As I had anticipated when asking her to take part, Val clearly put a great deal of thought into what she was writing and quoted from a wide variety of sources, including friends and colleagues, newspapers, the internet, books, films, social policy documents, etc. In her accompanying email she said:

(Val, 31.12.07)

... Christmas [the first since son H's death] *passed very quietly ... Because I had some time off work I was able to spend a day on writing my response to you – I thought I'd get as much in as possible before the first* [campaigning event] *management meeting on Jan 23rd and I have a lot of preparatory work to do for that, so my time will be more limited in future.*

Hope I haven't strayed too far off the point!

Val's 'Travel List' took up the last two pages of her letter; this included *"the places I really wanted to go to – and they all lived up to my expectations. Now although there are still places I'd like to visit, I don't feel the same compulsion."* There were 35 items on the list, from walking on the Great Wall of China to *"buying a ticket for the first commercial (affordable) space flight. I have a reservation with Thomson's but don't realistically think it is a desire I will be able to fulfil!"*

She ended:

"My list also included some lifestyle decisions which I've tried to incorporate ever since:
    Find a job I really enjoy
    Make time to read all the books I want (never going to achieve this!)
    Discover something new every day
    Enjoy every day – and celebrate every birthday I survive
– I feel I owe it to all the family and friends who are no longer alive not to moan about life. I can be sad (as over the death of H) but not whinge about the little things."

(Christine, 08.01.08)

So many things to comment on that I'm not quite sure where to start! It also brings up lots of my own stories as well ...

It's a bit of a paradox that the attention many women seem to want is mostly about being seen as sexually desirable – and that they apparently become 'invisible' without it. And this is not, as you say, just about older women.

Status does seem very important for many people ... since more or less retiring I've become more aware of who keeps in touch, who goes on valuing *me* rather than what I 'do' (or don't do, now!). Though I certainly don't feel invisible where I live.
What's your experience of this?

I don't link fertility with being 'a proper woman' but certainly didn't enjoy my menopause in my late 40s. Unlike you, I had many unpleasant symptoms and felt like going mad at times. I appeared very visible and capable in my work, but felt most of me was invisible, pretending all was OK whilst making bad decisions, especially around relationships with men.

I'm really happy to get your (very interesting) take on what's going on/being said on these issues, as well as your own personal experience. You're giving all kinds of examples, quotes etc. which are very relevant and helpful in this search.

You asked if I had 'a starting age' for becoming old – the answer is 'no'. I've been using the term 'older' which is relatively meaningless, especially, as you say, because the goal posts keep being moved ... 40 ... 50 ... 60 ... all seemed significant, but not 'old'. Becoming 40 was particularly important because it was the age my mother died – and I realised just how young it was, once I'd got there. 60 seemed very significant, but still definitely not old. Now 66 and still don't feel old ...not as much energy ... glad not to be working like I was ...but excited to have set myself this fascinating project.

Going on being interested and involved - sure it helps to maintain the 'sense of oneself', being visible to oneself.
Perhaps just another expression for 'self-esteem'?

... and there are important issues you mention of health, finance, relative privilege etc.

I have usually been good at looking and behaving in public as though everything is fine when it's not - and can remember feeling very pathetic and apologetic (and you being very supportive) when I felt like falling apart during those difficult times in my 40s – and you said: "You feel things more than I do". Strong visual recall of the room we were in – memory linked to emotion.

Is memory like that for you?
Your list ... hadn't realised how you went about making sure it all happened. Always admired and respected what I'm labelling being 'single-minded' in you - as well as finding it a bit formidable.

Do you know how it is that you are able to be so clear/single-minded?
Where did you find your sense of being entitled to your own opinions?

(Val, 01.02.08)

To some extent
everyone feels nobody knows
who they really are

I don't expect anyone to understand me totally
since I'm not sure I understand myself!

Been reading an article
about women suffering from
an epidemic of 'overthinking'
caught in negative thoughts and emotions
        Perhaps being depressed
        makes women feel invisible?

Never been depressed
and my instincts are always
to sort out any problems I have
        and plan a course of action

Have a friend who
needs to talk about everything
and never resolves anything
feeling she has no control over her life
I have great sympathy for her
and just thankful I'm not like that

Too many women
hyper-analyze the events in their lives
and come to negative conclusions
Many seem to feel
they need a man to fulfil themselves

If we aren't visible to ourselves
we will inevitably feel invisible to others
but some people
have taken self-awareness too far
        We've become a 'navel-gazing culture'
self-absorbed in pondering
the meaning of a twinge of sadness

It's no good agonizing
because someone hasn't done what you want
if they didn't know what you wanted
in the first place!
Much easier

to be straight
  and say what you think/feel/want

I don't like the idea of being formidable
even only a bit!
  In what way do you find me formidable?

And I would have said you are single-minded
You always achieve
what you set out to do
Or isn't that what you meant by being single-minded?

You always seem in control
because you are good at talking
about how you feel in a rational
rather than hysterical way

I've always been able
to control my emotions
  Only remember losing my temper
  once in my life
It's just the way I was made
It's not that I don't feel things deeply

  Very rarely think about the past
I couldn't write an autobiography
that covered more than a page
I do get mental images
they are usually snapshots
of good things that have happened

There's always been
a positive part of me
that no-one can touch
Is this what you mean by
a sense of self?

Always been my own best friend
I know what is best for me
  My inner voice is positive and rational

Being an only child
made me self-sufficient
and happy with my own company

More interested in the outside world
and other people
than thinking about myself and my life

Lucky to have been born
with an optimistic easy going outlook
to parents who loved each other
and me

     My parents had hard lives
my mother brought up in an orphanage
so awful she rarely talked about it
My father left school at 12
to work in a factory
eventually took courses
and introduced me to books

They never complained
or considered themselves victims
just got on with life
     and taught me the value of coping
     and taking responsibility for my actions

Did a Personality Assessor test
for fun
and scored low on neuroticism
high on conscientiousness and openness

I like a stress-free life
     good at reducing problems to lists
Don't let things go
round and round in my head
Commit them to paper
come up with a plan of action
and make sure I don't blame myself
if it doesn't work out

If I can't change something
I will change the way I think about it
Always believed
everyone is entitled to their own opinion

Try to make people feel better
about themselves
because I feel so grateful
    that I'm OK with myself and life

A poem learned by heart
made an impression
when I was about 12
and still think it applies
I'm sure you know it!

    If - by Rudyard Kipling

(Christine, 04.03.08)

I've quite often been depressed ... and worked professionally with many people who are. It's very difficult – can feel impossible – to sort out problems or plan a course of action. Sometimes being invisible is then exactly what I want ... not to have to respond to anybody. I've mostly been able to develop a sort of 'visible persona' to put on and go out into the world – people don't see the depressed me behind it.

One of the things motivating my research is anger at the way some older, successful, visible women seem to have turned on other women, writing articles and books, telling them they're doing it all wrong.
    What are your thoughts on this?

You're very good at being straight with people – it's one of the things I've always admired and respected (and part of what I

occasionally find 'formidable!). I can understand not liking the idea of being 'formidable' – though it's not intended negatively, more about the impressive *way* you do things – remaining very clear, logical and rational.
What does it mean to you?

I'm told some people find me formidable – especially when being passionate, enthusiastic, determined about things.
Did you hear 'single-minded' as negative?

Sure I could equally be similarly labelled – though think I tend to approach things in a rather roundabout way, which is perhaps why I see your rational approach as much more overtly single-minded than my often circuitous route!

Fascinating to hear you articulate what I have imagined to be so – about rarely thinking about the past and not re-living past emotions. Almost the opposite of me! Doesn't ruin my life in the present – and I don't spend my time regretting the past – but it's still there and very powerful – part of what makes me as I am.

I like your description of that positive part of you that no-one can touch – what I call a 'sense of self' ...
Do you have a sense of where the ability to retain that comes from?

You asked about learning to 'see' myself ... as a child, had very little idea of how to 'be' in the world – much disruption and loss, different countries, places, people. Became a sort of chameleon – good way to survive but a bit bewildering. Adapted to whoever I was living with, shutting my unhappiness away. The lesson drummed in was to put everybody else's needs ahead of mine ... or not to have any needs. So my time on my own in Villefranche – stopping 'doing' and learning about 'being' – felt life-saving to me.

Sounds as though your parents lived what they actively taught
you ... and you've chosen to learn and develop it in your own
way.

*What does your love of new information – and travel – give
you?*

(Val, 21.03.08)

You are very good at
concealing your depression
Do you know what causes it?
> *How do you overcome it*
> *as opposed to covering it up?*

Never considered you
as formidable
Far too approachable and empathetic
Perhaps people feel
envious/resentful/incapable/lazy
in the face of your enthusiasm and drive

Labels are always a bad idea
too simplistic!
> *I don't know how to be any other way*
than clear logical and rational
Don't feel single-minded
but if there is something I want to do
I will work towards achieving it

Men are better at compartmentalising
and can put doubt to one side
concentrate on something else
A lot of women will worry away
and magnify the doubt

I have no real sense
of where the positive part of me comes from

lucky genes - supportive parents

Optimistic by nature
Always expecting the best
but planning for the worst

I think high levels of neuroticism
infuse everything with suffering
Am intrigued by the way
other people think and act
especially the 'worriers'

So many people spend their time
telling themselves they are failures
and should always be doing something 'useful'
        I happily allow myself 'time off'
to indulge in 'doing nothing'
without feeling guilty

I make loads of mistakes
but don't have a critical
haranguing inner voice
        Don't give myself a hard time
or dissolve into tears
if someone criticises something I've done

I set realistic goals
very good at not procrastinating
Sense of achievement when I succeed
        a new challenge if I fail

H's death leaves an empty space
but I feel lucky to have had him
for as long as I did
and have many happy memories
to keep him alive

If I feel down
about any situation
give myself a pep talk
and get on with sorting it out

Always been fascinated
about the development of the human race
the rise and fall of ancient civilisations
Walking on the Great Wall of China
and seeing the pyramids
    connected me with my past
    and with past civilisations

Travelling to places
I had read about in school
and meeting the ordinary people
gave me an enormous thrill
and increased my awareness
of what's going on in the world

I'm still travelling
in terms of exploring the world of knowledge
through reading

    'A thrill beyond description'
is exactly how I feel on discovering
a new way of looking at things
when isolated pieces of information
fit together to make a coherent whole

My only sadness is there will never be time
to read all the books I want to!

(Christine, 24.04.08)

I'm very much enjoying engaging with you in this – gathering so
much – a wonderful growing folder of 'stuff' which is amazingly
rich.

Good at 'concealing' my depression because I've lived with it
for so long. Never sure what 'causes' depression, having
worked with it professionally for a long time. Maybe forms of

inherited tendencies? Certainly contributory was the death of my mother and other early losses ... nothing ever talked about or explained. I had a long-lasting sense of being unimportant, unworthy – left me with a strong need to 'understand' things ...

I think my enthusiasm and drive are the 'up' side of my depression, one of my ways of dealing with it and the allied lack of self-worth ... something I can tap into ... energise myself ... then try and share it with others ... perhaps sometimes I do this too energetically for some people ... a bit too 'manic'.

Is it only women who magnify their doubts?
I know plenty of men who worry away and magnify things, too!

I agree about labels being potentially simplistic – though also a helpful form of shorthand sometimes, as long as it's not just put-downs, prejudicial language.

> Struggling to understand what it's like to feel 'clear, logical and rational' – I think people value this highly in you, and want some of it ... *What's it like to be with people who aren't like that?*

Aware of how different your 'achieving' what you want to do sounds to my own approach.
Can you say how you 'work towards achieving it'?

Am definitely neurotic, with that 'critical haranguing inner voice'! It's sometimes very powerful and needs a lot of countering. Seems to come from the same place as my depression – the not 'mattering' part of me. The strongest voice is 'You don't know what you're doing and they're going to find you out' with lots of potential shame attached – needs lots of contradicting!

How do your pep talks work for you?

Your approach to H's death sounds very rational and reasonable. I know you feel things deeply, too.
   What's it like for you when other people get openly upset about H?

I've been aware of your fascination with the development of the human race for a long time, but realise I've rather taken for granted your social concerns and commitment and would be very interested to know more ...

Do you know your family history around education and rights, particularly for women?

I wish I knew more about my family history on these issues – and there's nobody left to ask now. I admire the women who fought so hard for the right to be 'seen' in all kinds of ways in this country – and it's a continuing struggle here, never mind so many other parts of the world where even basic women's rights to exist are still in question.

When Val and I discussed her being one of my co-researchers, she was enthusiastic but made it clear that it would not be an open-ended correspondence. She had limited time because of other commitments, including months of preparation for a major fund-raising event.

Sending her my fifth letter in April (above) I said:

(Christine, email 24.04.08)

> *No doubt you're well into the fray now, so I won't expect any*
> *further letters from you for a while. When you have time for some*
> *reading, here's my next letter. It's great grappling with all of this!*

She responded in July:

(Val, email 11.07.08)

> *Very sorry for the long silence –* [the event] *just absorbs all my free*
> *time … Now all I have got to do is write all my reports and then I*
> *can reply to your last response!*

Her fifth letter arrived later that month, when she said: *"I hope this*
isn't too scrappy but I do feel I'm running out of insights to give
you!"

(Val, 29.07.08)

It has been fascinating
    but I'm coming to the end
    of what I can usefully say about myself

I don't go in for self-analysis
but over the months
have tried to take a
good look at myself and my motivations

Can only conclude that
I don't have a lot of the emotional baggage
some people carry around with them
So it doesn't leave a lot

to talk about!

   Find talking about myself boring
Waste of time?
Unproductive?
More interested
in what other people do and think

It's really sad
that your early life
has influenced the rest of your life
so adversely

   Impossible to change something
   that has already happened

I like to 'understand' things too
but are we talking about
the same 'understand' and 'things'?
   I want to learn about everything ...

The men I know
seem much better at taking action
than most of the women
who seem to become victims of unfolding events
spending time ruminating over events/problems

   Only theoretical knowledge
   of what it's like to be depressed

Don't understand
how you can summon up enthusiasm and drive
and still be depressed
If you feel a lack of self-worth
where does your confidence
to share your ideas with others
come from?

Can't think of any other way to explain
what it's like to be me
and be clear logical and rational!

Just normal living
but a lot of my friends aren't like that
and it's fine
though thankful I don't have
what they put themselves through

Sometimes find it emotionally exhausting
just to listen to them
agonizing over a situation
Can't imagine what it would be like
to live with a constant internal version of that

I decide what I want to achieve
do any necessary research
look at all the options
pick the best one
often 'gut feeling'
then act and evaluate the consequences
          Don't like putting things off

I don't have lots of regrets
or 'if only' thoughts
screwing up my life
As long as I've done my best
it doesn't matter what other people think

Who do you think is going to find you out?
When I don't know what I'm doing
the best thing is to ask for help

Don't understand how a pep talk
can reinforce your sense of being rubbish
          Change your script writer!
My pep talks are designed to help me
get my head sorted out

Everyone has their own way
of dealing with grief
H died knowing he loved
and was loved
          no arguments unresolved

harsh words or silences to regret
I hope others might learn something
from my experience

I'm great at making lists
and prioritising
It's important to be in control of my life
as far as possible ...
    in control of my reactions
    to events I'm not in control of

Always felt the same way
about social commitment
as far back as I can remember
though not always had the chance
to express it

Born with a book in my hands
Both my parents loved reading
and we all made good use of public libraries

It's a very selfish hobby
Now that I have more time
I can be as self-indulgent as I want
    read anything and everything
and just see where it takes me

    I know very little
    about my family history

My fraternal grandmother
was a ward orderly
and loved jigsaws
which we did together
but she never read books for pleasure
My mother was a Barnado's orphan
with only a basic education
Like my father
she carried on educating herself

This was Val's final letter and I sent a brief email response:

(Christine, 29.07.08)

> *Many thanks ... it wasn't scrappy at all, but it sounds as though you've had enough now ... all sorts of things I'd love to say in response to your various comments and no doubt we could do some of that when we meet.*

We met the following month and acknowledged that we had reached the end of our email 'conversation'. Val agreed to be part of a limited email contact with the other six women co-researchers, saying: *"I don't want to have to write too much – really not got anything more to say".*

7.4 Alison

Transition seems to have been
a constant in the last few years

(Alison's autobiographical letter dated 18.04.09 at the end of our
correspondence)

I am a 65 year old woman
living in south-east London

Still 'on the cusp'
of working life and retirement

I live alone
but people often come and stay
visitors to the
Buddhist Centre
round the corner

Sharing my house with others
is a pleasure to me

My garden is important
though it doesn't always get enough time
I love the process of gardening
as much as the results

Walking and singing
are enjoyable and fulfilling
parts of my life

Following a Buddhist path
is the most important aspect
of my life

I continually reflect on ways
to devote time and energy to that
while spending time
with 'old' and newer friends

Alison and I met in the mid-1990s as part of a team on an innovative programme at King's College Department of General Practice, working to support and develop GPs in 'difficult' practices in south-east London. With previous experience of working within the NHS, we were recruited to facilitate Action Learning Sets and other developmental initiatives with GPs. We both continued with individual and group support work in general practice and remained in contact with each other over the years.

Among her other professional talents, Alison is a writer on mental health issues and has published two well-reviewed books. One is based on her own and her interviewees' personal experiences of the suicide of a family member and her latest is about recovering from a subarachnoid haemorrhage.

She quickly agreed to become one of my co-researchers and said it would be good to be 'interviewed' for a change. *"I am ready and willing to engage in email discourse! … and feel honoured to be a participant contributor ."*

In sending her my initial letter, I said:

(Christine, email 15.01.08)

> *There really aren't any 'rules' to this – it's not the usual sort of academic research and I'm pretty much making it up as I go along, so am very happy for questions, challenges, or whatever else occurs to you!*

Alison responded the same day, after having had *"a quick look"* at my letter, saying *"thoughts started to emerge … it seems like the kind of thing which needs to sit in my head for a bit while I see what rises to the surface"*. Her first (five-page) letter followed a couple of weeks later.

(First letter from Alison, 29.01.08)

I found your questions helpful
and welcome the opportunity
to reflect on my life now
        and where it might be going

How did I get to be 64?
I don't feel it
        though how is one supposed to feel?
Sixty-four doesn't feel old
but I'm aware
that my mother died at seventy

I live in my own house
with a garden – my first
on a small South London council estate
Moved here in 2003
from a flat in fashionable (?) Islington

In socio-economic terms
it's a mixed area
changing all the time
Hear a Babel of tongues
Struggle to feel at ease
in an often noisy
litter-strewn community
        where I sometimes feel invisible

Can't see myself living here
as a 'really old' woman
but most of my closest friends
are in South London

Just finished writing a book
and wondering what to do next
Not yet ready to give up paid work
Three words come to mind
        transitional ... uncertain ... unclear

The Jamyang Buddhist Centre
round the corner
is another tie
I attend teachings
volunteer
and sometimes just hang out

Going to India
on a pilgrimage
as part of a group
Thinking about committing myself
to following the Buddhist path
Going with an open mind
to see what comes up
        Maybe this will be a transition?

Transition seems to have been
a constant
(if that's not a contradiction in terms)
in the last few years

A brain haemorrhage in 2001
followed by a second one
where I was close to death
        survived knowing my life had to change

Couldn't go on being work – work - work
I had to face the fact
that life can change very suddenly

Not comfortable
living with the feeling
life is constantly changing

        Impermanence is central to Buddhism

Family are important
but in a 'difficult' way
Spend a lot of time worrying about them
and feeling I 'should' be making things all right

My sister took her own life in 1979
Her daughter and son
are important to me
in a positive way
> *They don't make demands*

My parents died in the 1980s
My brother recently had a stroke
then left his wife
and is very dependent on me

> *Very strong bonds with close friends*
There is the 'gang of six'
known for 50+ years
We were at boarding school together
and meet as a group and individually
We are diverse
but with a shared past
and know each other well

Don't always share the same values
but when we meet
there is much laughter and joy

Met my closest London friends
in our early 20s
living in a University Settlement
They are supportive
we are single
do things together
and are all growing older together

My home and garden
are important to me
a refuge and sanctuary
offering peace and silence
> *I find noise difficult now*

I want to be in a place
where I can connect with aspects of myself
that are more than the workaday

Trying to live with fewer and fewer objects

I enjoy gardening
a chance to think
let my hands touch the earth
watch the minute creatures that inhabit it

Took my brain for granted before 2001
(shorthand for the brain haemorrhages)
        Try to be compassionate
        towards my mind
when it doesn't work as well
as it used to

Much more 'cognitive' since 2001
and feel less at the mercy of my feelings
especially depression

Currently struggle
with what kinds of clothes to wear
        and perhaps how visible I want to be
Does it matter if I 'look good'?
I often still struggle with self-criticism

Important things in my life

Jamyang Buddhist Centre
friendly and warm
calming even when busy

Gone back to singing in a choir
and want to do more

Walking is very important to me
for its physical and mental benefits
sense of achievement
being around 'things of nature'
Regularly walk ten to twelve miles

My bed
for rest – sleep – lounging around – reading
watching television – listening to the radio
Maybe when I'm very old
I shall live in my bed 24/7?

Just back from fifth annual visit
to Cortijo Romero centre as a volunteer
I paint walls
It's in my mind a lot of the time
The wonderful mountains
the peace of the place
the sunshine and good air

Proud of my new book
but wary of looking for glory
      not very Buddhist!

In her final paragraph, Alison said: *"I've written this from notes. It's taken about two and a half hours of writing more or less non-stop. I'm not going to go back and edit it ... feel free to move my answers around ... I look forward to our continuing correspondence"*.

In my response I started by saying: *"I note that it took you two and a half hours to write* [your letter]. *I really appreciate that amount of time and effort – and hope that you won't feel that it need necessarily take up that amount of your time for each response."*

(Christine, 13.02.08)

I'm delighted this is a 'welcome opportunity to reflect' – an unexpected aspect of these conversations for some. As you know, this is intended to be a two-way conversation, so I look forward to questions back from you – and will certainly volunteer information as part of what we're doing.

Interested in how feeling 'transitional – uncertain – unclear' influences your sense of visibility or place in the world.
Is there any tie to your following the Buddhist path?

'Difficult' family relationships ... it appears that a lot is expected of you.
What would it be like for them if you weren't available?
How do you think your family see you?

What you say about friends sounds really strong and I like the importance of laughter and joy ...
What supports your sense of yourself in being with friends?

Most of the 'things' you mention as being important to you apply to me, too. Always enjoyed walking and have been in singing groups for years now – re-discovered parts of myself emotionally and physically through these sorts of activities – almost like becoming visible (to myself) in a different way. Part of what I'm learning through doing this research is the many shades of meaning of visibility/invisibility
Were these activities part of your life before being so ill?

I like the sound of your bed as a place of refuge and also recreation.

A lot in what you're writing about the importance of maintaining health and tranquillity through the things you do and the way you do them.
How did you learn about this?
What does 'serious walking' on your own give you?

Tell me some more about the experience of being surrounded by 'a Babel of tongues' where you live and sometimes feeling invisible because of it. One of my needs – more so in the past – was about 'belonging'.
Is it anything to do with that for you?

Glad you are able to be proud of your new book. You never struck me as somebody 'looking for glory' ...
　　but is this part of you at all?

Most of us have hankered after a bit of glory occasionally!

In Alison's second letter, after a month in India, she picked up on an earlier point: *"Please tell me if you'd prefer shorter replies. At present I'm happy to spend whatever time it takes, so that's my choice. I do write at length ... so hope you'll edit whatever you need."*

(Alison, 21.04.08)

　　I was in India for the whole of March
　　　　an extraordinary visit
　　　　for a Buddhist pilgrimage
　　which will contribute
　　to my continuing reflections

　　Am aware
　　of needing to hold the word 'visible'
　　in mind when writing
　　Started thinking
　　how I could be visible
　　　　in my presence- actions - behaviour

　　What do you think it means
　　to be 'visible'?
　　What might be going on
　　for the person doing the seeing?

Someone in India
mocked me (quite gently)
when I read aloud
from a radical political hoarding
in what they heard as
        my upper middle-class voice
Well ...
that *is* my voice
and whether it is visible
doesn't bother me

Would like to be much more visible
in the way I dress
Usually wear clothes
        which enable me not to be noticed

Admire the clothes you wear
which are often striking
Always notice what you are wearing

Highly visible in India
often the only white westerners
on the 'Buddhist trail'
Them staring at us staring at them
It felt very comfortable
a mutual interest or even curiosity
        Does being part of a group
        confer individual invisibility?

Work helps me feel visible
in the world
Being asked to do some work
seems to confer 'visibility' doesn't it?
Work in the future is unclear
it matters to me
        and will be felt as a major loss

After my two craniotomies
I sat up in bed and told a visitor
'When I leave here
I'm going to be a Buddhist or a Quaker'

Needed to rethink my life

More certain now
that I want to follow the Buddhist path
It's about how you use your mind
Mayhana is about benefiting oneself
and all sentient beings
> *Offers a coherent set*
> *of moral and ethical values*

We all seek happiness
and happiness does not depend on material wealth

Growing older
I like the focus of being mindful
of inevitable death
not frittering time away
> *being responsible for ourselves*
> *and how we live our lives*

My brother says
'Life is BAD
but I try and think of good things'
Talked to him
about how to deal with all this cognitively

I have created his dependency
taken on the role
and am learning about
the Buddhist concept of
'compassionate detachment'

My friends know me
have 'seen' me over many years
I can be 'me' – be myself
spontaneous – genuine - real
accepted warts and all
in contrast to my tendency to be
> *highly self-critical and uncompassionate*

On further reflection about my bed
it can indeed be a refuge
I still experience overwhelming mental fatigue
However in the last year
I've had some difficult times at night
worrying about anything and everything
         Perhaps because of depression
         am a lark rather than an owl

Often make myself visible
by talking a lot about myself
Can be witty and amusing
but it's not congruent
with being a Buddhist
cherishing of others and less of self

If I was more self-confident
and compassionate towards myself
maybe I would be less gabby about myself
         Would this mean being less 'visible'?

Do sometimes feel 'invisible'
particularly when out on my own
in my increasingly multi-ethnic neighbourhood

This is an issue for many people
but I think it's about being
middle class and English
Perhaps also about being single
         Does being with others confer visibility?
A neighbour's child was puzzled
that I don't have children or grandchildren

I think it *is* about a sense of belonging
and feel I 'belong' in our row of six houses
where we all know each other

My book is in my voice
and includes excerpts from my diary
after 2001
and will make me highly visible

I do look for glory
sometimes
but hope my book fits
the Buddhist idea of
      benefit to all sentient beings

In my next letter, I told Alison: *"I'm happy for you to send me replies of whatever length you choose – and will, of course, be doing a lot of editing eventually. But I'm delighted … that you're happy to spend whatever time it takes – and at the moment I'm very happily gathering stories without currently thinking much at all about the theoretical dissertation. It's become simply (?) my inquiry, with other interested women, into what's important, what we're discovering, at this stage of our lives."*

(Christine, 17.05.08)

The word 'visible' has begun to mean so many different things to me (and my correspondents) that a definition has almost become irrelevant. Being 'visible' is not just about being seen by others but also by ourselves – knowing enough about ourselves and being able to live with that knowing, in whatever way we choose (or find) to do this. So the most important 'person doing the seeing' becomes oneself, rather than external onlookers – *it's not about the eyes of the world.*

What a lovely thing to say about what I wear. Clothes matter to me – always have done – though I was brought up to believe that was wrong, almost sinful! I notice your clothes, too, and think they really suit you – long skirts, jackets in lovely materials. Never thought you not noticeable.

What would you like to change about your clothes?
What difference might that make?

You would, of course, have been highly visible in all kinds of ways on your pilgrimage in India. I have always found staring and being stared at very uncomfortable - and interested that you didn't
   Is that usual for you?

It brings out all my inhibitions and embarrassments. Being part of a group does seem to confer individual invisibility – which can be both positive and negative, depending on who's there, who's doing what and why etc.
   What are your thoughts on this?

Work does seem to provide a very powerful form of 'visibility' – found it very affirming during my years of self-employment to eventually stop having to seek out work and be sought instead. Been surprised not to miss it or the apparent status, perhaps because I took the decision to stop. Miss the money but wouldn't want to work like that any more. Many people find it incredibly painful to leave that 'world of work'.

   What will be the major losses for you when you do retire?

Very interested in what you're saying about Buddhism and your decision to follow this path after your major brain surgery.
   How did you go back into the world after your craniotomies?
   How visible did you feel?
   What helped and what didn't?

Buddhist concepts ... practising 'compassionate detachment' ...
   Does this help with the ongoing 'mental fatigue' you mention?
   What are the other ways you use this towards yourself / your worries?

You have talked about your home as a refuge and sanctuary –
and also seem able to be very hospitable, inviting people to
stay in an open way. I'm very protective of my space and need
to know that I can be alone when needed. So I'm wondering ...
how do you manage sharing your space with others?

(Alison, 23.06.08)

> The physical act
> of looking at myself
> is always strange
> Stare in the mirror
>> *and not sure what I'm seeing*
>
> Reminds me
> of seeing the image of one's brain
> on the monitor of a scanner
> how the mind can watch the mind
>
> Frequently feel very anxious
> about growing older
>> *and whether my mind*
>> *is ageing at an 'appropriate' rate*
>
> Caught up in worrying
> how other people see me
> Nearly always assume
> a critical kind of 'seeing'
> by others
>> *Perhaps I could see myself*
>> *more compassionately?*
>
> But comfortable being stared at
> in India
> as part of a group
> Being white
> and with a colonial history
> did I just feel slightly superior?

I'd like to look more elegant
but clothes would have to be comfortable
Don't think I could ever spend a lot of money on clothes
Most of mine come from charity shops

    Quite like being visible in groups
to be more in the forefront
Often want to be the organiser
Could be a better listener

Feel very visible in my work
Really hard to figure out
what the major losses will be if I wind down
reduce or even stop paid work completely
    Money 'coming in' matters a lot to me

How would I want to spend the days
now occupied with work?
Have I earned the 'right' to retire?
Would voluntary work
give me the feeling of being wanted and needed?

I'll return to your questions later about
going 'back into the world' after major brain surgery
So many issues ...
physical appearance
self-confidence
    What helped were my 'tools for recovery'
It's all in my book

Since finishing the book
    I sit and wait for 'desires' to arise
Don't cope well with mental fatigue
and sometimes get very bad headaches

Am trying to follow Buddhist practice
and treat myself and my mind
sympathetically
and be gentle with myself

Part of this is
    learning to say 'no'

With house guests
most of the Buddhist folk are fine
When people leave
I reclaim my house for myself
Asked to have permanent lodgers
recently but firmly said NO!

A final – new? – thought
Gone back to my 'Can't Sing' Choir
and would love to be able to sing as well as before
Gone from alto to ?? tenor??
Perhaps this is a loss of ageing

(Christine, 31.07.08)

Back from two weeks in the US for a big family celebration –
cousin's 50th wedding anniversary. She and I lost touch over
the years, met up again in the 1990s after 40 years and been
in regular touch since – she feels like the sister I never had.
There's a large extended family I'd heard about but never met
before. It was an emotional time – lots of stories to tell and be
told – as I get older, saying goodbye to people who live a long
way away gets harder ... *a whispered thought that it might be
the last time I see them.*

It's brought up lots of different thoughts about visibility and how
important it feels to actually *see* the people I care about – no
doubt because of my family history of people regularly going
away.

Back to your letter – and thank you for your thoughtful
responses to my questions ...

I don't really believe people who say they're not concerned about how they're seen, or bothered by critical 'seeing'.

How could you see yourself through more compassionate eyes?

About the advantages of sometimes being less visible – I certainly don't miss the unwanted verbal and other attention from men as I get older – seems like a real advantage of *not* being seen in that way.

What's your experience of this?

When we first met, I found you very confident and outgoing. I used to be a real shrinking violet in groups and was full of admiration for (as well as quite resentful of!) people who could speak out. Certainly experienced the pleasure of being visible as I grew more confident and could do previously unthinkable things – but still sometimes feel overwhelmed and want to vanish.

What do you get from 'being in the forefront'?
What does being 'a better listener' mean to you?

Your thoughts on work and possible retirement – positives and negatives – are very pertinent at this stage of our lives. I really like that idea of 'waiting for desires to arise'.

My desires have certainly changed since more or less retiring from paid work – but there needed to be the space to allow that. Made a bad decision to take on some well-paid consultancy work at the start of the year – mostly to pay for the time in the US – but my gut reaction was that I didn't want it – and I was right – it was awful, with a very difficult group, totally exhausting and very negative all round (despite the money). I was recently offered some more of the same and I very firmly said NO!

Do you pay attention to gut reactions?

I can understand your not liking it when people assume your fatigue is due to ageing – assumptions are not usually helpful. However, I find it quite useful to remind *myself* that I'm 66 and it's normal to get more tired than I used to – perhaps a bit like the seeing oneself through more compassionate eyes?

About the generous way you share your house ...
How to you go about reclaiming it for yourself?

I find ordinary invited guests difficult enough now and don't want to constantly have to pay attention to other people's needs. Having spent most of my life putting everybody else's needs ahead of mine (resentfully, of course) could have something to do with it! Discovered that being quietly in my own space is one of the ways in which I maintain my visibility/sense of self.

Always loved singing – about connectedness within myself as well as with others – the sound of voices harmonising – being able to play about with it. I've also gone from alto to tenor from choice and am really enjoying it. The community choir I'm in does 'busking' performances on the street for charity or whatever – so I suppose it's also quite a visible thing to do. But it's much more about the absolute pleasure of it – physical and emotional.
Have you always sung?
What do you enjoy about it?

(Alison, 03.09.08)

Lovely to hear about your US trip
and meetings with extended family
Made me feel quite envious!
How wonderful to have these experiences
set against your early losses

How did you keep it together as a child?

When we first met
thought you incredibly confident
clever and successful!

Sometimes feel like a small child
    Look at me ... notice me!
People may admire or respect me
but do they love/like me?
Don't remember
feeling particularly loved
as a child

Am trying to work on my more negative qualities
envy and clinging attachment
and also reflect on my good qualities
    my generosity for example

Recently had a new haircut
and bought a very pretty blouse
with a plunging neckline
Quite unlike me but I love wearing it!
Thinking about buying
non-charity shop clothes
perhaps softer swirlier skirts?

Never sought or attracted
the 'wolf whistle' sort of male attention
but now quite like being offered
a seat on a crowded Tube train

    A summer of 'no desires'
no energy or enthusiasm
for usual pursuits
like reading – gardening – concerts – galleries
Walking is the only thing I've wanted to do

Reclaim my house
by stripping the beds and
doing the laundry

as soon as guests have walked out the door
Enjoy having the space back for me

Drawn up a kind of plan
of Buddhist practice
for next few months
hope I'm not becoming a 'Buddhist bore'

Some post-book publication depression
and continuing struggles
with work or not-work
Want to stop when I decide
not when work dries up

Check my bank balances rather obsessively
and miss the whole sequence of
a) asking to do some work
b) doing it on time
c) being paid

Trying to work out
what a meaningful existence might be
for my life as it is now
retirement as opportunity
rather than threat?

Sung in school choirs and church
Can't remember why I stopped
Music can be fun
and very moving
Energy - enjoyment - relaxation

(Christine, 07.10.08)

Glad you enjoyed hearing about the US trip and all that family stuff. From our 'group' emails, you will have gathered that 'visible woman' Sara is the cousin who had the 50th wedding anniversary in the US. She's a year older than me and our fathers were brothers and both of them absent (in different ways). Been a real delight to get back in touch and slowly begin to get to know each other as adults, mostly by email.

Not sure how I kept it together as a child ... mostly by retreating into my head ... a very full fantasy life ... invented alternative family histories to replace what was actually happening. Better when my two older brothers were around as I felt part of a unit of three – but every time they went off to boarding school it was yet more loss.

> *How did 'not feeling loved' manifest for you as a child?*
> *What's it like for you not to be noticed?*

Sounds like some physically visible things are going on!
> *Any non-charity shop 'softer swirlier skirts' yet materialised?*

I like your ability to feel good about being offered a seat on the Tube, as well as being able to laugh at the 'older woman' part of it.

Very interested in your thoughts and reflections on Buddhist practice and don't at all find you becoming 'a bore' about it – sounds such an important part of your life now that it fits absolutely with what I'm asking you to write about. This includes your approaches to work/not-work – especially the idea of retirement as an opportunity rather than a threat. My own experience leads me to believe it can be – but know it doesn't feel like that to many people.

> *Could you say more about your 'post-book publication depression'?*

(Alison, 31.10.08)

Been more or less housebound
with sciatica
and wondering
are the illnesses of old age invisible?

Not been clothes shopping
So few attractive clothes
for older women
Are we meant to be invisible/dowdy?
Confused about how I want to look

Not sure what 'love' means
for children or adults
Perhaps for children
it's about attachment?

Mother not very demonstrative
and her mother didn't like babies or children
Father had a domineering controlling mother
and was like that himself
unpredictable – sudden rages

Homesick when first
sent away to school
but what was I missing?

Find it hard
to put my own needs/wishes/agendas to one side
and focus on the other person
Still puzzled about that
*but don't know what it's like
not to be noticed*

Post-book depression
a gap of a major focus
Hard to accept as 'true'
the positive feedback from friends
Lacking feedback from professionals
but now … Yippee!

a very nice review (attached)
>   *Trying to hold on to*
>   *the positive comments about me*

Trying to believe
voluntary work at the Buddhist Centre
is as much needed and appreciated
as writing a book

When I told a GP friend
about a hospital appointment mix-up
she said
>   *'Why didn't you tell them who you are?'*
Was this an injunction to make myself more visible
rather than letting them
shove me to the back of the queue again?
I laughed and said
>   *'Well, who am I?'*

In late November Alison sent me some information and postcards of paintings from the 'WOW!! Wild Old Women' art exhibition in London from November 2008 to January 2009 (see 'Examining the Bones' above).

(Christine, 28.11.08)

I hope your sciatica has improved – along with the restrictiveness of being housebound and inactive. Had a painful experience of it as one of the unexpected (and unseen by others) consequences of being pregnant. I don't think the apparent invisibility of certain conditions just affects older people – but your 'wondering' about this seems very pertinent as there are many invisible ailments connected to getting older – loss of hearing, reduced vision, all sorts of aches and pains – demoralising as well as disabling. Many older people tend to 'grin and bear it' in silence – so others don't think about why they're moving so slowly – not getting out of the way quickly enough – and just get impatient.

Enjoy the visibility that comes with dressing as I like – as an older woman have felt more confident about how I look. Didn't know how to find my own style when young and brought up to think it was wrong to bother about it.

What's your clothes history/story?

Your question about what you were missing when you were homesick at school is fascinating and poignant ...
Have you experienced those kinds of feelings since then?

When I went to Australia (aged 20) couldn't wait to get away from my family – when I felt 'homesick' occasionally, didn't have a clue what I was missing – it certainly wasn't places. Now think it was the *idea* of companionship and love, which I was always seeking and very seldom experienced.

Intrigued by your saying you don't know what it's like not to be noticed. Find it almost impossible to imagine – getting attention always made me feel embarrassed or guilty – or both!

Have you always experienced being noticed?

Fantastically good review of your book and I hope you're still holding on to the positive comments – you write so well.

How do you 'measure' your voluntary work?

Loved the WOW!! stuff and hope to be able to go and see the 'thrillingly, vividly visible' works.

Alison sent me a card at Christmas saying: *"I've really enjoyed
writing for your thesis this year – the next letter will hopefully be
written late December."*

(Alison, 11.01.09)

> Made time during my week in Spain
> to draft this reply
> I was in a rather irritable
> 'grumpy old(er) woman' mood
> > *Didn't want to be part of the group*
> at Cortijo Romero
> usually the highlight of my year
>
> Been feeling like this
> for some weeks
> Not sure what the causes are
> but over Christmas
> and the run-up to it
> > *everything was too much*
> > *and too little silence*
>
> Too much planning
> cooking
> shopping
> eating
> too many presents
> > *oh how ungrateful I am!*
>
> My episode of sciatica
> re-awakened memories
> of my recovery in 2001 – and beyond
>
> Swallowing pills
> Painful broken nights
> > *Not being part of Well-Land*
> Nice social occasions cancelled
> and a sense of being 'excluded'
> Took a week to get proper pain relief

Don't want to be one of
the 'invisible' older patients
a burden and not very interesting

Positively ...
the same trio of good friends
came round and shopped and cooked
Folk from the Buddhist Centre
offered visits and help
        Perhaps a rehearsal
        for the infirmities of old age?

Thanks for your question about clothes!
        Evoked memories of childhood
Dearly loved tartan trousers
Pink velvet party cloak
My sister and I
were close in age
and often wore twinnish clothes
matching dresses with lace collars
cardigans with silver buttons

As an adult
not much of a story with clothes
        No energy currently to 'dress up'
Hope this depressed phase won't last
Surprised that a friend said recently
she thought I dressed with style

My feelings towards my family
have generally been
wanting to keep them at arm's length
as they have often been a source of suffering

My Buddhist teacher
has been talking about love and compassion
which has helped me understand them better
        Sort of made sense to me
'Love' as wanting others to be happy
'Compassion' as wanting to lessen their suffering

Wanted to push people away
during my week in Spain
and do things on my own
      Difficult to feel loving
      or compassionate

Still struggling hard
with accepting that voluntary work
is as much needed
as writing a book

Feeling depressed that this book
will not have the same impact
as my previous one
nor lead to the same invitations
to train – lecture - appear on TV

      Sorry this is rather grumpier than usual

(Christine, 15.02.09)

Been really ill with chest infection and didn't go out of the house for two weeks. Can't remember when that last happened – and still dismayingly low in energy. Finally emerged clutching David's arm and feeling like an old woman ...not an experience I wish to get used to. Still feel an edge of childish resentment at hearing people talk about how good things/events were that I missed out on! Talk about feeling invisible...

   What does being part of Well-Land mean to you?

Everything you said about Christmas and the 'too much of everything' makes absolute sense to me – including (and especially) the 'too little silence'. Decided years ago to stop most of the Christmas 'stuff', including all that over-eating and giving and receiving mostly unwanted and certainly not needed presents. I was surprised (and delighted) by the positive response from almost everybody.

How do you get the silence you need at these times?

Enjoyed your clothes stories from childhood – and interested that you're still surprised by being told other people think you dress well – and in the contrast between your childhood stories – vivid, colourful, lively, evocative – and your adult one of not having much of a story.

Any further thoughts on this?

You wondered about your irritation with some people whose appearance seems deliberately 'in your face' visible. I could feel a strong personal response – wanting at this stage of my life to be allowed to feel intolerant and impatient sometimes – having gone through my life trying very hard to be understanding and accepting!

Love ... and compassion ... so many different definitions. Used to believe in romantic love – it was very painful when it kept not working and I would struggle to keep hold of something and suffer when it eluded me again. Seems simpler and also much more complicated now, with a better understanding and experience of loving real people (including, of course, my son – a powerful, astonishing kind of love) rather than this elusive thing I longed for.

Who really knows what love is?

And about your book ...
    What were your hopes?
    What does this mean about your own 'visibility'?

You seemed more honest than grumpy ...

At the end of this letter, I mentioned starting to write my dissertation ... and getting stuck ... and my supervisor reminding me to look at 'the spaces between'. I told Alison: *"I'm looking for the 'spaces' in which to start writing about all the stories I've been so happily gathering ... it feels as though it's about finding silence as well."* Shortly afterward, we agreed that her reply would be the end of our correspondence.

(Alison, 03.03.09)

> *Had my 65th birthday in February*
> a day to remember
> not because of my age
> but for snow snow and yet more snow
> My planned supper with friends
> was cancelled
>
> Everyone seemed to be enjoying themselves
> with snowballs and snowmen
> (but what about snow-women?)
>
> One friend insisted that 65 was really important
> and I felt quite irritated by that
> We don't all think and feel the same!
>
> My grumpiness is still around
> but ...
> > *some wants and desires are emerging*
> Now really know
> I want to do more singing
> and must figure out how
>
> Regained some enthusiasm
> for gardening
>
> Being part of Well-Land
> > *means being part of what's going on*
> not having to miss out on things
> because of illness

Had to cancel
so many things
because of my sciatica
Used to hate people who 'stood me up'
but am a bit more accepting these days

A common thread
       Back problems and brain haemorrhages
       are both semi-invisible 'conditions'

Would love to be able to have
a 'slimmed-down' Christmas
but can't imagine it going down well
with family and friends

Find it hard to keep 'difficult' family
at arm's length
Most people find my wish to do this
very strange and not very nice

Get the silence I need
by mostly living alone

Although silence can be external
there's also
what goes on in my head
       Sometimes too much going round my mind

I loved your saying
you just want to be allowed to be
intolerant and impatient sometimes
BUT get very low
realising that as a Buddhist
       this is not the way
       I want to think - feel - behave

With my previous book
       all that visibility was great fun
very affirming
I've no idea where this one has gone
or who reads it

Perhaps some more publicity
would have been a bridge
between full-time work
and something approaching retirement?

At the end of our correspondence, Alison and I had a series of email exchanges which seemed an important continuation of that exploration of meaning and the 'spaces' between us - an integral part of this co-researching with all the women involved.

(Christine, 15.02.09)

> I really enjoy your letters and your ability to reflect, occasionally chuck things back at me or choose not to go down an alleyway I've signposted, whilst coming up with a variety of stories, images and memories. So thank you, once again.

(Alison, 03.03.09)

> I felt quite – what did I feel? – reading that comment. How hypersensitive I am being! The little-girl Alison is saying: "I've tried my best". I mention this as it was a spontaneous reaction on my part ...
>
> Writing today, I realise how hugely I've enjoyed being part of your dissertation research because it's given me the chance to be heard – by you – and possibly by others? A wonderful exercise in visibility and focusing on myself!

(Christine, 13.04.09)

> *Before ending this bit of the co-researching, I want to come back to ... what you called your 'hypersensitive' and 'little-girl Alison' response ...*
>
> *Looking at what I said ... I hope it's OK if I more or less repeat it, adding that your 'best' has been not just very good but exactly what I wanted. I have really enjoyed your letters, your ability to articulate so fluently and in such a reflective way, and your honesty and strength in choosing which questions of mine you wanted to answer. I genuinely appreciate how you've done this and really did mean what I said at the very beginning* [about choosing to answer or not answer questions] ...
>
> *Let me know if there is anything else we need to explore around this – or any lingering difficult feelings.*

(Alison, 18.04.09)

> *I want to say ... how much I appreciate your comments about my written contributions to your dissertation. I think the issue you raised about my 'little-girl response' is worth a bit more from me. (That's probably why I've been mulling over what you said since your email arrived earlier this week.)*
>
> *I think the 'little girl' bit relates to me and my father and how difficult it was (and still is, though he's been dead nearly 20 years) to be my own person and do my own thing. Perhaps one of the ways I've coped with that has been working for other people and therefore pleasing them – and perhaps I've wanted to please you as part of that! So no hard feelings at this end – really!*

7.5 Cindy

I love not knowing things
and exploring new places and ideas

(Cindy's autobiographical letter dated 19.05.09 at the end of our
correspondence)

I am a 53 years young professional
in California near San Francisco
A licensed narrative therapist

Student Advocate
a friendly name for therapist
in a large high school
for over a decade

Previously
worked in computer industry
building facilities - managing budgets
and before that in construction

Part of a happy family
with two adopted Chinese girls
a lovely Italian/American wife
and our dog Marley

We are political
and we are busy!

Soccer
track and field meets
violin recitals
running and tennis lessons
working in the garden
making arts and crafts
school projects
meditating
lots of reading

homework
seeing and writing to friends

Typical family activities too
like cooking and doing dishes
laundry and other stuff
Lesbian families
can be just as boring
as anyone else!

Working on my EdD degree
for the last four and half years
Recently finished
and will be able to return to surfing
and being a beach bum
someday soon

Cindy and I met in November 2004 as 'new students' on our first three-day taught unit of the Narrative & Life Story Research EdD programme at Bristol University. I felt nervous and inadequate in the group of 16 – from various countries – who seemed at ease in this academic research world. Cindy appeared confident and was very articulate, though she later told me she, too, had felt nervous *"not knowing anyone or where I was ... I thought ... I can never keep up with these people."*

We both settled down and enjoyed this and subsequent units, attending all but one at the same time. I was always pleased to see Cindy's name on the list of students, enjoying her openness in the groups, her energy and engagement in debate and discussion – and her ability to think clearly despite the jet lag. As we got to know each other better, we began to share parts of our life stories in addition to those that emerged in group discussions during each narrative session.

She willingly engaged (by email) in 'conversations' for my Narrative Interviewing assignment (Bell, 2007): *"You are on – sounds like fun. I never get to be the interviewee."* After that we continued to correspond, our letters growing longer and more personal, with past and present stories, poems, thoughts, reflections, questions ...

In my invitation to Cindy to take part in this co-research, I said she seemed a natural choice *"if you don't mind being classed as an 'older woman'"* (she was then nearly 52).

(Cindy, email 06.08.07)

> *Our correspondence makes me write – which makes me a better writer – so sure – I'll help with your project ... I get pushed around for being lesbian in a mixed race family but not so much because of my age – that I can tell. I'm not sure I'm a good fit for you, but I'm willing and happy to play.*

(Christine, email 10.08.07)

> *So pleased that you're willing and happy to play ... this doesn't just have to be about age or about being pushed around ... it's much more to do with being a woman over 50 and going on being who you are, whatever that means and however you feel about it.*

Following our earlier correspondence, Cindy and I exchanged more than 20 letters each way, plus poems and other reflections, over the time she agreed to take part in this 'visible women' co-researching. We both roamed far and wide in our narrative responses and questions to each other - so I have weaved together relevant sections from our correspondence over the period July 2007 to the end of 2008, rather than focusing on individual letters in date order.

(first 'weave' from Cindy, July/August 2007)

Excited about being
in the old lady category!
        Permission to be snippy

Don't feel old very often
though folks sometimes ask
Are these your grandchildren?

        Always told I look young for my age
Maybe it's not true any more
Mentally don't feel any different
except perhaps a bit wiser
and am getting better at rest

Physically there are a few clues
Both started getting grey
when we had the girls
        Still like to play and be silly

When did you go white?
I like it
Wouldn't colour my hair if it was like that

Have enjoyed young people
for as long as I can remember
an ability to connect
in a way many other adults cannot
        believe it is my love of life

Often enjoy M's [wife] family
more than mine
They are so Italian
and really enjoy life
At her mom's 90th birthday
celebrated with all the family and friends
They sure know how to throw a party!

Had a complete hysterectomy
aged thirty

Always wanted to be a parent
We tried to adopt locally
then heard about the millions of baby girls
abandoned to orphanages in China
filled in mountains of paperwork
and waited

Not sure the girls really get the idea
of extended family

Moving in with Nonna
so she won't be lonely
Watching M reconnect
with her childhood neighbourhood
        Can't imagine those kind of roots

We moved so often
when I was a child
The oldest of five
and feel the responsibility at times

When I visit
am getting better
at just letting my parents have their own life
        without trying to figure out what they need
My parents are both musicians
We seem to get along fine
        as long as I'm 3000 miles away
In many ways
they are proud of me
even if they don't understand
me or my life

They're very Southern
polite
Conservative
racist
religious
Completely given over to Christianity
in all their thinking

After my dad died
and my mom remarried
          the rules kept changing
my step dad
would not let us do anything
other than go to church on Sundays

M is baffled by how
I ever came out of that household
          because I am SO completely different
She and my mom do not get along
and visits together can be bumpy

Come from a line of fisher people
Grandmother would take me deep sea fishing
          Guess you could say
          I'm a beach bum
I like to surf
My family went to the beach
every summer when growing up
The sea means wholeness
health
endless possibilities
connection to life

          Still feel connected to my father
though he's been dead for forty years
Being on water
brings back the sound of his voice
a way to be close

M and I plan to spend
our golden years
looking for the world's most perfect beach

Looking forward to our 18th anniversary
We make a good team
          It's the safest place I've ever found
We've built a nice home together
and cherish each other

Moving has meant
    coming out all over again
    to a new group of people
We'd been in our area for so long
I'd stopped thinking about it

This confident loud person
is the opposite of what the
Southern young lady
is supposed to be

How did you grow your back bone?
Have you always known what you wanted?

    This idea of women as visible
My feminist heart starts beating faster
just thinking about
how objectified women are
every day

(Christine, July/August 2007)

Started going grey in my twenties ... after colouring my hair for
years, discovered it had pretty much gone white so cropped it
very short (it's very curly when it grows) and left it white ... a
new me! Began to feel that colouring it was all part of going
along with that 'being objectified'.
    Refusing to believe that being white haired makes me
    invisible?

    What 'visible' things matter to you?
    Has this changed over time?

You asked about yoga – not now in a class but have evolved
my own morning routine and been doing it for years – my body
is more awake afterwards.

Like you, I love being by the sea – though imagine we might do quite different things there! Enjoyed your stories of being on water and the importance of it for you – used to sail when I was young, but not a surfer and don't sunbathe because I burn too easily (and already have too much sun damage). Enjoy looking, listening, sitting, swimming, walking along the shore and the cliffs here ...it's a very therapeutic place for me.

Talking about moving often ... lack of roots ... really resonated with me ... not knowing what 'home' is. Now feels at least as much about people as place – though have come back to where I was as a child, the nearest place to 'home'.

Where is 'home' to you now?

You sound like a good and dutiful daughter – and it sounds like hard work. My father was a distant person, even when there ... but many of my values (political and social - not religious) have been influenced by his. Recognising this over recent years has helped me feel closer to him now than when he was alive – something about him being more visible to me, maybe?

You mention rules changing in your household. In my extended family (and the various people who looked after my brothers and me) there were lots of different rules about behaviour.

How do you feel about rules now?

It has always seemed obvious how much you love both your daughters – you talk about them very freely – they seem always with you. Which is the amazing thing about children – even when not there physically, they are still there in heart and mind - and sometimes a worry as well as a joy. I can feel G [son] as an active presence even if I'm not consciously thinking about him.

How do you cope as a parent? Are you a worrier?

Enjoyed your story of how you and M got together ...

As for my story of falling in love again ... that will have to be a separate letter! D and I met in our mid-fifties. He and G get on very well – really like each other – which is a delight for me. G insisted on 'interviewing' D very soon after we'd met because he knew how bad I'd been at picking partners previously! I was very touched by that – and so was D.

About backbone ... possibly inherited? Always been independent, determined and stubborn, despite being shy and lacking confidence. Often reacted against what I was being told to do – or be.

What about you?

(Cindy, September/October 2007)

> Preferred to be numb
> for much of my youth
> A wild child
> living as much life as I could
> > *Never thought I'd live past 35*
> Now I'm 52
> a nice number
>
> Could write a book
> about what visible 'things' matter now
> Used to be a big deal to get new things
> after growing up with not very much
>
> Been a big shift around 'stuff'
> and how little it matters
> What has grown over the years is

finding ways to express myself
in music and words
    also 'being' more than doing

Directing my expressing to others
is about being able to connect
    and being real about why
It's really scary
to give poems to people
you don't know very well

Still get very disappointed
when can't do the things
I used to physically
but appreciate now
being able to sit in meditation

    Being 'out there' is easier
but I want to put a nice face on it!
Seem to be more aware
of how I look now
than when I was younger

L's [daughter] new teacher asked
"How are you all connected?"
and we calmly explained
she has two moms
The teacher's eyes got big
and the lights came on

Not a worrier
most of the time
M loves to worry

I miss our old house
and am having to make adjustments
around living with Nonna
M is a strong person
    and we both feel better
    when I stand up for me

(Christine, September/October 2007)

It's a very big thing you've done, going to live with Nonna in M's old childhood neighbourhood – leaving the home you and M had made together with the girls – and loved.
How do you find your own space there?

You asked if I had spent time wondering what it would have been like if my mother had lived ... and yes, I certainly did – and still do sometimes. A lot of silent longing and imagining things differently as a child. Later I began to talk about her, even though nobody else seemed to want to – trying to make her more 'real' rather than the perfect person she had become in memory.

Did you do this with your dad?

Tell me more about 'being numb' in your youth.

'Stuff' – and caring about it – was seen as immoral in my family. So of course I went through a period of wanting to rebel against Baptist Protestant guilt – be a consumer, try out 'bad' things – seems fairly innocent and naïve now, but felt daring in the early 1960s!

Very much more important now – and for a long time – is having my own space. Always ('selfishly' I was told) needed lots of time on my own – not so much unseen as not wanting to see or be with others. Not a very patient person ... except professionally, interestingly.

Talking with the women in my singing group about our generation's different ways of dealing with getting older ... the clothes we wear ... our physical selves ... expectations from others ... choosing not to disappear ...

And talking about being objectified ...
> *how do you deal with the way so many clothes are now for young girls?* ...

turning them into fashion objects, everything in pink with sexist slogans ... makes my blood boil!

See we have our birthdays in the same month – two Virgos! Really enjoyed my 50s – when I properly came into my own.

> *Why didn't you think you'd live past 35?*

Used to do a lot of letter writing and journaling – much less now. Was one of my ways of doing emotion, I think. Maybe now I'm able to express how I feel so much better, I don't need that outlet as much?

> *Tell me a bit more about 'standing up for me'.*

In October, I told Cindy about being very affected by the suicide of a woman I had been mentoring as part of my work with an NHS team over three years. Her death came at a time of year I always find difficult, especially with the 60th anniversary of my mother's death in November.

(Cindy, November/December 2007)

> Sorry life is throwing you
> a curve ball right now
> What do you typically do
> around your mother's death?
>
> Had a big party for my dad
> when I passed him in age

He was 35 when he died
I have the same blood disorder
    so figured my time was limited too

Sending a separate piece
on my maternal grandmother
We called her Granny Flash!
    Encouraged me by her example
Until I was in my thirties
she was the most stable part of my life

    Grew up singing
and really miss it
just don't have the time
Must get back to exercise routine

Life has been crazy
increased hours at school
more shopping and cooking
construction work on the house

Thanksgiving was wonderful
M's oldest brother and sister-in-law
came with a car load of goodies
and took good care of us all for a week!

Miss my house and neighbourhood but ...
the girls seem really happy
Nonna and I get along fine
She has a lot to teach me
    I enjoy learning from her

Do have some time for myself
meditating while the toast is toasting
walking in the evening with M
or on my own listening to my ipod

Standing up for me
means saying/doing what I want
    regardless of the effects
Sometimes results in a good change

Not always a good thing
Still feels risky

We let the girls decide what they wear
for the most part
though we do draw the line when buying
If L wants to wear pink all day everyday
so be it
We talk about it
        so they know the choices they are making

It's really disgusting
what the stores carry for young girls
Some of the stuff makes them look like hookers

Really appreciate our conversations
Never connected the dots
of capitalism and what they push on us
Often said retail therapy was fun
        Whole new meaning for me now

Thought kicking women
was just a sexism/gender thing
Now see it's part of our consumerism

Cindy and I regularly sent each other writing drafts of academic papers, articles, poems, etc. for comment. Around this time she emailed a copy of her dissertation proposal (on 'Absent Parents') and an abstract for her paper at the 2008 Qualitative Inquiry conference in Illinois.

(Christine, November/December 2007)

When I'm depressed and can't quite see the point of anything (including writing assignments!) it's difficult to know what keeps me going. Takes me into a 'needing to make a difference' place ... Told Jane [supervisor] about feeling low – and very stuck with final assignment. She suggested an un-assignment ...which strangely unblocked me!

Have personal rituals around my mother's death and her grave ... gather pebbles from the beach ... sit and talk .. and weep ... sometimes still angry with her for dying when I was so young.

I didn't know about the rare blood disorder that you share with your dad.
    How do you cope with that now?

Loved your grandmother stories – what great memories – so fun and alive.

In your proposal, I enjoyed the way you describe *how* you intend to tell the stories about 'absent parents' ...
    Are you going to say why as well?

Really enjoy singing – brings different parts of me alive. Sometimes we 'busk' on the street for charity – very visible but good fun.
    How could you find time for singing again?

    How are you surviving the 'craziness' of your busy life?

Consumerist stuff makes me angry ... there are huge connections between those pressures and how we feel about ourselves. Gender politics seems to be *about* visibility/invisibility.

    What would you say you and I are doing here?

(Cindy, January/February 2008)

Flew back for sister's 50th
and to put my eyes on my mom
     all five of us 'kids' together again
I'm the bossy oldest
who moved away to the 'left coast'

One of the sweetest things was
my Bible-thumping right-wing Christian brother
inviting me to dance
We often don't get along
     It really touched me

Would never take the time
to reflect on my family
without your good questions

Not sure why my view of the world
is so different from the rest
Would like to give credit to my dad
who was kind to everyone
     I know the 'box' is not for me

Figured my time was limited
like my dad
but have never let the doctors
play with me like they did with him
Too many red blood cells
     some day it will catch up with me
but I'm really fine

     The act of buying things
     gives me a sense of power and control
but currently in a low stuff mode
My mother is a 'shop-a-holic'
Nonna lost everything in Italy during the war
and only spends if she must
M is so tight she squeaks when she walks

The house is now functional

Looking forward to sleeping in
and exercising every day
in my week off
SO busy at work
it's hard to fit in an 8-hour day!

      I was so angry and lost at high school
hoping to keep that misery
from a few young people

First time I went to counselling
in my thirties
my mom was so upset
she sent me a get well card
every day for a month!

It works for me
our writing together
Interesting and engaging
Look forward to hearing from you
and writing back
We are so different
yet share many of the same values
      feel closer to you since we started

(Christine, January/February 2008)

Enjoyed your family stories and the 'sweetest thing' of that
dance with your brother. There are definitely times to ignore
differences and celebrate what brings us together. I loved your
expression 'put my eyes on mom'!
    Is that you making her visible?

Yes, I do see my two older brothers – more now as we get
older. Love them dearly, though not sure I know them very well
and we've lived very different lives – but gone on sharing the
same sort of values. Younger half-brother lives in the US and

we meet once a year or so. I've always been the noisiest about my feelings!

Christmas was good, with G and girlfriend staying for a week. I love spending time with G anyway – he's interesting and challenging (of course!). Lots of time to walk and talk, eat and drink, play games etc.

Definitely know you better and feel closer since starting this. Find our correspondence fascinating and also sometimes need a space before replying … a bit like deciding not to answer the phone and listening to the message later.
Do you ever feel like that?

Aspects of 'visible women' seem to emerge from just about every part of all our conversations for this co-research.
How are things 'emerging' in your research?

Just had a couple of days in London, seeing the Louise Bourgeois exhibition … she always has a big impact on me … angry, often depressed, difficult and determined not to disappear in her 90s.

Do you know her work?

About to hand in my dissertation proposal – being self-indulgent and subjective is part of my criteria – copy attached.
Any comments when you have time.

Cindy added a paragraph dated 26 February to a letter begun on the 15th, letting me know that Nonna had been in hospital for 10 days or so and just been diagnosed with cancer. She said: *"I've really appreciated Nonna over the last 19 years and I know this will be hard on the kids … Everybody will be devastated … I'm REALLY*

*glad we made the decision to move down with Nonna – she is really
going to need us now."*

Nonna died at home on 11 March.

(Cindy, March/April 2008)

> Nonna died in her own room
> in her own house
> with all three of her children
> with her
> > *That's the way I want to go*
> surrounded with all the familiar noises
> and smells
>
> Now everyone has left
> things are calming down
> the phone has stopped ringing
> flowers and food have stopped coming
> people no longer just drop by
> and dinner has returned to just the four of us
>
> > *Makes room for the sadness*
> but glad to be back to some 'normal' time
> whatever that is
>
> Mostly don't want to do anything
> Would be happy to sit
> and watch movies all day
> or just go stare at the ocean
>
> Need to snap out of it!
> Way too much to do
> > *but no desire to do any of it*
> Difficult to manage
> my work load at school
> and no support or supervision

On the inside I feel so shy
constantly worried
about making a fool of myself
I like your saying I come across as friendly

Did missing your mom
play into your wildness as a youth?
        Missing my dad added tons to mine
No one talked about him
and I wanted to know everything
Wonder if he felt shy like I do?

        Tell me more about self-indulgence
I love that you have this
as part of your criteria

Seem to be writing in mosaic pieces
about 'absent parents'
different in colour and tone
not sure how they're connected
        need to find the right glue

Attached please enjoy my poem to Nonna *'Are you ready?'*
I read it to her and M's oldest brother put it in her casket

Cindy was looking forward to a three-day workshop in April with Michael White, with whom she had done her Narrative Therapy training in Australia. On the second day he had a heart attack and died within a very short time. She emailed: *"This seems really hard now on the heels of Nonna's* [memorial] *service and we are just getting our heads round the fact that she isn't coming back. I'm hoping a beautiful poem will rise out of all this shit – like the flower garden after being fertilized."*

(Christine, March/April 2008)

Your poem is very moving ... about Nonna and about you.
Great to be celebrating her life – and taking care of others, but
...
> *Who says you need to snap out of it?*
> *What about going gently?*

It's been hard. Maybe just staring at the ocean is what you
need to do at the moment.

Basically I'm a shy and introverted person ... always worked
hard to present myself as confident ... fooled lots of people, just
like you did!

> *What are the really positive things your dad gave you?*

It's great telling my stories to people who really listen – and not
being therapied!
> *Imagine this happens between you and M?*
> *and also did with Nonna?*

Spending a lot of time on 'visible women' writing and reading
...it will be hard to stop 'gathering' stories. I really appreciate
your enthusiastic engagement.

> *How is your mosaic doing? Do you really need 'glue'?*

Shocked that you have no supervision at work with all you do
...
> *Could you set something up informally – peer supervision*
> *maybe?*

Self-indulgence ... well, it's as a positive rather than negative
concept ... setting my own criteria, being subjective, not

pretending to be objective, allowing my own biases and opinions to count ...

(Cindy, May/June 2008)

Returned to meditating daily
before anything else
Seems to help make more room
Less likely to hurry
feel more aware of things
that push me around

Sometimes just get so overloaded
I don't want to do anything
Have now set up weekly co-supervision
for support at work
Thanks for driving that home

Back to exercising
so all around I feel better
Got to the beach in April
        spent some time staring at the water

Reconnected with some wonderful folk
from the narrative training
after Michael died
        It helps a lot
to hold on to them in my thinking

Hope we keep this letter writing up
long enough
to get to some of the growing-up stories

Hard for me not to follow the rules
but am going to 'indulge' myself more
and see where it goes!
M and Nonna been great listeners
        and I learn lots about myself

forming answers to your questions

Some of my dissertation stories
are like shards
ragged ... incomplete ...
> *but you're right*
> *I don't need any glue!*

Presenting some of it at QI [conference]
was actually fun this time
and received wonderful feedback

Planning on graduating
next summer
making a Bristol trip with the whole family
then on to Tuscany to meet some of M's family

Now M is working hard
on getting us ready
for our month in China

(Christine, May/June 2008)

So glad you've set up your exchange of supervision with R – and meditating and generally finding room and space for yourself.
> *How can you hold on to this?*

> *What's your version of self-indulgence?*

Used to get overloaded – and panicky – and have to appear calm and in control. Not quite sure what happens to time now – it just passes – whatever I'm doing expands to fill the time available. Like my *Magic Summer* ...

I'm happy to keep going for as long as we're both happy to write – and not just for my dissertation.

Does this fit for you, too?

I look forward to hearing about your long-awaited family visit to China ...

Cindy and family have been learning Mandarin (spoken and written) over the years. They spent four weeks in June/July 2008 re-visiting the two orphanages and the areas where their two Chinese daughters originally came from.

From her 'China files':

> *"We've come a long way for this visit ... it's an effort to help [daughters] have more of their story ... before they were part of our lives. We are looking for pieces of their story in these places and with these people."*

David and I spent two weeks in the US in July at a big family celebration for my cousin Sara's 50th wedding anniversary. There were many exchanges of chatty emails between Cindy and me before and after our travels.

Once back from China, Cindy and family began getting ready to move back to their old house and neighbourhood, which they had all missed whilst living with Nonna. They were also planning a second wedding in October because of possible Californian State legislation changes.

(Cindy, 03.08.08)

> *The time change from China is really hard – plus we were on the go so much over there that I think we were worn out! Right now we are packing and working on the house ... for our return ...*
>
> *We are planning our wedding right now ... just need to get married again before the election in case the vote goes against us ...*

I have so much to say and so much to share – it's overwhelming ...

(Cindy, 26.08.08)

Thought you might like some of the writing I did in China ... [China files attached]

We are moved in – more or less and it's wonderful to be home. I sleep SO much better ...

(Christine, 26.08.08)

I LOVE your China writings ... a sensitivity of language that felt very appropriate to your emotional story ... Your writing has changed over the time I have been reading your stuff – it seems like you're allowing more of yourself to be in there, which I like a lot ...

How are you feeling about the letter-writing? ...

(Cindy, 26.08.08)

I do want to continue our conversation. I love writing to you and I love hearing from you. I find it really helpful. It keeps me in my writing and your questions help me see things differently, or something you've said gives me new ideas to consider.

(Cindy, September/October 2008)

Finally at a place where I can write again
School started back
my office and forms are ready
and being back home
has increased the depth of my sleep
ten fold

Travelling with my family this summer
could not have been better
Loved being with them
and exploring China together
  Too many pleasures to number

My upbringing was so negative
about pleasures
that it still feels like self-indulgence
hanging out with friends

Been having the best time
playing with the photos from China
By the fourth day there
realized I didn't have the vocabulary
to express what it was like
  Would love to get to a place
  where I could capture
  some of the unworded times

So relieved to know
my China writing was effective
M just loved it
Having you think it was beautiful
really means a lot to me

  Lost all our earlier letters
from my computer
so upset having them vaporized
Thanks so much for re-sending
Each time a batch arrives
it's like a visit from a friend

Been having these 'Foucault moments'
about how power is constructed
by our languaging

Can't wait to finish writing up my research
Still so much to do
I'm up to 25 different stories
One thing I seem short in - time
    Always want to do
    more than I have time to do

Writing about my mom
and the times in my life
she has been completely absent
even though she's still living

Been nice to connect
with the rest of the 'visible women'
How did you find
such a nice group of women?

Cindy and M got re-married on 25 October and we exchanged more emails:

(Cindy, 31.10.08)

> *Please go to this link and check out the wedding* [photo] *collection*
> *...*
> *We had a complete blast. It was great fun to have so many people from all different areas of our lives there to celebrate together ...*

(Christine, 4.11.08)

> *Great photos! ... Everybody looks very beautiful and very happy ...*
> *... also keeping our fingers crossed for your* [presidential] *elections*
> *today.*

(Cindy, 5.11.08)

> *I'm completely pumped!! I even wore my Obama T-shirt to work*
> *today!!*

> *Still a bit blue that I may not be married for much longer – due to*
> *prop 8* [legislation] *passing – it will be another court battle now.*
> *But it can't hold a candle to how happy I am to have Obama as our*
> *leader!!*

(Christine, October/November 2008)

> Already exchanged many emails thoughts about the wedding,
> but I really hope you get to stay married this time ... I very much
> enjoyed the photos – and what a lovely, funny, moving poem
> for M on your wedding day.

> Enjoying the various 'group' emails – glad you are too – and
> was pleased to see such strong, interesting responses to your
> wondering 'what to wear as an older woman' at your
> wedding.

> Lots of resonances for me around forbidden pleasures and
> 'self-indulgence'
> > *How do you deal with those 'shalt not' prohibitions now?*

> Beautiful photos from China ... and your 'voice' comes through
> so clearly in your journaling ...

Has this helped with your dissertation writing?

Despite my reservations about Foucault, he did write some fascinating stuff about power and its uses/abuses.
    Tell me more about your 'Foucault moments' if you can bear to!

Enjoyed the seminar in Bristol ... Jean Clandinin saying stories aren't smooth, there are cracks and borderlines – spaces in-between.
    We seem to have been exploring lots of these ... ?

About the vegetable growing – a horrible summer has made it even more hard work, but I still get enormous pleasure from it – very therapeutic.
    Tell me more about your 'tales from the garden'.

(Cindy, November/December 2008)

M and I say
we'll keep getting married
until the State gets it right
        We had a complete blast!
Fun to have so many people
from different areas of our lives
to celebrate together

For my dissertation
I'm enjoying 'work' books
that feel like pleasure books
        *Getting permission to just
        write from the heart*

The 'Foucault moments'
are about people who have influenced my thinking
I'm writing them 'letters' or 'postcards'

saying how and why

Lots of ideas for my writing
just need to be still long enough
to write them down

Cindy and I continued – still continue – to write email letters to each other, though we agreed in early 2009 that these were now for ourselves rather than my co-research. Exploring with her the 'cracks' and spaces between has contributed enormously to my delight in this journey.

Her (and my) 'tales from the garden' became very much part of our letter-writing as she completed her dissertation and discovered the delights (and disappointments) of vegetable growing: *"... think I might have put my tomato plants out too early. Who knows ... M keeps saying – did you research this?!?!?! Oh well – either way it's fun!"* (Cindy, 07.04.09).

(Christine, email 13.04.09)

I've so much enjoyed this part of the research that I'm reluctant to stop, but am sure that you and I will continue to correspond anyway ... thank you so much for your fascinating and enthusiastic contributions over such a long time ...

(Cindy, email 20.04.09)

Yes, I'm very glad to keep writing with/to you ... just returned to work after our Spring Break ... and I feel SO much better and well rested ... The garden is coming along ...

At the end of April 2009, Cindy came to Bristol for her viva, which she 'passed' with traditional flying colours. I was able to join her and Jane, our supervisor, for a celebration afterwards – and she flew back to California the following day.

(Christine, email 01.05.09)

> *LOTS of congratulations again and I loved reading your whole thesis on my journey home today – sitting on the train (and the bus) with the occasional tear in my eye ... delightful to be able to spend time with you both yesterday ...*

(Cindy, email 03.05.09)

> *I'm still about 10 feet off the ground and I'm loving the smile on my face that has yet to fade ... what a perfect way to celebrate! ...*
>
> *Thank you for coming so far out of your way to see me ... made me feel very special.*

7.6 Marie

I am big and untidy
as are my belongings

(Marie's autobiographical letter dated 18.04.09 at the end of our correspondence)

Current age 70
Born Chelmsford
1938

Father steel contractor
Mother employed by Bata shoe manufacturers
and then on to teach flower arranging
a domestic goddess of the old school

Grammar school education
(where Miss Brown announced to my peers
that I had somehow
managed to attain
the lowest maths marks ever
in my first year exams)

University of Essex
degree in Linguistics
1986

Employment
apart from a short spell with Which? magazine
with the NHS
from 1973 to retirement in 2004

Moved from London to Bath in 2005
and became an observer of folk

Married 1960 to R – marine engineer
Divorced 1984
Two sons

A married with two children
D married with no children

Likes
theatre – language – film
West Ham – England cricket matches
Tom Stoppard plays and the U3A poetry group

Dislikes
craft work
and driving (because I can't)
fruit salad for pudding
people who don't listen
(because sometimes I don't)
and long conversations on the telephone

Marie and I met in the late 1990s when we were both working within NHS primary care trusts in south-east London. At the many seemingly endless meetings we both attended, I greatly appreciated her ability to listen, straightforward and 'sensible' way of talking, obvious deep intelligence and sense of humour. We got to know each other better through our involvement in a programme to support French GPs coming to work in London practices.

In 2005, after her retirement, Marie decided to move from her flat on the outskirts of London to a terraced house in an elegant Georgian crescent on the edge of Bath; the 'college' was built specifically for *"single ladies in reduced circumstances, without male support"*. As she said, this was *"the potted version of the original criteria needed for entry"*. Her decision to move was motivated partly by financial circumstances and a desire to retire to pleasant surroundings, with a small garden; in addition one of her sons and his family had recently moved to the area, with other family members already living nearby.

After agreeing to take part in this co-research, Marie responded to my query in January 2008 as to whether she was ready to start the 'conversation:

(Marie, email 08.01.08)

> *I expended my remaining energy organising a party for* [the college] *on New Year's Eve. We had quizzes and pass the parcel, Call My Bluff and charades. What larks – 20 old gals making a last pitch at glamour with dangly ear-rings and high heels. We could have made the Bath Chronicle …*

> *I am conscious of being a visible woman … probably not at my most creative but if you outline again what you need and when I will do my very best.*

I sent her my 'first letter to visible women' in mid-January.

(Marie, email 29.01.08)

> *I find my thoughts and reflections come easier in a journal/diary format when writing and I hope to get some initial response to you soon. We can then discuss whether it works or not, or if there is a better way of doing it.*

(Christine, email 01.02.08)

> *Your thoughts in any form are totally acceptable!*

(first letter from Marie, February/March 2008)

Resident since 2005
in Georgian almshouses
close to the city of Bath
with twenty five ladies
from 60 to 88

We are viewed as an entity

Visible behaviour
        is not actively encouraged
though we speak up
at our three-monthly resident meetings
Expectations are not greatly different
from inception over 150 years ago

We are the 'College ladies'
we get invited in groups
to local events
        Most of the time
        I feel institutionalised

At the centre
of this privileged domain
is a chapel
which we attend at least twice weekly

Our chaplain is 83
Along with the handyman
he is the only male presence
entitled to regular visits
and unquestioned access to our homes

        We have all brought with us
        remnants of our former lives and occupations
Among us
a wartime aircraft mechanic
a Wren
one missionary
3 nurses
2 headmistresses
a Sotheby's valuer
and 2 Sisters from Holy Orders

Our only constant link
is that we are no longer
or never have been
married
paradoxically a key concept
in the loss of perceived individuality

As a single woman
the proximity of family
was appealing
in my decision to move
    offering a semblance of family unity
    and freedom in retirement

Some friends
of many years standing
feel I have become less accessible
as though the exclusivity of almshouse-living
is a barrier to communication

The past year
was not a time for complacency

My grandson started school
and his mother
was diagnosed with advanced lung cancer
after a routine health check
    Within hours
    the ground had shifted

The minutiae of this new life
made a mockery of what we had previously
held important

Chemotherapy began
and in the gaps
my daughter-in-law
started to impose some structure

S has immense courage
and resilience
She talks of her hopes and fears
for her children
answers their questions
as best she can
They are laying down memories
and building blocks

I understand the role
she wants me to play
should I outlive her

Approaching 70
I am not sure if I am capable
Sometimes ashamed
of the despair I feel
thinking of the impact
of the loss on her young children

Where it matters
I am visible
My presence makes a difference
to these four lives
I have a voice
to talk to my son
and his wife and children

I can respond
to my 3 year old granddaughter K's demand
to 'cheer me up, Baba'
when we are having a bleak day

To my mind
this is the most enduring quality of all
and a privilege to be part of
what lies ahead

But that's on a good day

(Christine, 10.04.08)

Your description of life at the college was wonderful ...funny,
insightful, poignant, rather like Jane Austen ... though can't see
you being a 'College lady'!

What's it like being 'viewed as an entity' ... who by?
How do you maintain your own sense of identity?
Tell me more about feeling institutionalised ...

What you write about S – and your own feelings – is very moving. I don't want to over-psychologise, but ...
perhaps you're feeling the despair S understandably can't or won't ?

You referred to my childhood experience ... only after I reached the age my mother was when she died (40) did I begin to let myself wonder what it was like for her, slowly dying with three young children she would never see grow up. In my family, as you know, it was never spoken of – never a chance to learn to live with the loss – to 'lay down memories' – just a terrible, black, silent hole.

What you all seem to have done so well – with S's lead – is to make it all very visible and able to be talked about, however painful.

You are regularly in my mind, very visible in the way you are telling about your life and all that is happening. Your 'having a voice' – and your listening – is a vital part of how your family will all live with this.

If you can (or want to) tell me some more about the bad days ...and your despair ...

We spoke on the phone occasionally about the impact of S's illness and Marie's concerns for the children (then aged 3 and 5). She was also worried about not fulfilling her 'obligations' to me and sent a card by post, with her next letter:

(Marie, 25.05.08)

> *I hope I am not proving to be a bad choice – couldn't bear not to come up with the goods for you … I value what you are doing and most of all your patient friendship.*
>
> *… I find it* excruciating *to spill my thoughts on paper, thus the formality of the attached. Maybe it's a melting down process and no. 3 might reveal the sinews softening!*

(Marie, May 2008)

> Things with S's condition
> are so much better at the moment
> with no active malignancy now
> I am taking a step back
> Reshuffling my priorities
> > *focusing on what it is I want to do*
> > *from the place in which I find myself*
>
> I continue as before in my role
> of 'College lady'
> attending chapel
> maintaining my garden
> opening my house to inspection by the Trustees
> when required
>
> My first faux pas on arrival
> was to query
> (politely)
> a guest speaker's idea
> of 'ladies' enjoying a life
> 'just pottering'
>
> > *Suppose I now conform*
> > *because that was part of the deal*
> Our benefactor laid down 'rules'
> to last a life time
> She genuinely wanted the best place

in a carefully chosen location
for the less fortunate to live
when women were dependent
on male relatives for survival

Some identities are being maintained
but we find it difficult to understand
the terms of engagement
even between ourselves

    Knowing how to be is complex
Conversing or not becomes significant
Signs such as leaving our back gates open
are used as an indicator
of a willingness to 'receive' visitors

Not inviting friends to visit because
    I do not regard this as my home
If they come
I 'show them around town'
rather than draw them in as I did in previous homes
I seem to have ground to a halt
in adding to our experiences together
both in physical and emotional terms
    I do care about that very much

Have lived here
as long as I attended university
but am still bewildered by my surroundings
    and think I have learned little
The answer could lie in
accepting the way it is
and believing that one day
I might just walk the edgy streets of Bermondsey again

Am seeking inspiration from
a book on fascinating insights
about the energy of connecting through language
the key to interacting with the world
listening and responding to what is being said

My 70th birthday came and went
A feeling of absolute unreality
Celebrated on the river
in a narrow boat
with eighteen extended family
and a few old friends

(Christine, 02.07.08)

I certainly don't find you a 'bad choice' – quite the opposite – you write so well. As you know, I enjoy 'spilling my thoughts on paper' and hope that you do – or will be able to – find it other things as well as 'excruciating' ... and you could also decide not to do this at any time, if it proves too much.

How are you starting to reshuffle your priorities?
Do you feel any clearer about what you want?

What you don't seem to have lost is your very clear individuality – or your sense of humour and ability to spot a euphemistic put-down.
How are you managing to retain these qualities?

Does writing about it help that 'energetic connecting'?

What you say about the founding principles of the college is a good reminder of just how much 'women were dependent on male relatives for survival' – and often still are in so many parts of the world.

Sounds very difficult to be living somewhere that's not 'home'. Brings up all sorts of memories of not feeling at home where I lived – and having very little sense for years of what 'home' looked or felt like. Home began to be wherever I 'hung my hat' – even if not exactly where I wanted to be.

What are your needs around 'home'?

I wonder why you believe you're no longer adding to shared experiences with friends ... it sounds like such a big loss for you. *Have you had any 'feedback' from friends about this?*

An interesting comparison of the time spent at university and the college! Though somehow doubt you've 'learned little'. *Did you find university bewildering, too?*

I didn't go to university but emigrated to Australia instead, aged 20 – and learned loads – some of it not what I wanted to learn!

What will you take back with you to 'the edgy streets of Bermondsey'?

Because of the difficulties and demands of Marie's family situation, there were frequent gaps in our correspondence. We discussed the possibility of her withdrawing from this co-research and agreed she would continue to write as and when she felt able to do so.

(Marie, 29.08.08)

A valedictory letter from Bath
Leaving three years to the day
from first taking residence
    Years which did not bring me
    the tranquillity I thought I was looking for

Not solely due to family circumstances
more because I have felt myself
gradually fading into the landscape
of these impressive grounds

Surprisingly
Eros has shot a couple of bows this summer
alas missing me
but striking two of our kind

I watch in wonderment
the transformations that have taken place
in these women
They are out
proud
and extremely visible

Absolutely the same effect
as my youthful forays
with teenage friends
to the Kursaal in Southend

>   *Feel my own sense of freedom once more*
>   *in my plans to move*
and the thought
that changes may be taking place
in the lives of others here
pleases me no end

Chosen to live
in the heart of the village
where A and family are
to be on hand in emergencies
        and feel in control of my own life

Buses to Bath
are reliable and mainly on time
and I shall continue
with regular trips to London
and old comrades

It's a slightly odd feeling
to be leaving the ladies behind
even though we have shared our comings and goings
for a relatively short time
        I did ultimately connect with most of them

We plan to celebrate my departure
with a party
Some of the most reticent
have expressed regrets at my going
One told me of her 'devastation' at the news

So I am puffed up
with a strange sort of bemused pride
I am an Essex girl after all
in culture and approach
a long long way
from the world of Austen gentility

Organising yet another house move
is not to be recommended
independent as I like to think I am
I want to pare down 70 years of living
which demands a degree of self-discipline
and the shrugging off of many memories

I had offers of 'help' of course
but the first team has long since run out of patience
with the task of persuading me
to sanction what goes into the black sacks

Find it interesting to think of
personal belongings becoming
part of a stranger's set of attachments
Beautiful table linen that my mother left
soon to absorb other conversations

> *I need these anchors in my life*
> *to counter the apprehension*
> *about what lies ahead*

Try not to anticipate the future outcome
for my son and family
but if I have any influence at all
I want my grandchildren to have some fun
and look forward to sharing
just a little bit of time

exploring the future with them both

Not going to be a smooth ride
and can easily imagine a foggy November morning
'stranded' in a small village
But in the past three years
have become fractionally more creative
with using my time
and involving others

The theatre remains
my constant source of escapism
If I could take away with me any building from Bath
it would be the wonderful Little Theatre
where I claim a single armchair
with a glass of wine
and watch films all afternoon

In late August, Marie said she was happy to be included in the 'group' emailing: *"I think contact with others (as you say short-term) a good idea and will round things up in that I am sure we all had different experiences about how we felt writing about ourselves ..."*

She negotiated a short lease on a (very small) flat in the village where her family lived, six miles outside Bath, and moved in mid-September. We had little contact for some weeks while she worked out new routines with her son, daughter-in-law and two grandchildren. Her internet connection was also problematic and, although she wished to continue with our correspondence, we agreed that I would not send another letter until she had the time and energy for it.

(Christine, 23.10.08)

Your move sounds successful – and a brave thing to have done. I'm interested in the experience of paring down and letting go of 'stuff' ... no doubt very therapeutic in some ways but also sounds demanding. All that 'shrugging off' of memories ... and the 'devastation' for others of your leaving.

How do you feel now about the 'paring down'?
What difference do you think you made to the lives of 'the ladies'?

Your description of 'gradually fading into the landscape' gives a strong sense of what living at the college has been like for you.

How do you feel about your visibility (to yourself and others – including your family) in the village?

I enjoyed your telling about K wanting to be 'a different sort of girl' ...
and wonder how you are getting on with being a 'different sort of grandmother'?

You seem very good at maintaining your 'anchors', even though you said recently you'd not paid enough attention to your friendships since being in Bath.
How do you think this might be different in your new environment?
What do you think are the expectations of you there?

I've done quite a lot of 'joining' in Bridport – which is an interesting one for me. Never been much of a 'joiner', unless it's something that has really fired me up (like CND and other political stuff). I now 'belong' to various groups – singing, books, environment, film – and am on the fringes of various other things. The spin-offs and social expectations in this small community mean being clear about saying 'no' – choosing when to be available. Maintaining the level of visibility that works for me at this age and in this place is an ongoing project.

Marie wrote letting me know that her daughter-in-law needed yet more treatment:

(Marie, note 6.12.08)

> ... S has to have some additional radiotherapy sessions before Christmas and we have all had to re-arrange diaries. She is deeply disappointed that her chemo programme has not staved off secondary tumours as we had all hoped. The treatment means intermittent stays in hospital and there is some urgency ...
>
> I will be in touch in the New Year ...

We had some contact through occasional phone calls. At the end of January she sent me her fourth (and what turned out to be final) letter, saying *"... never feel it's quite fit for purpose but trust you completely to pick and mix at will."*

(Marie, 28.01.09)

I write this looking over
a Camberwick Green view
of Post Office and Chemist
both set in Cotswold stone

When I moved
from the clipped lawns of the College
thought the novelty of village shops
within leaping distance
would hold me captive
    But novelty and convenience
    quickly become routine
and the infrequency of the bus service
takes my attention

It is nevertheless
a welcoming place for newcomers
with neighbours locating me
as 'living in Roger's flat'
a new building
considered not quite up to scratch
in a village with 'protected' status

The flat is bright clean and small
    I am big and untidy
    as are my belongings

My next door neighbours
live in what is the grandest House
in the old market square
and invited me to their
New Year's drinks party

I am probably viewed
as a potential property owner
biding my time
In reality I am still living out of boxes
and supplementing my income
from meagre savings

Not convinced I have achieved
very much of what I set out to do
    Did feel I could make a positive difference
    to the lives of my grandchildren
but it is particularly important to their parents
that things follow a routine pattern
for as long as possible

S's most recent scan
showed that her cancer has spread
and her treatment increased
Our proximity and increased intimacy
has not worked to strengthen our friendship
and there is little scope for general discussion
or for differences of opinion

For my part
I have to question my self-appointed role
as overseer of the family's wellbeing

Other family members have become
confidantes of choice
ostensibly to save me 'the worry'
because I am alone
        I am filled with a primal surge of rage
        when I hear this

But how much access to other people's emotions
and confidences
can I legitimately claim?
In Austen parlance
        I feel like the mop-squeezer

I hear agonising
over possible guardians
and Wills being amended
Talk of contesting decisions
made behind closed doors

It is exhausting and messy
but is the backdrop to our lives
The challenge has to be
to find a level of equilibrium
day by day

I am not good at it
        and accept that I have been trying too hard
Finally realise it is not within my power
to make things as I would have them
nor should it be

        Where and what next I don't know
The College was kind enough
to say there would always be a home for me
within their protected walls
It is the only return ticket on offer
but the thought of two singles

still holds enough mystery
to keep me moving

I will be available if called upon
but am no longer hovering
on the outskirts of responsibility

(Christine, email 28.01.09)

> *Thank you so much for this, including your howls of rage – it all sounds traumatic and is obviously taking its toll on you … want to say how much I appreciate your sharing all this with me in your own very particular and impressive style.*

We exchanged emails during February, as Marie decided whether to stay or go once her six months' lease at the flat ended. During this time we agreed by phone that the main letter-writing part of our co-research had come to an end, though we would continue to send potentially relevant emails that could be included, in addition to the occasional 'group' correspondence.

(Marie, email 25.02.09)

> *After much time spent deliberating and scouring for alternative accommodation I have accepted an invitation to take up residence once more at the College.*
>
> *I know, I know, but times and situations change and this has become not only the devil I know but offers a good house on the south side of the terrace at an affordable rent and a bit of sun at the back.*

(Christine, email 26.02.09)

I shall look forward to meeting you again once you're back in 'the cloisters' ... imagine they'll be welcoming you back with the traditional open arms, given the send off you got – and really look forward to seeing and hearing how it goes for you.

It has sounded like an extremely difficult few months.

Marie moved back to Bath in March and we met at the college in early April 2009.

(Christine, email 13.04.09)

It was so good to see you again and to note how well you have made your re-entry. What a victory of visible woman-hood that has been ...

As you know, I'm now at the stage (sadly) of bringing to an end the letter-writing stage of this project, as I move into 'writing up' (or down as the case may be). I'll really miss doing it, as I've been in love with my research and don't want to let it go. Thank you so much for your wonderful contribution ...

I have one final (for now) request. When you have time, could you let me have any brief, background autobiographical information that you would be happy to see as part of your 'story' in these writings ...

(Marie, email 15.04.09)

... as little as I contributed, I too feel a sense of loss to think I didn't ask you any questions at all and just wanted to get out the starched tablecloth and move the best china around on the page. Which does reflect on the topic of 'academic writing'. It took me

three full years to meet the requirements at Essex but then the door slammed shut and I couldn't get out.

I don't know if I will ever be able to just let words and thoughts flow anymore without censure but I did want to say that 'your writing' in place of 'dissertation' captures the essence – you only ever do your writing, without self-conscious adornments or jargonese, and I so look forward to reading the final version ...

Within the next couple of days I will send a bit of background as asked but never mind if you feel you have to say 'not what I'm looking for'!

On 18 April Marie emailed me the autobiographical letter at the start of her story here and I replied the same day: *"My usual many thanks – for your usual wonderfully concise piece!"*

7.7 Sara

It feels great to be this age ...
So much more free than I've ever been before

(Sara's autobiographical letter dated 12.06.09 at the end of our correspondence)

I'm 68 now
Can't believe the years go by so quickly!
So much goes on
and I don't seem to have the time
to savour some of it
     Perhaps I try to cram in too many things ...

We live in an old house we rebuilt ourselves
in Middleburg
a small town in Florida

I'm a doll and puppet maker
and sell my work in our shops
at Renaissance Festivals
around the country

We spend the year moving between
time at home and at festivals
So we go to Texas for two months
then home for two
upstate New York for two
and home again
off again to Pennsylvania
and Louisiana
then start all over again

It certainly never gets boring
and with our nice big travel-trailer
home is always right behind us!

The travel helps us stay in close contact
with our three children
eleven grandchildren
and four great-grandchildren

It really has been an interesting life!
Being born during an air-raid
in the middle of a war
does tend to set things up

I was supposed to arrive in London
but the bombing was so bad
my mother went to stay
with family in Bridport
which promptly got bombed

My father went to India
after evacuation from Dunkirk
and apart from a few days at home
never returned to live with us
My younger brother and I thought
he'd taken one look at us
and decided we just weren't good enough

My mother went out to work
my brother went to prep school
and I went to live with maternal grandparents
over their shop in London
until I was 14

Met R my American sailor boy
the love of my life
and we got married
aged 17 and 18
MUCH TOO YOUNG (everyone said)

Went to live in the US
and I followed R's squadron around
with the children (as they arrived)
until we found this wonderful house

Mother came over to live with us
when she retired
She became more and more dependent on me
as her health declined
and she died eleven years ago

R was at sea much of the time
until he retired and said
"It's your turn now"
and I started my small business
He builds the shops
and keeps our vehicles on the road

Celebrated our 50th anniversary
last year
with many of our large extended family

     It's such a great time now
working as and when and where I want
being with different parts of the family

There have been some really hard times
and sad times
but don't think I'd want to change it

I feel very fortunate to have all this

Sara and I are cousins, our fathers the youngest and oldest (respectively) of three siblings. My father and his sister became missionaries, like their parents. Sara's father, the tall, handsome, charming 'black sheep', deserted his family after leaving the army at the end of World War II to live in Australia with another woman – and was almost never spoken of.

Sara grew up in Crowthorne and London, where her two sets of grandparents lived. Her pregnant mother was evacuated from London in 1940 to stay with my mother's sister and GP husband. Sara was born and spent her first few months in the small Dorset town where I now live (and spent part of my childhood) and our families occasionally met during school holidays. We never had the opportunity to become close but got news of each other via family letters. When she and R married, I was 16 and living in Trinidad and we had not then seen each other for some years.

We finally met again after 40 years, in 1995 when I went to visit her and R (and her rather demanding mother) in Florida. Since then, we have become 'sisterly friends', with a few visits back and forth and many, many email letters and family stories exchanged. We have offered each other warm support via letter at various difficult times for us both; especially painful for Sara was when her younger brother (and only sibling) P, who lived in Australia, took his own life in 2004.

Her family in the US has been – and continues to be - central to everything Sara has done over the past 50 years. She is at the heart of a large and extended network of in-laws, grandchildren, step-grandchildren and now great-grandchildren. She was fascinated by my ideas around visible women and enthusiastically took part (with Cindy) in 'conversations' for my pre-dissertation un-assignment.

(Sara, email 07.08.07)

I'll be glad to be your willing victim! Just let me know what you need and I'll pitch in.

(Christine, email 09.09.07)

I'm delighted you're prepared to be a willing victim ... and am attaching something [first letter] *to start the process off ...*

(first letter from Sara, September/October 2007)

It feels great to be this age
So much more free than I've ever been
   Can really come and go as I please
The only restrictions
are ones that I put on myself

Always set my own goals
With R at sea so much
had to make my own decisions
about everything

One thing that is weird ...
sometimes a person
usually younger
will walk towards me
   and look right through me
   as if I'm not there!

The first few times this happened
I was startled
then thought I was just imagining it
so purposefully made eye-contact
and nodded or smiled
Sometimes there was a response
and sometimes I was ignored again!

Very odd
Can't explain it really
except it's only happened
in the last five or so years

Perhaps a 'cloak of invisibility'
starts descending upon one
on turning 60!!
Oh well ...
   I can certainly live
   without the acquaintance of people
   who choose not to see me!

Nice to have lots of family
in one's life
but sometimes also nice
    not to be responsible for them all

I really like being a great-grandmother
Involves holding and admiring babies
Being pleased with lop-sided cup cakes
and scribbly drawings
No work involved ... lovely!

Feel like escaping sometimes
away from all responsibilities
but ... there are only so many days
in a lifetime
and I don't want to waste any of them
    Too many things I want to do yet

I like doing Renaissance Festivals
such an interesting group of people
very talented
highly educated
artisans and entertainers
choosing to live somewhat unorthodox lives
'under the radar' in many ways

    I like being 'mother hen'
to some of the very young women
living on their own
being very independent
Some have been 'on the road' from an early age
because of family problems
so haven't learned at home
how to cope with life's bumps and jolts

They will turn to an older woman
to take the place of an aunt or grandmother
Not a role I look for
but feel I can be of help
because of my own experience

People were quick to say
I was much too young to marry at 17
After 50 years
guess I knew what I was doing!

R went to sea
two months after we first came to America
    I was pretty lost and scared
not knowing anybody
or where to turn for help
and had to work things out for myself
Being pregnant put a stop to getting a job
and didn't have many qualifications

    I've always sewed
Nanna had been a dressmaker
and taught me when I was five
Made all my own clothes
then clothes for the children
and toys as they grew up

The local historical society
asked me to make period costume dolls
Started selling them at local craft shows
and ventured out more and more
as the kids needed me less

    It was good to branch out a bit
once R retired
and was willing to help with Mother
as she became ill
and very dependent on me
I felt smothered much of the time

    I'm happy making dolls
very rewarding
inventing and creating new ones
and running my three little shops
at the festivals around the country

It's a wonderful chance to see
my children and grandchildren
as some of them become involved

Really fun to be enjoying
a grown-up relationship with the children
there's companionship
not conflict
in how we work together

Sara and R travel around the US for much of the year, often with family members of various ages (including step-grandchildren), as they camp at the different Renaissance Festivals, meet friends and sell her dolls and puppets.

During our correspondence email contact was sometimes difficult for Sara and the frequency of exchanges depended on internet connections as well as time available. Between September 2007 and March 2009 we sent 12 'visible women' letters each way – Sara's often written in what she described as 'episodes' over a period of weeks – and I have stitched these together to form the fabric of our conversations.

I have omitted much of the lengthy personal family history shared - without, I hope, detracting from the strong sense of connectedness we both gained from these exchanges.

(Christine, October/November 2007)

Enjoyed your 'telling' about your current life and how you got there – your sense of freedom now – the very creative way in which you've made yourself visible through your work. I like the way you have decided not to be bothered by the odd occasion when somebody seems to look right through you.
Do you have any further thoughts on what this might be about?

What does being a 'visible woman' mean to you now?

Interested in what you say about the 'unorthodox' way of life at the festivals – and your enjoying being a 'mother hen' to the younger women. You seem so good at this – very much part of your particular 'visibility' ...
What is rewarding about it for you?

Not having been much mothered, was never sure I could do it – or even wanted to – and was surprised by the power of my feelings for G [son].

Your mother seemed a very strong woman – interesting but formidable, and extremely visible! Didn't know her well, but she was so much more fun than most people in the family. I see you as strong and independent in a different way. Impressed by your energy and skill – including inventing a career for yourself.
What's it been like, becoming successful in this way?

I found it strange, especially after becoming self-employed, selling a 'talent' for something ... but also learned I enjoyed being 'on show', despite my basic shyness.
Do you enjoy this 'public' part of what you do?

(Sara, November/December 2007)

> Visibility
> seems to have something to do
> with those who 'see'
> being somewhat respectful
> of older people of any gender
> Maybe it goes back to
> the tribal/village way of life

where elders were encouraged
to share their knowledge

Not afraid to speak up
and go for what I want or need
        which probably helps to be 'seen'

With the younger women
perhaps I'm just passing on
the love and support I was given
I think having strong women
Mother – Grandma - Nanna
in my life
helped me to stand on my own two feet

Growing up without a father
is not as hard as growing up without a mother
but still not the best
        It sticks with one
        doesn't it
        not having a parent around

My mother was a very strong woman
which stood her in good stead
when our father dumped her
but she was also very domineering
and wanted to be in the spotlight
with all the attention on her

She could be kind and caring
but did need a lot of pampering
When she came to live with us
she expected me to be
companion - care-giver – housekeeper

In my forties
with the children grown up
and needing my total attention less
Mother seemed to need it more and more
With few - if any - marketable skills
I began to feel

(as I realise now)
almost invisible
not like a real person
     as if I had no place in the world

Thinking about all this
realise I unconsciously decided
to invent a career for myself
as a doll-maker
in order to have an area
in which I could at least participate
and found I could really thrive

Having people look
at work I created myself
and take it home with them
     says that I'm a real person

I like travelling
seeing different parts of the country
Have a hard time
staying put in one place
so going to these Festivals is perfect!
And I enjoy
displaying and selling my work
     all part of being visible

Happy with the work I'm creating
always seem to have new ideas
which makes me feel more and more alive

R is happy that I'm happy
and doesn't mind travelling
as long as we're home
every few months for a while
He likes being busy and useful
and there's always something that needs doing

The festival business
can be very demanding and difficult
Sales depend absolutely on the weather

then there's the economy of the region
and so on and so on
Always a bit of a 'crap-shoot'
    We certainly never get bored!

(Christine, January 2008)

Loved hearing your various takes on being visible/invisible – especially the very creative way you made yourself visible through your work. It must have taken a lot of courage to get out there and sell yourself.
    Do you still find that difficult?
    How did you and R work out the 'transition' when he retired?

You mention being more 'in control' when you're working and needing your own space. That's very important to me, too – both the control and the space – for me I know it's connected to my depressive feelings and needing to be able to retreat.
    What does it mean to you?

You seem to be very good at 'keeping going' even when things are tough – another thing we share! Agree about the importance of having strong women around ... we shared an amazingly feisty grandmother ... and aunt.

Good to hear about your 'companionship' with your children. Parents very often seem to have unrealistic (and rather selfish) expectations of their children.
    What was your experience of this as a child?

I never felt 'good enough' for my father – or seen as myself – so was constantly trying to be something/someone else to gain approval. My brothers say they had the same feelings of inadequacy.

Always remembered you as seeming very confident and sure of
yourself when we were children – and being slightly envious
because I felt the opposite.
   What are your memories of how you felt then?

(Sara, January 2008)

   Perhaps 'keeping going'
   is a visible act
   whether we realise it at the time or not?

   Creating things with my hands
   that I've thought up myself
   does make me feel visible and alive
   Feel more in control
   when I'm working
           not just doing something
           someone else wants me to do

   Like being busy
   not just to fill time
   but because there are so many things
   I want to do
           Can't imagine
           having nothing one wants to do

   It is important to have some control
   over at least part of one's life
   I've been a bit demanding
   in having a work-space
   that's just for me
   Even more important
   now that B [younger daughter] and the boys
   are living with us again

Looking back on taking care of my mother
felt in some ways that I was the child again
          taking orders and doing as I was told
while having to make adult decisions for her care
I was very frustrated
Couldn't do any of my own work
as she panicked if I wasn't constantly available

Don't think I really felt confident as a child
I was devastated when our father
returned from the war
and then left after a few days at home
Remember hearing that he wasn't coming back
          Only saw him four times in my life

Nanna gave me all the mothering I needed
and I was blessedly happy
living with her and Grandad in London
until Mother wanted me back in Crowthorne
to help look after my father's parents

          R has been a good father
though away so much
Was afraid he would be bored silly
when he retired from the Navy
after 32 years of a rigidly disciplined world
but he's made a visible place for himself
at home and at the Festivals

He's very practical
good with the children
and actually a good teacher
known for his building abilities
and being able to coax
many a decrepit motor into giving a bit more service!

What a lot parents miss out on
when they're 'disappointed' in their children
Is that because the parents have failed
not the children
I wonder?
          Thought for another time!

(Christine, February 2008)

Been thinking about the 'keeping going' and wonder if sometimes it can be a rather mechanical way of appearing to be 'seen' – more of a front ...
> *an avoidance of being really seen?*

Perhaps it comes from fear of being found wanting? I've done that ... constantly busy ... trying to be 'superwoman' ... Sometimes I'm surprised to have survived at all! As a child and young adult, certainly felt I wasn't 'normal' and needed to pretend to be all right when I felt anything but.

Appreciating all your family stories – learning so much more about you and what happened in all those years we didn't know each other. The demands of starting a new life at 17, pregnant, on your own in a new country; the children and all of those stories; the constant 'following the fleet' for so long; then the years with your mother .. and for much of the time R being away so much ...
> *How do you feel about yourself when you look back at it all?*

Been wondering what it's like having to adapt your space yet again. You seem to have spent a lot of time being generous and hospitable with something you like to have control over.
> *How does this work between you and B* [daughter]*?*

As a child you seemed to have found a way to appear sure of yourself. Though in Trinidad and out of touch with you at the time, I heard about and admired your determination to get married at 17 – your certainty it was the right thing for you – despite people's objections.
> *What enabled you to do that?*

Sara and R invited David and me to be part of a family gathering for their 50th wedding anniversary in July 2008. It felt important to be there – to celebrate and to meet more of this family I didn't know.

Sara emailed in February: *"I'm so happy you're planning to join us this summer."*

(Sara, February/March 2008)

> I wonder why some people
> want to 'hide'?
> Afraid of being themselves
> or not knowing who they really are?
>
> Think my brother had begun to feel
> his life had lost its meaning
> after he lost his job
> couldn't get another
> and his (second) wife eventually leaving him
>
> We used to talk on the phone
> but he seemed disconnected from everyone
> even his four sons
>   *Wish I'd been able to help him more*
> Perhaps he had been 'hiding'
> for a while
> but no one knew it
>
> Wonder if any of us are really normal ...
>   *what's normal anyway?*
> Wish I'd known you
> perhaps have been a friend
> when you really needed support
> It's hard when one is isolated
> not to try to be 'superwoman'
> It's scary when there's no one to count on
> but yourself

Don't know very much
about our family history
Would love to sit down
and talk with you sometime
and find out more

Not sure what kept me going
when first on my own here
Learned to cope
by solving one thing at a time
Tend to be methodical
        learning to trust one's own strength

Always pretty determined
I could do a thing
if I just stuck with it long enough

When R and I met
we knew almost instantly
that we would spend
the rest of our lives together
        He was exactly what I wanted
though don't know
that I'd ever thought about it before!

Everyone thought we were just idiot children
but we kept on insisting
that we would get married
R put in for permission to marry
EVERY Monday morning for four months!!

Plenty of times when it was extremely hard
but we never doubted each other
or our ability to cope together
        We've made a good team

Some of our children's life choices
have been very challenging
but decided to let them make their own mistakes
We thought we were old enough to choose
when still teenagers

and felt we could do no less
for our children

In the long run
they've all done well
and grown into interesting grown-ups
people we enjoy spending time with

Started this in February
at a Festival in Texas
called Four Winds
for very good reason!
On a ranch
with lots of horses
and long-horn cattle
in the cold and wind

Finishing it in March
and it's warmer with no wind
but we had SNOW on Friday!!

(Christine, April 2008)

About 'hiding' – perhaps the fear is of discovering things we don't want to know (for ourselves or others). For me it was about not being able to bear (or imagine anybody else could) my own difficult feelings ... being unacceptable ... putting on a front ... it's a very lonely place ... becomes important to just 'get on with it' ... a lot of the time didn't think I wanted any help.

Beginning to understand more about myself helped to understand more about H [first husband] and why he drank and behaved as he did – why people do things that seem so destructive – and why I was attracted to that, too.

Love your stories about how determined you were (and are)! I'm pretty determined, too – can't say I've always been right in what I've been determined to do, but have certainly learned from it.

How did you know that R was what you wanted?
What stories do you tell your children about that time?

You seem to have done such a good job with your children and all their families – and become this 'matriarch' and mother to everybody.

How do you see yourself in that family role?

Getting to know you better through these letters is so interesting. It would be lovely to sit down and talk about our family history – though I don't know that much. But I do know (or have gathered) that we have some amazing (and very visible) women – mothers, grandmothers, aunts – so let's include ourselves in that band!

(Sara, April 2008)

Another episodic letter ...
Back home
unpacking kept getting more involved
Done now
and whatever still isn't in its right place
too bad!

I like your thoughts
on why people 'hide' themselves
I suppose the taking of drugs
alcoholism
hoarding stuff
constantly buying things one doesn't need
etc
are all ways of hiding from oneself

not really being in the world

Understanding behaviour
studying how and why people behave
the way they do
is important
        Always had common sense
must be my Essex forebears
but definitely learned a lot as I grew older

R is one of the most sensible people I've known
always so practical
really clever at mending things
fabricating parts to fix things
Like to think I'm practical and sensible
but he thinks I'm a bit flighty!

Both pretty determined people
but each has given the other
the opportunity to realize our dreams
R to stay in the Navy as long as he wanted
and me to have my own business

R and I met by chance
far too young
to think about the rest of our lives
Sounds weird now
but there was never an idea
that we would ever part
Always been like that
        even the times over the years
        when we didn't much like each other

Telling the children about it
is a double-edged sword!
Because it worked for us
they have no qualms
about getting into a relationship
at an early age
Unfortunately they've not always been right
but I do like the way they've all matured

Always felt I had such a tiny family
isolated from everybody else by distance
The idea that R and I
have caused this huge extended family
to come into being
amazing and exciting!!!

> *One really marvellous thing*
> *about getting older*
> *is not having to do all the work*

I can sit back and enjoy them all
hold the babies
play with the little ones
talk to the bigger ones
love the older ones
just be with them all

I so enjoy
being Sara – Mum – Granny
to them all
Can't wait for you to meet
at least some of them this summer

When we started this correspondence
I believed that my visibility was
at best
fading

Now it seems
as if I just wasn't really looking
Feel much more validated

We are a group
of very visible people
aren't we
the women of this family
on all sides?

(Christine, May 2008)

People's behaviour is always interesting – even if apparently inexplicable or dysfunctional. Believe there's always a reason for the strange things people do – even if I sometimes struggle to understand my own 'hidden' feelings and behaviour, never mind anybody else's. ...
Are there parts of you like that as well?

You seem very practical and sensible – as well as having imagination and vision – the ability to create things. I know you are other things too ...
What does being 'a bit flighty' mean?

Can't tell you how delighted I am to hear what you say about your changed sense of visibility ... very validating for me, too. Started this without knowing where it was going to take me (which I believe is what research should be about) ... and been learning what a wide variety of personal definitions there are of visibility/invisibility.

Older women so often seem to have gone along with the 'myth' of becoming unimportant, no longer counting or being seen – by themselves as well as others. Definitely not just about a physical visibility – internal as well as external process – being able to have a sense of one's own self *for oneself* – working out how we want to be in the world – what sort of contribution we want to make in society, etc.

The way you've developed your 'mothering' roles within the extended family (and elsewhere) sounds like a very important part of finding your own way of being who and what you want to be.
Does this make sense to you?

Still amazes me – that certainty you and R had – knowing what you wanted so clearly, so young. In terms of relationships with men I kept on getting it wrong for such a long time – can still feel real shame around how I let myself be put down or not well treated. Thought of myself, even when young and lacking in confidence, as quite feisty and having clear opinions and views – but that would vanish around the men I fell in love with. Another form of invisibility! Don't think I knew what 'love' looked or felt like.

(Sara, June 2008)

> Isn't it interesting
> how little we know of those around us?
> > *People keep all sorts of things*
> > *to themselves*
> I'd rather people think of me as calm and organised
> but sometimes am rather snarky and impatient
> Wish I wasn't
> but there you are!
>
> Used to hate having to tell my mother
> something I knew she wouldn't like
> > *She was very vocal when displeased!*
> I'd put off telling her until the last minute
> which only made matters worse
>
> Tend to go 'off with the fairies'
> sometimes
> drift about
> in a bit of a fantasy world
> then R has to come and sort me out
> Do this when I have an idea for a project
> and need to work it out
> so I forget to put the dinner on!

Still find myself rather invisible
in some situations
    but am learning to ignore
    those who ignore me
instead of worrying about it
Much more satisfactory I think

For a while
felt as if my role in the world
was becoming redundant
    so felt more invisible than I really was
Your idea of finding one's own space
and knowing who and what one is
makes perfect sense to me

My 'mum's-in-charge' bit
just evolved
Wasn't always very good at it
and made mistakes all over the place
but if one just keeps plugging away
it works out.

Thanks for telling me
so much of your story
about falling in love with the 'wrong' men
I don't think anyone knows
what love really is at first
how it feels
what it looks like
Love doesn't just happen anyway
it evolves and changes all the time

Hope we can find some time
to tell some more of our stories
while you're here

It's going to be
an amazing summer
I can't wait to see everyone!
So many family are coming
We'll have a bunch of babies to play with!

Sara and R had arranged the celebration of their 50th wedding anniversary in July to coincide with the opening week of the annual Sterling Renaissance Festival in upstate New York. There was a big extended family gathering over the week, including David and me. Family and close friends came from around the US, the UK and Australia.

(Christine, email 25.07.08)

> *What can I say? What a WONDERFUL party – or series of parties. You really pulled it off! ... so much enjoyed meeting so many of the family ... it did my heart good to see so much fun going on ... and you and R looking so relaxed and loving and happy ... lots of photos to remind me ... Still feel a bit tearful every time I think about saying goodbye to you ...*

(Christine, July/August 2008)

> Writing this soon after leaving the party ... still feeling emotional ... it was really hard to say goodbye to you ... Feel that through our exchange of stories we've become differently visible to each other and to ourselves.
>
> In my family it seemed like everything was hidden – not spoken about. Very hard to even ask questions. Not surprised about not wanting to tell your mother difficult things – think I was a bit scared of her when we were kids.
> *Do the children in your family talk to you about 'stuff'?*
>
> Having now seen some of this huge extended family – and got a sense of your place within it – I'm even more astonished at what you've achieved!
> *How does it feel to be this amazing matriarchal figure?*

Grew up with a need to be OK whatever happened – a sort of inner rebellious strength. Often wanted to disappear as a child ... being depressed was like a way of escaping ... a place inside me where nobody could go but me.

In August I asked all my co-researchers if they would be willing to take part in some 'group' contact in order to share their experiences of our exchanges. Sara's response was: *"Yes, you can share my email address with any of the group. I'd love to correspond with your other participants."*

(Sara, September 2008)

> Another episodic letter
> I like doing it this way
> don't feel rushed to get it done in one go
> can take my time writing each bit
>
> We're at another festival
> near Pittsburgh
> Lovely site
> beautiful and peaceful
> but sales are very slow
> and we've decided to sell the shop here
> It's getting hard to do this
> right after Sterling
> and then Louisiana coming up in November
>
> We had such fun at the 'do' in Sterling
> even though we got pretty knackered
> what with all the partying!
> > *Everything we wanted it to be*
> A huge family get-together
> with kids and food and games and chatting
> just wonderful!!

Expect I have a much higher opinion
of my helping powers
than the kids/grandkids do!
They talk more easily on the phone or by email
than face-to-face
Glad to help
even if it's only a sympathetic ear

Became so used to looking after the children
that wasn't sure what my role would be
as they grew up and moved out

Mother became more and more
dependent on me
wanted me to look after her all the time
Very insistent I care for her at home
I felt rather trapped
in the role of care-giver
          sort of became invisible

Tend to drift off
when thinking up something new
and get rather impractical
Spend hours
scribbling or sketching or just thinking

          Do enjoy drifting about sometimes
like lying on one's back on the grass
when we were kids
and watching the clouds
The rest of the time
I try to be sensible!

So impressed by your strength and determination
Your description of depression
is profound
It sounds as if
you found a safe place to 'hide out'
probably not a bad thing

Rather enjoying
learning about your life
and sharing some of mine

(Christine, October 2008)

Your episodic letters seem very 'immediate' and chatty – I hear your voice coming through. Email can be a wonderful thing! So good getting to know you differently through this. Have the sense of re-discovering the cousin I felt fond of but not close to (and slightly in awe of) ... and becoming a sort of sisterly-friend. Recognising the strength in each other has been part of this ...

Go on being amazed and impressed by the complicated family dynamics in your huge family 'tribe' – how all the 'steps' and 'halfs' (as it were) have been integrated into the whole.
How on earth do you all do it?

You might be surprised at what your kids/grandkids really think about your 'sympathetic ear'. As mother of a grown son, been careful not to give advice – because of my experience of unwanted interference. Very nice sometimes to be invited to 'interfere' – touches me hugely as well as making me feel very visible. What a lot you did for your mother ...
How did you manage it and not get resentful?

I've sometimes (guiltily) allowed myself to wonder what it would have been like if my mother had lived and turned out not to be such a perfect mother after all ...

This 'drifting' sounds like a lovely place to get your ideas and inspirations ...
Do you really feel you ought to be 'sensible' all the time?

(Sara, November 2008)

Started writing this at home
and continued
in Louisiana

When I left England with R
was so excited to be escaping
the kind of life Mother had planned for me
I wasn't even sad

Both R and I had
really great grandparents
who took us in when we needed it
Our parents weren't very good at grand-parenting
so we decided to make up for that
and we've been really tested!

Another great-grandchild has just arrived!
Adorable of course

Thinking about the components of this tribe
guess we just don't worry
how they came into the family
Accept each person for who they are
and love them all

Your kind words and thoughts
were very helpful
when I lost my brother
It was extraordinarily difficult
to talk about P
for the first couple of years
after he took his life
Still hard to think about him
I wonder why it still feels so raw?

(Christine, January 2009)

Used to worry about not having a proper 'home' or roots like other people. Never knew what to say when asked 'Where are you from?' – often made things up. Then realised it didn't matter that I don't 'come from' somewhere – carry my roots around with me, bit like a pot plant.

How interesting – your excitement at 'escaping' from England ...

What do you think was the life your mother had planned for you?

Was very excited at the idea of going to Australia on my own and couldn't understand why people kept trying to talk me out of it ... a big adventure!

Pleased to hear that you both at least experienced good grand-parenting ... and the way you've been able to set up your own family dynamic based on acceptance and love. What a gift to everybody ...

Did you feel loved by your mother? Do you think P did?

Good to know you found it helpful to correspond with me about P's death ... and that you still feel able to talk about it. We go on missing people ... don't believe in 'getting over' death and grief ... they remain as part of us and our experience. Grief and loss change us ... I think that's how it should be.

Perhaps your rawness is partly connected to the way in which P chose to take his life - and how that impacted on others?

Noticed that both our letters are getting longer ... telling our family histories to each other is really enjoyable and it's quite difficult to stop writing once I get going! I'm beginning to move toward the time when the 'co-research' correspondence will need to end, but look forward to our chats continuing.

(Sara, February/March 2009)

> Always enjoy writing to you
> makes me think about
> what I'm saying!
>
> Just had an opportunity
> to buy two acres of overgrown woodland
> next to our place
> May even borrow a goat
> to eat the undergrowth ...
> and it's firewood for years!
>
> Love having this place to come back to
> > *but moving around*
> > *never has bothered me*
> Always have a few books
> photos and odds and ends
> that go everywhere with me
> including pot plants!
>
> Neither of us wanted to stay in one place
> R left his home on the farm at 17
> and joined the Navy
> We met a year later
> and left for America
> a year after we were married
>
> > *I was glad to have the opportunity*
> > *to lead my own life*
> though don't think I realised
> America would be so different
> or that R would be sent away to sea
> so soon after we arrived

Don't think Mother ever planned
to 'let me go'
She thought I'd always be there
        ready to do whatever she wanted

She made it clear
I couldn't expect
to be able to come home again
if it didn't work out

As children
P and I didn't spend much time together
but were always really close
I'm sure Mother loved us
        but I think she liked us better
        when we weren't there!

We were both quite sure
that our father didn't love or like us
he left to be with another woman
and NEVER supported us at all

Wonder if my ongoing sadness
over P's death
is partly because he was the last
of my 'original' family?

Started this at home
as we packed for Texas
then nearly a month went by
before finishing
It's been a bit crazy
but the Festival is going well
now we've got some decent weather

It's so nice to fill in the bits of our history
as we go along
        It's difficult to stop writing to you
I enjoy it very much
even though it sometimes takes me forever
to get finished

We agreed that this would be last of our correspondence for the co-researching – and that we would continue to email each other personally. The ongoing sharing of past family history and our current lives is a 'project' that we are still engaged in.

(Christine, email 13.04.09)

> *I'm about to send out a brief letter to all of you, individually, letting you know that I'm now at the stage where the 'research phase' letter-writing is coming to an end as I begin to concentrate on pulling the whole thing together. However I'd really love to keep writing with you as part of our ongoing getting-to-know-each-other thing ... so hope you're up for that!*

> *I so much enjoy your letters and thank you for all that you've contributed so far.*

(Sara, email 13.04.09)

> *I certainly plan on staying in touch and 'chatting' with you ... this is such fun exploring oneself and all the people who surround one ... though it sometimes takes me an age or I can't get an internet connection, it's great that I can just take my time writing ...*

> *Look forward to reading all our stories when you've finished!*

7.8 Jane

The ways I now feel visible in the world
are so incredibly comfortable

(Jane's autobiographical letter dated 17.04.09 at the end of our correspondence)

I am 61 years old
and living very happily
with my civil partner N
in a house in Hampshire

Retired early
from a very busy and demanding
professional job
having been part of the health professions
most of my working life

Most of this time
was spent operating out of my left brain

After being fortunate enough
to spend some months
in a Retreat Centre
in the Mid-West of the USA
I found my right brain again
which opened a whole new world!

Have found a love affair with fabric
and stained glass has also fascinated me
so retiring early
has given me the time and space
to develop my self-taught fabric creativity

Now call myself a fabric artist
and work on commission basis
creating large wall hangings
that look like stained glass

I also enjoy
creating more earthy and ethnic pieces
which honour my South African origins

Jane and I met as students in 1993 on an innovative and experientially-taught two-year MSc programme, Change Agent Skills & Strategies, with the Human Potential Research Group at Surrey University. Jane, who lived within commuting distance of the university, very kindly offered me accommodation during the five-day taught modules each month.

We grew to know a lot about each other, both during the intensive experiential group sessions and the evenings spent reflecting together on the day in our very different ways (often knocking back large quantities of red wine at the same time). One of my ways of reflecting became known between us as "colouring in" because of my propensity for drawings and diagrams using multi-coloured pens.

Jane was then in a high profile, very stressful post in the health professions and experiencing severe back problems. Shortly after the end of the MSc programme, she decided to take early retirement on medical grounds and concentrate on developing other aspects of her life and interests. This has included completing an MA in Religion at the School of Cultural Studies at Southampton University, when she undertook an exploration of how art facilitates spiritual meaning in death and dying. Jane also made numerous visits to Rockhaven, a creative retreat centre in the US, where she eventually met her American partner.

We have maintained contact over the years and I have followed her transition from stressed executive to creative fabric artist and loving partner with great delight.

(Christine, email 02.01.08)

I was wondering if you now feel ready to engage with my visible/invisible women project?

My ideas, of course, keep changing, but then that's part of why I'm doing this ... It feels all kinds of things, including exciting and challenging – and I'm planning quite a lot of colouring-in!

(Jane, email 05.01.08)

We seem to have a fairly busy time planned – it just sort of happened! ...

Yes of course I can endeavour to engage in your project – just make it simple and remember I'm a bear of very little brain!!

(Christine, email 07.01.08)

Many thanks for saying you're ready to have a go ... and as for the bear of little brain, I shall just ignore that one! ...

I'm attaching my first letter and can only repeat the 'no rules' bit in it – which is that you can answer or not answer the questions I've asked – you may well have better ones you'd rather write about ...

(Jane, 18.01.08)

I shall peruse your questions
as a useful starting point

Just coming up to my 60th birthday
and life is great
Better than it's ever been

A clear sense of 'this is who I am'

Living with my civil partner N
from the US
We got 'married' last September
One is not meant to use that term
but for me that's what we did
and I refer to her as my wife

Our lives revolve
around friends in the UK and US
all people who accept us as a partnership
and probably equally spread
between straight and gay

Always aware of feeling more comfortable
with women
but did not come to terms with my sexuality
until I was 50 years old
          Now feel freer than I ever have

Creativity is now an important aspect
Since retiring 12 years ago
I opened to another part of me
my right brain
which had been rather under-used

Fabric and colour really excite me
now a fabric artist
an enormous change from my career
in nursing and midwifery

I loved the job I had
AND it was the most demanding ever
Retiring early
felt like the end of the world
at the time

The stress was a contributory factor
to my intractable back condition
Experienced a lot of anger
about how this was dealt with

Physical pain was part of my life
until having major reconstructive surgery
after retiring

Also gifted myself with retreat time
looking at childhood issues
and ways of actively changing
conditioning that no longer served me well
from a background of emotional and physical abuse
Witness to extreme parental violence

Opening the lid of that box of unknown
was an enormous risk
but such a worthwhile risk
My life is now just so rich and so real ...

(Notice that your letter was called 'no. 1' ...
you're obviously hopeful of more ...!)

In an email accompanying this letter, letting me know that she and N would be away for a couple of weeks, Jane said: *"I'm giving your questions a go ... do feel free to question further about any of it ... Hope my ramblings will be of some use to you."*

I responded a couple of days later: *"I really like your 'ramblings' – they're very you! Which is exactly what I want – the real voices of real women and not what 'they' are telling us we're thinking or feeling as we get older."*

(Christine, 14.02.08)

Letter no. 2 – and yes, I am hoping for more!

So many things in your letter I could comment on or ask questions about ...

What does 'married' and 'wife' mean to you particularly?
Sounds like good 'being visible' stuff – or maybe that's just my
bias! Dislike that word wife – for myself – and resist using it.
Perhaps a hangover from my first marriage ...

Not sure I've ever asked ...
    why you feel so excited by fabric and colour ...??

I appreciate what you're saying about your sexuality. It
seemed very difficult to even broach the subject when you so
generously shared your space with me – though we talked so
freely about so many things.
    What is your memory of that?

What you say about both physical and emotional pain reminds
me of how much you have coped with over the years.
    How did you learn to 'accommodate' pain?
    What turned this into 'fighting' for what you needed?

I remember you seemed like quite an angry person a lot of the
time – not towards me but about work and with certain people
in the group. Almost certainly recognised it because of my own
anger, which was bursting out in all kinds of ways, sometimes
not very appropriately (but wasn't it wonderfully energising!) ...

Interested to hear more about the 'end of the world' feelings
around retiring early ...
    How would you now describe being 'visible' in the world?
    *What's different from your eminent, high-profile
    professional self?*

(Jane, 26.02.08)

Your questions and comments
are helpful
and also very insightful

Married
to me
means intentional commitment
> It is really important
> to have equal choice
to live together legitimately
which same sex couples
were precluded from before

The 'wife' bit is interesting
and also your resistance to using it
Could have something to do
with the association of ownership
by the guy of HIS wife
and her using his name

We choose to use 'wife'
as a term of endearment
and not as a definition
of our relationship
> Yes it is good visible stuff!

Really bright and vibrant fabric colours
are exciting to me
I love the textures
Being able to actually FEEL the colours
via the fabric
put them together
as other artists mix paint

Around my sexuality
it was very frightening
to contemplate inviting disapproval
It was difficult to separate
my professional from my private life

I was reluctant to own who I was
even with people who might not disapprove

Always had to accommodate pain
as part of my life
Learned quickly
what is acceptable behaviour
  As a child I just closed down
  in order to survive

Asked to be sent to boarding school
at eleven years old
and it was one of the happiest times
in a beautiful peaceful location
surrounded by love from the nuns
Learned to play the piano
and spent hours immersed in music

Had a quiet determination
about where I needed to go or be
from quite an early age
Hated going 'home' for the holidays
and came to England
to live with grandparents
two days after finally leaving school

'End of the world' feelings
on retirement
related to the lack of identity
outside my professional role

How was I going to have
any sense of social acceptance
if I wasn't contributing anything
to society?
Had to learn to simply say
I was just Jane
And you know ...
  the world didn't stop
  and I wasn't rejected!!

Being visible in the world now
feels incredibly comfortable
> *Happier as I approach 60*
> *than I ever have been before*

Jane attached what she called *"a few bits and pieces"* to her letter, with two poems about grief, pain and healing written during her retreat times and photos of a recent fabric 'stained glass window' commission.

(Christine, 13.03.08)

> I loved the photos of your work – and of you – and the way N 'got' you with all your bracelets on full display, your colourful clothing alongside the colours of your 'window' ...
> > *If it's possible to put into words, can you say more about the whys, whats, hows of your feelings around colour?*
>
> About intentional commitment – I feel much the same way. D and I decided to get married for that reason, despite having both said we were never going to do it again.
> > *What made you so sure about 'visible commitment' to N?*
>
> The way I often hear the 'my wife' and 'my husband' bit between couples seems both about owning and being owned. Maybe I'm being over-sensitive because of my previous experience ... Sounds like your use as a 'term of endearment' is about acknowledging the strength of your commitment rather than laying claim to each other ...
>
> Your poem *Dark Side of the Moon* is very telling about the deepness and darkness of your pain – and your fear of revealing more of yourself. It seemed very hard for you to have much of a personal life then ...

Maybe you were always so incredibly busy partly so you didn't have to think about a personal life?

How might you have felt if I had asked more about all this at the time?

Agree that most people who've had painful childhoods learn to 'get on with it'. It's a 'good' way for children to survive – but not a good way to carry on living as an adult.
Where did your 'quiet determination' come from?

Your story about discovering being 'just Jane' and not your role in the world sounds like a very important milestone ... reminds me of learning to see myself during my 'magic summer' ...

What was it like, not being rejected for just being you?

(Jane, 24.04.08)

Not being rejected for just being 'me'
was like being given
the best present I didn't know I wanted
Opening page one of the book called
'The Art of the Possible'
        A *gift of being visible to others*

Needed your sense
of not going further in asking me questions
in those earlier times ...
I was still so closed to myself
about my sexuality
and so afraid of 'coming apart'

Remembering an image
when working on my 'child' stuff
of being totally surrounded
by a wall of thick ice

Fear of it melting
and people might get to see me
which seemed more fearful
than people being able to get closer

I would hate to be 'owned' or 'owning'
and think you've totally got
what I mean by our 'term of endearment'
Hadn't even thought
of making this sort of commitment before
Very quickly an incredible degree
of 'comfortableness' with N
as though we'd known each other for years

Standing outside my American 'dream house'
in Defiance (wonderful name isn't it!)
and knew
I wanted to spend the rest of my life with N
Later that night
realised it wasn't the house
        it was N that was the dream

Difficult to describe
my love of fabric
but I'll have a go ...
When right into choosing colours
trying them out
I'm in a different place
kind of cushioned by the colour
Time disappears ...

        Deep sense of being 'inside me'
soul – mind – body connection
Enormously happy
once I find the desired colour and texture

A big sense of completion
when a project has taken a long time
but also a sense of loss
and letting go

This is me as an adult
Didn't get to express too much
in the world of painting and drawing
as a child
My younger brother and sister
were far more artistic than I was
Learned to sew from a very early age
had my first sewing machine at ten
which I loved and used a lot

Just been out to South Africa again
Some of my delight in strong bright colours
may well be rooted there
    Loved reconnecting
      to large colourful African art
the expansive country
and big tropical flowers
growing wild and in profusion

Jane attached a photo of her first fabric 'window', created as part of her MA research into art facilitating spiritual meaning, together with an extract from her thesis showing her reflections on the process.

(Christine, 27.05.08)

You certainly look different to me now – it's a delight to be allowed to 'see' you in all kinds of ways. Been thinking about times in my life when I've appeared very visible from the outside but was actually hiding a lot (from myself and others) ... having to learn about really being seen ... when that was safe ...

    What's it like for you, this 'gift' of being visible to others?

'Comfortableness' doesn't seem a word you would use often or lightly ...

What does it mean to you?

Really enjoyed your reflections on my questions about your love of fabric and colour ... descriptions of how you work ... being 'cushioned' by colour and how supportive that sounds ... the synthesis of soul-mind-body connection and internal happiness. Being able to find this very different kind of work – and also 'find' N - seems part of the way you are now different from that stressed, over-worked, unhappy person you were and have described ...

Does that fit for you?
Am I being over-analytical?

Appreciated seeing the picture of your first window and reflections on it –fascinating – and a real insight into your process.

Can understand your delight in reconnecting with the vividness of the colours in South Africa. Find it interesting you've chosen to stay in England – so often described as grey and wet. Remember my almost shock at seeing how green and 'tidy' it is when returning from living in very different countries and climates.

How does it feel when you return?

You said N had not been out of the US before you met – and you seem to be doing a lot of travelling together now. As a very independent person, used to whizzing about the world, doing your own thing ...

I wonder how you're finding it – both travelling with and living with somebody else?

Interested in your sense of both completion and loss when you finish a piece of work. Wanting to finish something and yet not wanting to let go ... I'm already experiencing the end/loss in advance of my correspondence with this amazing group of

visible women. Feels like real in-depth 'story telling' that allows
me to put myself in there alongside the people whose stories
I'm gathering. The sort of writing I've always wanted to do ...

(Jane, 21.07.08)

This being visible to others
is so incredibly freeing
          So different not having to hide ...
          from myself more than anything
To feel able to say and be who I am

Some of that comes
with an increasing degree
of comfort with self
that comes with age

When I used the word 'comfortableness'
it meant like sitting in a really comfy chair ...
sort of wrap around
supportive
holding and snug

          Being prepared to trust my own intuition
          in a more visible way

It finally dawned on me
how much more meaningful
good people are
than material things!

N has been here a year
and we have worked through various things
as you do when sharing space and life together
We did 'find' each other
and there is a lot of happiness together
AND we both need different individual space
within what was 'my' house

in order not to 'lose' our sense of self

When we were in the US recently
it was quite exhausting
So many people to see
after N's first trip back after a year
Wall-to-wall visiting and interacting with people

On our return
N had to settle in to England again
and found that no easy task
It's been quite a whirlwind for her
with all the travel we've done
in quite a short space of time
Now we both want some time here
        quietly being at home

Really delight in returning to England
looking down on the patchwork quilt
of every possible green
The ever-changing landscapes here
are connected to there being four seasons
In South Africa
it was raining or sunshine

Loved what you shared
about feeling loss in advance
and also the enjoyment
from in-depth story telling

Jane regularly gave me positive feedback about taking part in this co-research. At the end of the letter above she added:

"It has been such a good experience being one of your 'visible women' — your incredible insights and questions/challenges have been very helpful and thought provoking. So I want to thank you — all very revealing."

(Christine, 26.08.08)

> Thank you for your feedback. I'm loving doing this and delighted you're finding this such a positive 'visible' experience ... imagine it has a lot to do with your no longer hiding from yourself , which is so important, isn't it. Once we stop hiding from ourselves, it seems to become more natural (and obvious) that we won't want to hide from others ... gaining the confidence to be who we are without constantly striving for affirmation and acceptance from others ... choosing to be around people who can accept us as we are.
>
> *Perhaps we have to 'earn' this – through the knocks of life?*
>
> About 'intuitive knowing', had a sense of your beginning to try this out in the MSc group (all those years ago!) – but your work and other pressures seemed to make it difficult then.
> *How does it work for you now?*
>
> Sounds like the creating of different spaces for you and N within the house is an important stage within your relationship and your individual 'sense of self'.
> *How is this working now?*
> *What does it give you?*
>
> You seem to have done an extraordinary amount of travelling around in a short time ...
> *Was there a reason for doing so much at once?*
> *What's the settling back in been like for each of you?*

(Jane, 29.09.08)

> Yes you're right ...
> was beginning to try out
> trusting my intuition

all those years ago!
Difficult given my fears
about what the effects might be
of my personal on my professional life

This had an opportunity to grow
when I went to Rockhaven
and had the chance to experiment more
           in a safe place without recrimination
The whole thrust of the place
was about being real

Even so
it took some time
to come to terms
with the whole sexuality bit
and be visible
with that knowing sense of
           this is really me

Who would have thought
it would take until I was 50
to 'come out'
and that it would be
with a bunch of nuns in the woods!!

The journey to this place
can demand knocks and ups and downs
but it's so worth it
to experience that sense of freedom

No particular reason
for all the travel earlier in the year
just kind of came together
but good to be back
and busy on projects in the house together

           Continuing to make this place
           more ours than mine
Finding a way to create
different work spaces

is going really well
and it's made a big difference
for us both

As promised a photo of my latest 'window'
Chinese design of cranes and pine trees
to do with longevity

(Christine, 25.10.08)

Your crane 'window' is beautiful ... the sense of movement as
well as elegant arrangement of shapes and colours ...

Enjoyed your 'coming out with a bunch of nuns in the woods'!
Interested to hear more about what 'being real' means to you
...
*What were the ways in which you weren't being 'real'
before?*
Had there been other safe places?

Very interested in the way you're changing your shared space
– making it *"more ours than mine"* – and also what it means in
the way of those other spaces around, between and within ...
How do you two work this out between you?

When I feel intruded on (physically, psychologically,
emotionally), get a sense of being disregarded ... beginning to
disappear ... tend to withdraw in order to get some inner space
... in order to stay 'visible' to myself. I've had to learn to talk
about it, make it 'real', not pretend it's OK even if there's no
easy (or obvious) solution. It only works if both are really able
to 'see' what might be difficult for the other person.

Now have a Russian doll theory of visibility ... Lynn has lent me
hers (all seven of them) which I can play with and see how

neatly and cleverly they fit, one inside the other ... different ways of being seen ...

Lots of different images about how this dissertation will go – have a sort of 'colouring-in route map' but no doubt the journey will be different! Bit like not knowing if the world really IS round but planning a round-the-world exploration anyway – all the time slightly anxious that I might fall off the edge!

(Jane, 21.12.08)

Being real
means not having to think
about trying to act
in a way that is going to please
or be 'right'
    Being free
    to express an opinion that is mine

The places of not being real
were a carry over from work
having to please others ...
and of course much further back
with the mother
and needing to do it right
It was very well learned!

Starting to do it differently
without recrimination
was quite unbelievable
The sky didn't fall in
I didn't get beaten up
literally or figuratively ...
    and I just got braver and braver!

Withdraw when my 'expression space'
is reduced
    Guess that going all quiet

is like going invisible

Great frustration
at not being able to get what I need
and it comes out as anger at times
as don't always realise
what the underlying problem is

Became aware of conflict
deep within
about having created this space
and it being mine
then moving my vision
to look at it through N's eyes

It is a slow process
but once begun
it became easier
and I just wanted to do more and more
and of course
N was then able to enter in more easily

It is now so very comfortable
        a result of a lot of work
        on both our parts
in the acknowledgement
and open discussion
of different needs

Loved your 'round-the-world-exploration' image
and had wonderful visions of you
walking tentatively round the edge
My mind went back to that time
you and I sat overlooking the sea in Cadaquez
using the 'edge' to metaphorically throw over stuff
we didn't need or were finished with

I'm so much enjoying all this and have been delighted
with the bits of group emailing that have happened

Jane also loved my Russian doll theory of visibility: *"I have a little one ... all in slightly different clothes which seems very liberating ... If I can find it, will let you have it."*

Some weeks later a little package arrived with a note: *"At last have gotten into the attic and found this ... which I would love you to have. I actually bought her in St Petersburg."* There are five little dolls, the smallest of which is only 2cm high. They still sit on the windowsill in the room where I write, just behind my laptop.

I was quite ill with a virulent chest infection for most of January 2009 and did almost no writing at all. On getting back to work, I began negotiating the ending of this part of our co-research with those who were still corresponding.

(Christine, 12.02.09)

As you know, been well below par and incredibly low in energy – so quite happy with a relatively low level of visibility for the past few weeks!

A lovely memory of our throwing 'stuff' over the edge at the end of our MSc time – do you remember that Apollinaire poem? Went something like:

Come to the edge, he said
They said, we are afraid
Come to the edge, he said
They came
he pushed them
and they flew

Your comment about getting 'braver and braver' sounds very liberating – interesting that you were still feeling you had to 'get it right' when you seemed so vocal and able to speak your mind.

How did you experience yourself in that group?
Did you feel seen and heard?

I wonder how you went about making your space at home 'so comfortable' ...
> *When did it become 'visible' that you needed to make changes?*
> *What was it like, seeing through N's eyes?*

I know how interested you are in 'the process', so am sharing a bit of the story of the latest part of this particular journey ...

I have so much wonderful material from letters, poems and other gifts – and still LOVING gathering the stories and writing the letters – but towards the end of last year was beginning to wonder if I could ever turn it into a dissertation. Seemed both too difficult and a bit of a pointless academic exercise. My latest tutorial helped me get back to feeling connected to why I'm doing this – and finding some spaces to put away (not throw away) the bits I won't need for this particular task. My supervisor, as always, did a lot of good listening (she's also a therapist) – and suggested I get back to leaf gathering rather than trying to plant whole trees ...

And here I am beginning to bring this part of the leaf-gathering to an end so that I can move on to sticking some of them in my academic scrap book ... whilst paying attention to the spaces between me and you (and the other women) and how we have communicated within them ...

Am now clearer about how I can start writing my dissertation in a way that isn't about trying to fill all the spaces – but actually allowing them to be visible. Not sure if any of that makes sense!
> *Any comments/questions etc. would be very welcome !??!*

So intrigued to get the package in a little chocolate box – and the delight of discovering the Babushka, with all the smaller ones inside. She's sitting next to me now ... thank you once again ... she is already a visible part of all this.

Time to go off and do a bit of 'flying' – or hurling myself over the edge maybe!

(Jane, 02.03.09)

> The Apollinaire poem
> is a wonderfully simple thing
> to refer back to
> when we need a shove
> to take a new or different step
> > *AND with the positive outcome of 'flying'*
>
> Loved the bit about leaf gathering
> rather than tree planting
> ALLOWING VISIBILITY
> rather than
> FILLING SPACES
>
> I really understand this
> Seems like stepping back
> from the active
> almost contrived stuff
> Waiting for a spontaneous kind of happening
> or 'filling'
>
> I did feel seen and heard
> in that group
> but it was only one 'layer'
> the majority of which
> was my 'work/professional' self
> and was pretty disturbed

When I went to Rockhaven
it seemed much more about
    reaching other deeper 'real me' layers

Accepting that I needed to pay
more than lip service
to N sharing 'my' space
meant having to see it through her eyes

This is a permanent thing
that we have entered into
and each of us
needs our own areas of creativity

The resulting comfort
is about physical and mental space
    to be *separately when we want to*

I think 'flying' sounds so much more loaded with possibility
than 'hurling'
and I shall watch this space with much interest

In the early part of 2009 there were various exchanges of emails within the group as I asked for feedback on some of my ideas about the language for writing this narrative dissertation. Jane's response was typically robust and positive (see 'Writing in Visible Language' above).

(Christine, email 25.03.09)

Thank you so much – this is wonderfully supportive!

As you know, I am beginning to wind the letter-writing down now, as I have SO MANY stories … I think I could go on doing it for ever!

(Jane, email 27.03.09)

Glad you feel so supported by us all! Don't get lost in all the stories – it sounds pretty overwhelming.

(Christine, email 13.04.09)

As I'm now getting seriously into the writing, I shall reluctantly need to come to the end of exchanging letters with all my co-researchers. I have so much enjoyed receiving and sending letters and thank you once again for your wonderful contribution so far.

One final request (for now!) – when you have time, could you let me have any brief, background autobiographical information that you would be happy to see as part of your 'story' in these writings. Possible areas would be: age, current living arrangements, what you do now and what you used to do (work, play, etc.) anything relevant you want to say about family history, roots, etc. Hope that sounds OK and do-able ...

(Jane, email 17.04.09)

Herewith a brief background biography. Thank you for the guidelines – very helpful.

Although this brought an end to our letter-writing for my inquiry, Jane and I have continued to correspond and enjoy exchanging our stories more or less regularly.

CHAPTER EIGHT

THE VISIBLE GROUP

I believe ... we have connections
that cannot be investigated
but have to be relied on.
(Munro, 1985: 193)

8.1 Talking amongst ourselves

*We live our experiences through the stories we construct
in order to 'tell ourselves' to another ...*
                                             (Oliver, 2002: xxv)

This is a collection of the 'group' emails exchanged between the
eight women involved in these conversations.

(Christine, first group email to all seven women, 04.09.08)

Dear co-researchers

*Firstly, thank you all very much for agreeing to give brief 'group
feedback' as part of the ongoing VISIBLE WOMEN exploration
we've been on together. I've really been enjoying these
conversations, questions, occasional photos, poems and other
delights over the past months.*

*Having recently had another meeting with my wonderfully creative
and supportive supervisor, I'm slowly beginning to move towards
the next phase of planning the 'shape' of the dissertation. We
agreed that it would be a good idea to offer you all the opportunity
to give some feedback within the email group about your
experience of taking part.*

*Just to reassure everybody again - this can be as brief as you want
to make it, both in length and frequency. The names and email
addresses of the seven of you who have taken part are above – I'll
leave you to choose individually what to say (or not) about
yourselves.*

*Here are a couple of what one of you called my 'deceptively simple'
questions for starters:*

*a) What learning (if any) has there been for you in being asked
questions, thinking, writing about this issue of becoming an 'older
women' - both personal and in a more general sense?*

b) Has it felt like a 'conversation' of sorts? If so, have you felt free to question, comment, reflect on both sides of the conversation? If not, how else have you experienced it?

If any of you want to give a bit of brief biographical detail (or other relevant story) when replying, please do - and I'd also like to invite you to ask a question of the group (which may or may not get answered, of course).

Over to you ...

(Lynn, 17.09.08)

Hello. Sorry it's taken an age again. Constipation of the brain set in! I shall answer your questions in order.

A) I've learned a lot from your questions and my answers. As an older woman (although mostly I feel 15) I am far more confident and very cynical. Generally I find most of the women I meet over a certain age rather stuck. They wear drab clothes and appear to be drab in themselves. They've lost the joy of life and have forgotten how to play (if they ever knew!). Whereas others (like you) have changed enormously and yet still know how to play. I also feel that most of us have made the decision to grab back our own power. We have been lucky enough to live in a time of peace (relatively speaking) so our energies can be directed on ourselves, perhaps!!!! ... whatever it is I'm glad to be alive and have pink hair.

B) Yes. Your emails have been a conversation. With your amazing insight encouraging reflection I have felt as if I've done some therapy. Do you feel that? At all? With the amount of waffle I've thrown at you I'm astounded you can make sense of it let alone use it! How will you compartmentalise it all?

C) My question to the group is: Would you like to make contact? ... I feel it may be fun, with Christine as one of us, of course.

(Val, 19.09.08)

Hi Christine (and the group)

A) It has been fascinating to engage with you like this because I don't usually go in for self analysis. I'd also never considered whether I was a "Visible or invisible" older woman, so it was fun doing some research of my own (reading, internet, asking friends) and finding what a complicated issue it was. Some of my younger female (and male) friends actually said they felt "invisible" so it doesn't seem to be age or gender specific.

Our correspondence made me realise that I don't feel invisible and your careful questioning … made me evaluate why that might be. I think I'm just lucky to have been born with an optimistic, easy going outlook to parents who loved each other and me … I'm extremely fortunate because I'm still doing a useful job that I enjoy, working only the hours I want with enough money (just!) to do what I want, when I want, with my brain still functioning and with enough good relationships. I think financial independence and good friends help prevent women of any age from feeling powerless and invisible.

B) Our correspondence has felt like a "conversation" – but with a longer time lag than talking to the moon! Your comments have always been interesting and moved the discussion on and I've learnt a lot of things about myself - and you - that would not have been possible in "ordinary" conversation.

C) Lynn's suggestion of continuing with a group contact sounds great - but I'm sorry, as I explained when we started the discussion, my time is limited. I'm already a member of two online Study Groups so will have to say no. But I am looking forward to reading your finished dissertation – good luck with all the paper work!

(Sara, 21.09.08)

Hello everyone –

I'm Sara, the cousin in America. I've so enjoyed this correspondence with Christine; we weren't in close touch with each other for years and have now established a lovely close friendship that I really treasure.

I've thought about the questions she's posed, they've been interesting and insightful and I've discovered that I'm a lot more "visible" than I thought I was. I have learned about the family from whom I've been separated for 50 years - and want to learn so much more. I've learned about myself, too, and the surprisingly large family that my husband and I have helped to create. It's been an interesting journey - I hope it doesn't end too soon!

I hope I hear from some of you other participants about your experiences with this project.

(Alison, 22.09.08)

Hello Everyone

Thanks to Lynn, Val and Sara for their input already. My reply will be pretty brief – mainly, I think, because, though I've enjoyed participating in the research, I'm not sure how much energy I've got to write more!

I worked with Christine at King's College … for several years where we facilitated groups for GPs. I'm nearly 65; live alone on a quiet'ish council estate in South London, I still do some paid work, and I'm a Buddhist (have 'taken refuge' in June). I'm also a writer, researcher and counsellor – or was. 'Was' because work is dwindling and that's my main preoccupation at the moment as I don't feel ready for the loss of identity, role (and income) from being a worker!

This is a transitional time of life and being involved with Christine's research has helped me think through some issues in a

*more structured way – though still struggling with the next steps.
The back and forth emailing of letters has been brilliant. When
Christine asked me to participate, I panicked – assuming it would
involve being interviewed.*

*I've enjoyed the wide-ranging discussions - covering everything
from clothes, singing, working, travelling, falling over, etc .etc. It's
also been lovely to get to know more about Christine!*

Greetings to everyone

(Jane, 24.09.08)

Hi Christine and the other Visible Women

*Thanks for your inputs - have enjoyed getting to know a little about
the others in the Group.*

*I too have enjoyed the contact and the learning from Christine's
incredibly insightful questions. I believe a really big learning for
me has been the acknowledgement of how visible I am - much more
so than 12 years ago when I first had the pleasure of beginning a
friendship with Christine. We were on a Masters degree course at
Surrey University at which time I was in a very high powered and
pressured professional job in London. I've now been retired for 12
years although was just 60 this year. I live in Hampshire and have
developed an alternative life as a fabric artist, have been doing
some facilitation at a Spiritual Retreat Centre in the Midwest in the
USA and have recently had a Civil Partnership with a wonderful
American woman who I met at the Retreat Centre!*

*The exchange of letters with Christine has been a great
conversation and her questions are brilliant and helpful - I've
really had to think and tap into deeper places which has been so
constructive and enlightening.*

*I too will need to decline the offer of continuing group contact. The
idea does sound good, but like Alison I'm running short of writing
energy at the moment. I am also a Trustee on two Charities which
is demanding a lot of input at the moment. Am so looking forward*

to reading the finished dissertation too - how you 'sew all this info. altogether'.

Greetings and warm wishes to all the Group.

(Cindy, 25.09.08)

Dear Visible Women

It's very nice to hear from all of you and it's always wonderful to converse with Christine over email.

I'm delighted to hear so many of you are too busy to email back and forth – to me that means you are having fun somewhere else ... I'm a bit crazed at the moment – time wise that is – but something came up yesterday that was very visible about older women's invisibility.

I'm getting married next month – to a beautiful woman I have been sharing my life with over the last 19 years. We have two adopted children. Thanks to the Supreme Court of the State of California we can now legally marry. One of our close family friends decided that she would host our wedding at her house and she's making a big party of it! Yeah! I love to dance! But ----- What to wear!?!?!

So I started looking around and it's very difficult to decide or know what to wear. I turned to M last night and said – I don't like any of the clothing I see on TV – I keep looking, hoping to see something that would look nice on me. Her reply – 'Cindy, they don't have women our age on TV!' And she's so right – I never realized that I never see anyone my age on the shows we sometimes watch. How silly of me!

On the other hand most women my age have enough sense to stay away from TV all together! So I guess I get to make up my own look for the wedding ...

So – enjoy yourselves – and I'll write again soon I hope.
Best to all

Cindy's story about visible outfits for her and M's wedding sparked responses to (and from) her and became a relevant part of the group conversation.

(Sara, 27.09.08)

Hello Cindy, Sara here

I enjoyed reading your email about your upcoming wedding. Congratulations and best wishes to you and your partner, I hope your union becomes even more special with the wedding ceremony making it "official". I'm sure you'll find just the right dress, look gorgeous and have a wonderful day.

You are so right about women of "a certain age" not being seen on the telly, whether they're wearing plain or fancy outfits! The only ones one does see are portrayed as nuts or completely feeble, not functioning, professional members of society. Most of the stuff on the telly is just silly, anyway; only good for keeping up with the weather and so forth. The news is mostly so slanted it's useless for real information.

I'm really enjoying this group contact, it's fun to finally have a chat with some of you.

My husband and I travel around the country quite a bit; I'm a doll and puppet maker and sell my work at our shops in various Renaissance Festivals - Florida, New York, Pennsylvania, Louisiana and Texas. The travel helps us stay in close contact with our children, grands and great-grands.

Best to all

(Cindy, 29.09.08)

Thanks so much for the good wishes, Sara

I did find a fun outfit that looks pretty good. I had a friend go shopping with me and her directives were really helpful. In fact, I got several new outfits and cleaned out the old stuff I'd been wearing. Interestingly enough it was the 'fit' of things that mattered most and with that foremost in mind, and being with a 'shopper' – which I'm not – I did find some classic looks that make me look better without looking trendy as if I was younger than I am.

In some ways it was like having my own pep rally about my body and it really helped me feel good about myself. Since I've followed a life long path of not fitting in, or said another way, embracing my 'otherness', it was wonderful just to see how put together I could look without going to the dark side!

Interesting process, which we are still in the middle of - now we have to dress the girls, 9 and 12, and find that same balance. L, the 9 year old is into fashion forward, while G, the 12 year old would be happy in her jeans ... So we'll see how it all goes. In the stores for the girls, it's VERY hard to find dresses and nice clothes that don't look like grown up cocktail dresses or revealing hooker clothes. I have this hope that it's different in the UK – but maybe I'm wrong.

Anyway - thanks for your kind reply and I look forward to hearing more from the group.

Best

(Jane, 29.09.08)

Hi Cindy, Jane here from the UK

I was so thrilled to hear about your wedding plans and hope by now you have found some wonderfully expressive outfit to wear. I really understand how exciting this all is for both of you, having married my wonderful woman last year. We've just had our first anniversary. We got married here in England although it is called a civil partnership here but gives us complete equality with marriage 'rights'.

I know it is now legal in California and a couple of other States in the USA but do keep up the pressure wherever you can to get

Federal gay marriage. My wife is American but because I'm British and same sex she had to leave the US in order for us to be together. Same sex marriage in the US in the States where it is legal is not permissible for immigration purposes, so it precluded us. If we had been a heterosexual couple I would have been eligible for a green card by virtue of marriage to an American. We so wanted to live in the US but it is just not possible. Should the law become federal this may be possible. Anyway we are very happily married here and are so thankful that it was possible to be so in England.

I so hope your day is really happy and I'm sure you'll look amazing. I had similar problems to you and ended up making my own silver jacket for the occasion!
Have a wonderful wedding.

(Cindy, 29.09.08)

Way fun – thanks!

(Lynn, 07.10.08)

Dear Christine, Cindy, Jane, Alison, Val, Sara and Marie

The emails that have been flowing have been so free and easy considering most of us have never met, which is probably due to the tact and integrity of our leader.

I met Christine 13 years ago when we were training in Psychotherapy. We sat across the room staring at one another for a while. I love her humour, humility, intelligence, irreverence and general being.

Christine's doctorate has given me much to think about and I've discovered a few things about myself I didn't know. I'm enjoying being my age (64) apart from needing a full body-lift. It is so nice not to worry about so many things any more and to be able to think, feel and do what I want and not what I think I ought to be doing. I am not working any more (as a therapist) as I became very disenchanted with a lot of that world. Or I grew up!! Or I was cured!!

I am quite good at playing and your emails, and my answering of them, seems rather like a wonderful sharing game.

Cindy - Good luck in your marriage and a wonderful day.

Sara - Congratulations on fifty years.

If I go on it will be wittering I'm sure.

Take care

(Sara, 08.10.08)

Hello Lynn, thanks for your good wishes about our special day.

It was such a wonderful occasion, all the more fun with Christine and David there! It really was just what R and I wanted, a time with as many of the family as could be there, talking, playing, eating, laughing, being together. A day we'll remember our whole lives.

I've so enjoyed re-connecting with Christine; we were separated by distance and the circumstances of our lives for many years and now we're re-discovering so many things about each other and the family.

That's one reason I've enjoyed participating in this research project, it's been an opportunity to think about who and what I've been and become over the years and how events have shaped the lives of our family.

I'm still working - sort of! ... selling my work at 'Renaissance Festivals'.... is a lot of fun and so far has been reasonably profitable – until the last few months! Guess we'll just have to wait and see what happens next. At least life is always interesting!

Hope we can keep up this world-wide chat, it's fun.

Most of the women were still corresponding individually with me at that time. The group emails continued occasionally, usually prompted by a request of some kind from me.

(Christine, 23.10.08)

> **Subject: Naming the visible women**
>
> *Dear Alison, Cindy, Jane, Lynn, Marie, Sara and Val*
>
> *I'm just beginning to get to the point of doing some 'writing up' for my dissertation (although I plan to allow myself at least a year for this) ...*
>
> *As part of this stage I want to ask how you would like to be identified in the final text. There are various possibilities and I'll set out the ones that come to mind – if you have other ideas I'd be delighted to hear them:*
>
> *a) your actual first name*
> *b) a pseudonym (choosing your own, of course)*
> *c) just an initial letter*
>
> *There doesn't have to be general agreement about how to do this – as far as I'm concerned you can each be identified in the way you choose. When you've had a chance to think about this, let me know what you'd prefer. This could be another 'group email' or just individually to me.*

When I started re-writing for this book, one of the women requested a pseudonym. For my dissertation, however, within a few days of the email above all the women replied that it was fine to use their own names.

All but one of their replies were addressed individually to me and very brief. Cindy sent a group email with some interesting questions:

(Cindy, 23.10.08)

Hi Christine, and everyone else

I've been thinking about this most of the day and I think my name is a fine way to go.

I'm happy to answer questions about anything I have or have yet to share ...

I know this is a good ethical question and a way to protect folks from ??? Feeling taken advantage of? Not being honoured? Not being consulted about what Christine will and will not use?

I'm at a loss right this minute about what I would need protection from. Can we talk about it?

(Christine, 24.10.08)

Hello again ...

Cindy's point about the ethical question of 'protection' is a valid one – though I hope none of you do/will feel that I'm going to either take advantage of you or not honour what you're all contributing. I will certainly consult with all of you about what I will be using and you will all be given the chance to read whatever goes in about you.

I've already said all this, but maybe this is a good time to repeat it. Anyway, over to any of you who would like to join in a conversation about this – I might even have something more to say myself!

(Christine, 25.10.08)

I have now heard from all but two of you (neither of whom check emails very often) and so far the other five have said OK to use your own names – with Cindy's suggestion of having a chat about it. Anybody up for that?

P.S. Incidentally – since Cindy has already told you all it's happening – today's the day she and M are getting married (again) …

There were no direct responses to this, or engagement with Cindy's invitation to a discussion about what they might need to be protected from – though there were some good wishes for her wedding day.

A few days later Lynn confirmed by phone that it was fine to use her name. I also heard from Marie, who had just moved and had not so far engaged in any group emailing.

(Christine, 04.11.08)

Just to let you all know that I've now heard from Marie, who has not been able to join in any group emails as she's recently moved and has a very weak and intermittent internet connection, with email often not getting through.

Like the rest of you, she is happy to have her own name used.

(Marie, 04.11.08)

Thank you, Christine

Although a little uneasy about my 'weak and intermittent' connections, it was ever thus.

Glad to be on board and to respond as little or often as the mood takes. I am sure there have been some very interesting narratives and I look forward to catching up.

I wrote individually to all the women, adding in a group email:

(Christine, 26.11.08)

> *Thank you all very much for agreeing to my using your own name in my writing.*

> *This is very affirming (for me) of your all trusting me sufficiently – at least I hope that's what it is! …*

> *I'm currently experiencing a form of writer's block as I begin to get into trying to write the first 'chapters' for my dissertation. I think it's partly resistance to moving from sharing and gathering stories with you all (which I continue to LOVE doing) into the more 'tasky' academic stuff.*

The same day I also forwarded a letter from Lynn:

(Christine, 26.11.08)

> *Enclosed is a message to everybody from Lynn. Not quite sure about being what she calls the 'dear leader' (various rather unpleasant dictators come to mind) – but then maybe that's very appropriate! Anyway – any comments – responses – etc. welcome.*

(Lynn, 25.11.08)

> *Dear Visibles*

> *How are you all?*

> *In Devon it's dank cold windy and wet. We like to call it paradise!!!!*

> *It has been a busy year for some of us (not for me) so you are, perhaps, just coming up for air. My most interesting experience this year was to go to Canada and meet up with my cousin J (she is 77 yrs old) who I haven't seen for 52 years. Her morals, priorities, manner and character and looks were my Mother!!!!!! This was both lovely and disconcerting.*

As in most families there were idiosyncratic rules in ours and J still uses them. I only use some but was fascinated that I still recognised and knew them. You will be pleased to know that I did not show myself up by saying toilet or serviette. I know!!!! It takes so much energy to keep all the rules going and I fell by the wayside years ago.

Write soon. I'm sending this through our dear leader without whom we would not be a gang of formidable Visibles.

(Sara, 26.11.08)

I love the idea that we as a group (as well as individually) are 'The Visibles'!! … I do know that I really feel more 'visible' and more affirmed as such since we all started this journey together - and that includes our fearless leader! I'd like to reply to Lynn through you, if I may, Christine.

Hello Lynn and all the other 'Visibles'

I have had a busy year - most of them are, with a large family.

We're in Louisiana at the moment and it's been chillier this year than last but still lots of sun most days. We're getting ready for Thanksgiving Day, when tons of food is prepared for hours and hours, then devoured in nothing flat by all the hungry family and friends who show up. Then the men-folk sit around and watch football games on the telly and fall asleep half-way through!

It's fun cooking big meals when the family's all together and we do have so much to be thankful for, especially this year, with a son-in-law returned home safe from Afghanistan, a new great-grandchild, born just a week ago, the rest of the family safe and well - what a year!

Happy Thanksgiving to you all, wherever you are –

In forwarding this letter from Sara, I also passed on Alison's information about the 'Wild Old Women' (2009) art exhibition in London.

There were positive individual responses to the idea of being 'The Visibles' but no more group contact until my letter in March 2009 - and their responses – about not using 'academic language' (see 'Writing in Visible Language' above).

In April I sent the final 'group letter' in connection with writing my dissertation, attaching the Germaine Greer quote (see 'Fragments' above) on the *"positive aspects of being a frightening old woman"*:

(Christine, 10.04.09)

You may be pleased (and/or surprised) to hear that I've now really got going on the dreaded dissertation (though calling it 'my writing' in order not to frighten myself too much!). I haven't started on all your stories yet, but have written various introductory 'leaves', about why I'm doing this, what I'm doing and how I'm using writing with you all as a form of research.

I promise not to bombard you with endless drafts of all this, but have just come across what I think is a good quote from Germaine Greer, who I both admire and sometimes want to throw things at. Hope you enjoy it, too.

(Jane, 10.04.09)

I think this is absolutely bril.

(Cindy, 10.04.09)

Brava!

(Alison, 11.04.09)

Thanks – I love it!

(Sara, 11.04.09)

> *I really enjoyed the quote, thank you for sending it. I'm glad you're getting on all right with 'gathering your leaves' and beginning your writing ...*

(Lynn, 13.04.09)

> *The quote from G. Greer is brilliant. I find it so liberating to be this age and not care what most people think. At 15 years I wept when someone told me they didn't like me. How sad. I must have been a burden to others as well as myself.*

I sent each of the women a copy of their 'story' as it was written, for any comments or queries. They were all, in different ways, powerfully affected by reading their words in poetic form and none asked for any alterations (see 'Afterwords' below).

Once my dissertation was completed and submitted, in early 2010, I sent a printed copy of the whole thing to each of them – and all sent me extremely positive feedback about having been part of the experience. They were delighted by my successful viva in April 2010.

8.2 Afterwords ...

Writing is not complete
until the reader has responded ...
(McIntyre, 2008)

After compiling each individual woman's story for my dissertation, I sent a copy to the 'owner' for comment and/or correction. To my amazement (and slightly tearful delight), apart from one or two overlooked spelling mistakes, there were no requests to alter anything. These are the responses from each of the women:

(Lynn, 30.08.09)

> I like it
> makes me sound
> quite intelligent
>
> You were
> delicate
> tactful
> sensitive

(Val, 05.10.09)

> Enjoyed reading my story
> and loved the layout
> Looks like you have done
> an enormous amount of work

(Alison, 22.10.09)

> Been sitting and reading
> the 'Alison' section
>
> Am so very impressed
> by the way you've written this ...
> what a wonderful original approach

I hope you are 'well pleased'

Strange reading what I've written
Had to keep reminding myself
that is what I wrote then
Sometimes a wish to edit
but only when writing about
feeling miserable or grumpy

(Cindy, 27.10.09)

Really enjoyable
to see our words intermingled
Said as much about you
as about me
　　　Was it like that for others?

Like a mini flashback
to all major events in my life
in the last five years
So much happened!
To see it all gathered together
is amazing

I love that you have been
on this passage with me
and that herstories
provided the 'salt'

Surprised by how much
I've shared with you
how much of my life
documented

Really appreciate
how you have turned
the letters into prose
Your spacing and timing
and different line breaks
make the words really sing

Found it comforting
respectful
loving
that we checked in
with each other
about continuing
our email conversations

(Marie, 31.10.09)

The form portrays
perfectly
the fragments of a life
which is not sure
where it's going
and which hovers
on the ethereal side
of visibility!

Thank you
for the respectful way
you treated
my tightly wrung out musing

Am truly sorry
I could not bring myself
to say more at the time

(Jane, 15.11.09)

How you extract
these poignant things
I just don't know!
You are amazing

It sounds great
and I can't wait to see
the whole thing in context
when you've finished

(Sara, 20.11.09)

SO enjoyed reading it

Makes me sound
a lot more together
than I sometimes feel!

R says it does sound like me
and he's known me
longer than anyone

Thank you for allowing me
to take part in your project
It was a great experience
and very interesting

CHAPTER NINE

POSTSCRIPT

One way to subvert and rewrite
master narratives
so that women can be represented
is to change the conventional patterns
of narrative closure …
'writing beyond the ending'.
(Bloom, 1998: 66)

9.1 Beyond the ending

Although the virtual 'group' did not continue, there has been the occasional email:

(Christine, 01.10.10)

> *Hello again – another 'visible women' group email and another request ...*
>
> *I'm writing a chapter for a book being edited by Jane Speedy (Bristol Uni supervisor) on creative approaches to research. My chapter is about 'poetic inquiry' and I'm using extracts from my dissertation – and would like to include some of the 'poems' I created from your letters.*
>
> *I'd be grateful if you could let me know how you feel about this, including whether it would be all right to do as you all generously allowed in my dissertation and use your first names ... I'm happy to send you a copy of the draft chapter ...*
>
> *Just as an advance warning, I'm hoping to get my dissertation published – though need to do some work in order to make it into a book. So I'll be coming back for more permission sometime around that!*
>
> *There has been some very interesting feedback and reaction to my various sharings of 'Visible Women' so far – it seems to have struck a cord with lots of women, in particular, but there has also been some really moving and positive feedback from men. People have had things to say about how struck they were by your individual openness, honesty and willingness to engage with the issues that emerged for you. So it's gone on being a very powerful experience for me.*
>
> *Thank you all again for everything you brought to the work.*

The same day, I had a telephone conversation with Lynn, who said it was fine to use her poems and her name. Everybody else emailed:

(Sara, 01.10.10)

Wow! How exciting to be writing more about your research methods. Of course you can use anything you find useful in my story, name and all. I'd enjoy reading what you come up with whenever you're ready. And as for the work on The Book, you go girl!!

(Cindy, 01.10.10)

Of course yes – you may use anything you like for this and/or you future book.

(Val, 01.10.10)

It's great news your work will have a wider readership – you can use my contributions in whatever way you like – good luck with your book as well.

(Marie, 02.10.10)

As ever you have my 'consent' to use what you will from my modest contributions.

I am so glad you are getting the feedback you deserve – the poetry was yours.

(Alison, 02.10.10)

Yes – prolific writer! – I'm fine with that.

(Jane, 04.10.10)

> *The answer is positively yes to it all!*

Some of the women took up my offer to read the draft chapter on poetic inquiry and let me know they enjoyed it, liked my writing style and found it *"clear and interesting"*.

Early in 2011, I was delighted to get the contract for this book and contacted the group to let them know. They all repeated their enthusiastic permission to use their letters however I chose – and that they looked forward to reading the finished work. One person asked to be anonymous and we agreed a change of name and omission of one or two potentially identifying details. She left the changes up to me, saying: *"You can fill in the blanks with anything you think suitable – I trust you completely"*.

Writing the final section of this book, I have a profound sense of warmth and gratitude towards my seven women co-researchers for the extraordinarily generous way they have shared their memories, thoughts, experiences and feelings with me - and each other – and now with you, that other reader.

> *... oh, if only I were sometimes you and you were me*
> (Fisk, 2008)

9.2 My story – part seven:
seeing and being seen

All of us, female as well as male, fear the will of woman ...
female will is embedded in female power ...
(Dinnerstein, in Bly & Woodman, 1998: 51)

What do women really desire, above all else? In the mythic tale of *Sir Gawain and the Lady Ragnell* this is a life-or-death question. The correct, transformational answer in the story is one that would, I believe, ring true for all women: the power of sovereignty, the right to choose, to exercise our own free will.

There are still, tragically, too many places in the world – in any country – where women are not given sovereignty and, indeed, may be severely punished (even killed) for attempting to exercise their own free will. For those of us who are (at least physically) free to choose to be ourselves, it seems we too often go on being bound by the need for approval – conforming to external models of how we should look, behave, be in the world.

Whilst having some emotional and psychological understanding of this, I feel my earlier impatience with the stated need to be 'noticed' by men in order to feel visible . There are too many negative examples of this 'noticing' and few real positives. So I remain indignant about the ways in which those of us who *can* choose, allow ourselves (including my younger self) to be socialised into *wanting to be wanted*.

This is the central theme of Polly Young-Eisendrath's *Women and Desire*; she tells the tale of the Lady Ragnell, along with other mythical and contemporary real-life stories, to illustrate her argument about *"psychological and social constraints on female power":*

> We try to appear attractive, nice, good, valid, legitimate, or worthy to someone else, instead of discovering what we actually feel and want for ourselves" (2000: 2).

Being 'nice' – and all that goes with it - can feel like a full-time occupation. I've tried it, reluctantly though never very successfully. It takes all our energy away from allowing ourselves to feel and be the many other things we are. But certainly when younger, 'being nice' seemed to be what was demanded in return for my being allowed to simply exist in the world. My internal lists of 'dos and don'ts' – spoken or implicit – included:

> *DO ... smile; be grateful; ask permission before you do anything; always think of others; know your place; BEHAVE; be quiet; fit in ...*

> *DON'T ... make a noise; cry; EVER GET ANGRY; show off; ask questions; answer back; think about yourself because YOU DON'T MATTER ...*

One of the pleasures of growing older, becoming part of that bunch of fearsome old crones, is that I really don't need everybody to like me, or care what people think of me. Of course I care a bit - and am not at all free of vanity. I need loving relationships, respect, friendship, support from those who matter. But what a burden all that endless *wanting to be wanted* was! What a relief to be (almost) free of it.

If we older women, especially, can bear to be seen as we really are – warts and all, like the Lady Ragnell, Baba Yaga and all the other powerful 'hags' of myth in all cultures – then we can choose to be the subjects of our own desires instead of wanting to be objects of other people's.

> *Seeing and being seen*
> *certainly have something to do*
> *with the forming of the self .*
> (Wright, 1991: 55)

On becoming 70

REFERENCES

Allardice, L., 2011. **A Life in Writing: Interview with Margaret Drabble.** In *Guardian Review,* 18 June: 12, 13

Armitstead, C., 2009. **Invisible women.** In *Guardian Review*, 28 March: 8

Athill, D., 2009. **Somewhere Towards the End.** London: Granta

Atkinson, P. & Silverman, D., 1997. **Kundera's Immortality: the interview society and the invention of self.** In *Qualitative Inquiry,* 3(3): 304-325. Thousand Oaks: Sage

Atwood, M., 2008. **Close to home: a celebration of Alice Munro.** In *Guardian Review,* 11 October: 2-4

Bakewell, J., 2007. **The View From Here: life at seventy.** London: Atlantic

—. 2008. **Riding the elephant.** In *Guardian Review,* 4 October: 8

Barr, P., 1985. **A Curious Life for a Lady.** Harmondsworth: Penguin

Bawden, T. and Rogers, S., 2011. **40 years on, equal pay is yet to come.** In *Guardian,* 8 March: 11

Bell, C.J., 1995. **Creating chaos out of order: examining the relationship between change and the right brain experience.** MSc dissertation, Change Agent Skills & Strategies. University of Surrey

—. 2006. **Doing, undoing and redoing: a layered, experiential exploration of an encounter with art.** EdD modular assignment, Narrative & Life Story Research. University of Bristol

—. 2007. **Conversations with Cindy.** EdD modular assignment, Narrative & Life Story Research. University of Bristol

—. 2008. **Messy Texts and Visible Fragments.** EdD unassignment, Narrative & Life Story Research. University of Bristol

—. 2007-2011. **Personal journal.** [Entries made during this exploration]

—. 2010. **Visible Women: tales of age, gender and in/visibility.** EdD dissertation. Graduate School of Education, University of Bristol

Bernadac, M-L., 1996. **Louise Bourgeois.** Paris, New York: Flammarion

Berne, E., 1968. **Games People Play.** London: Penguin

Bidisha, 2010. **A culture of contempt.** In *Guardian G2,* 30 July: 18, 19

Bird, J., 2004. **Talk That Sings: therapy in a new linguistic key.** Aukland: Edge Press

Bloom, L.R., 1998. **Under the Sign of Hope: feminist methodology and narrative interpretation.** Albany: State University of New York Press

Bly, R. & Woodman, M., 1998. **The Maiden King: the reunion of masculine and feminine.** New York: Henry Holt

Bochner, A., 1997. **It's About Time: narrative and the divided self.** In *Qualitative Inquiry,* 3: 418-438

—. 2000. **Criteria Against Ourselves.** In *Qualitative Inquiry,* 6(2): 266-272. Thousand Oaks: Sage

Bond, T., 2002. **Naked Narrative: real research?** In *Counselling & Psychotherapy Research,* 2(2): 133-138

Bourgeois, L., 2000. [Exhibition]. **I do, I undo, I redo.** Installation in the Turbine Hall, Tate Modern Gallery, London 12 May-17 December 2000

—. 2007. [Exhibition]. **Louise Bourgeois retrospective.** Retrospective at Tate Modern Gallery, London 10 October 2007-20 January 2008

Brady, I., 2000. **Anthropological Poetics.** In Denzin, N.K. & Lincoln, Y.S. (Eds), *The Handbook of Qualitative Research,* (2nd edn): 949-979. Thousand Oaks: Sage

—. 2005. **Poetics for a Planet.** In Denzin, N.K. & Lincoln, Y.S. (Eds), *Sage handbook of qualitative research,* (3rd edn): 979-1026. Thousand Oaks, London, New Delhi: Sage

Braidotti, R., 2006. **Transpositions: on nomadic ethics.** Cambridge, Malden: Polity Press

Brooks, X., 2010. **The queen of Cannes.** In *Guardian G2,* 28 May: 12-15

Bruner, J., 2002. **Making Stories: law, literature, life.** Cambridge MA: Harvard University Press.

Caremark, 2001. **Health after 60 – Interview: Doris Lessing on Aging.** [Online]. Excerpt from Rountree, C. *On Women Turning 70.* [Accessed 14.04.09]. Available on: https://www.caremark.com/wps/portal/HEALTH_RESOURCES?topic=lessing

Carson, A., 2010. **Nox.** New York: New Directions

Casement, P., 1985. **On Learning from the Patient.** London, New York: Tavistock Publications

Churchwell, S., 2010. **Mothers I'd like to show their age.** In *Guardian,* 24 July: 27

Cixous, H., 2004. **The Writing Notebooks.** Selected and translated by Sellers, S. London, New York: Continuum

—. 2005. **Stigmata: escaping texts.** Abingdon, New York: Routledge

—. 2011. **Philippines.** Cambridge: Polity Press

Cixous, H. & Calle-Gruber, M., 1997. **Rootprints: memory and life writing.** London: Routledge

Clandinin, D.J., 2008. [Seminar]. **Narrative Inquiry.** Graduate School of Education, University of Bristol. 18 September. [Verbatim notes]

Clandinin, D.J. & Connelly, F.M., 2000. **Narrative Inquiry: experience and story in qualitative research.** San Francisco: Jossey-Bass

Clark, A., 2011. **A Life in Writing: Interview with Jane Gardam.** In *Guardian Review,* 8 January: 10, 11

Clark, M. C., 2001. **Incarcerated Women and the Construction of the Self.** [Online]. [Accessed 14.02.10]. Available on: http://www.coe.uga.edu/hsp/monographs1/clark.pdf

Cochrane, K., 2010. **It's not finished, it's not uncool.** In *Guardian,* 24 July: 28

—. 2011a. **Standing up to the BBC was the right thing to do.** In *Guardian G2,* 12 January: 6-9

—. 2011b. **Ann Oakley interview: 'She was too visionary'.** In *Guardian G2,* 8 July: 16, 17

Crawford, J. et al, 1992. **Emotion and Gender: constructing meaning from memory.** London, Newbury Park, New Delhi: Sage

Davies, C., 2011. **Celebrations across the globe, but 100 years on, so much still to be done.** In *Guardian,* 9 March: 2

Davies, L., 2011. **New wave of feminists head to 'boot camp'.** In *Guardian,* 6 August: 15

Davies, B. and Gannon, S. (Eds), 2006. **Doing Collective Biography.** Maidenhead, Berks: Open University Press

Davies, B. & Harre, R., 1990. **Positioning: the discursive production of selves.** In *Journal for the Theory of Social Behaviour,* 19(4): 43-63

Denzin, N.K., 1997. **Interpretive Ethnography: ethnographic practices for the 21st century.** Thousand Oaks, London, New Delhi: Sage

—. 2000. **Aesthetics and the Practices of Qualitative Inquiry.** In *Qualitative Inquiry,* 6(2): 256-265

—. 2005. **Emancipatory Discourses and the Practices and Politics of Interpretation.** In Denzin, N.K. & Lincoln, Y.S. (Eds), *Sage handbook of qualitative research,* (3rd edn): 933-957. Thousand Oaks, London, New Delhi: Sage

Derrida, J., 1973; first published 1967. **Différance.** Illinois: Northwest University Press

Drabble, M., 2003. **The Seven Sisters.** London: Penguin

Drewery, W., 2005. **Why We Should Watch What We Say: position calls, everyday speech and the production of relational subjectivity.** In *Theory & Psychology*, 15(3): 305-324. Thousand Oaks: Sage

Dube, L., Leacock, E., Ardener, S. (Eds), 1986. **Visibility and Power: essays on women in society and development.** New Delhi: Oxford University Press

Duffy, C.A., 2009. **Premonitions.** In *Guardian Review*: Sisters in poetry, 2 May: 2-4

—. 2010. **Poetry archive.** [Online]. [Accessed 13.01.11]. Available on: http://www.poetryarchive.org/poetryarchive/singlePoet.do?poetId=11468

2011. [Book Festival]. **The Bridport Open Book Festival and The Bridport Prize.** 25 November. [Verbatim notes].

Duncombe, J. & Jessop, J., 2004. **Doing Rapport and the Ethics of 'Faking Friendship'.** In Mauthner, M., Jessop, J. & Miller, T. (Eds) , *Ethics in Qualitative Research*: 107-122. London: Sage

Dunmore, H., 1995. **Burning Bright.** London: Penguin

Edemariam, A., 2009. **Hilary Mantel interview: 'I accumulated an anger that would rip a roof off'.** *The Guardian* [online], 12 September. [Accessed 20.09.09]. Available on: http://www.guardian.co.uk/theguardian/2009/sep/12/hilary-mantel-booker-prize-interview?INTCMP=SRCH

Ekman, J. (Ed), 1994. **Louise Bourgeois: the locus of memory, works 1982-1993.** Exhibition at the Brooklyn Museum with The Corcoran Gallery of Art, Washington, DC, 1994. [Exhibition catalogue]

Enright, A., 2008a. **The Gathering.** London: Vintage

—. 2008b. **Author, author.** In *Guardian Review,* 22 November: 15

—. 2009. **Author, author.** In *Guardian Review,* 3 January: 13

Ephron, N., 2007. **I Feel Bad About My Neck – and other thoughts on being a woman.** New York: Doubleday

Estés, C.P., 1993. **Women Who Run with the Wolves.** London, Sydney, Auckland, Johannesburg: Rider

—. 1994. **The Gift of Story.** London, Sydney, Auckland, Johannesburg: Rider

Faubion, J. (Ed), 2001. **Michel Foucault: Power: the essential works, volume three.** London: Allen Lane

Fisk, M., 2008. **The October Garden.** *Michigan Quarterly Review* [online], October 2008. [Accessed 27.11.09]. Available on: http://findarticles.com/p/articles/mi_7663/is_200810/ai_n32298660/?tag=content;co11

Fontana, A. & Frey, J., 2005. **The Interview: from neutral stance to political involvement.** In Denzin, N.K. & Lincoln, Y.S. (Eds), *Sage handbook of qualitative research,* (3rd edn): 695-727. Thousand Oaks, London, New Delhi: Sage

Fromm, E., 1985. **The Art of Loving.** London: Mandala

Geertz, C., 1983. **Local Knowledge: further essays in interpretative Anthropology.** USA: Basic Books

Gold, T., 2011. **Inequality? Let's not have legislation, ladies, let's lunch!** In *Guardian,* 8 January: 27

Greer, G., 1992. **The Change: women, ageing and the menopause.** Harmondsworth: Penguin

—. 2011. **Review of Tracey Emin's exhibition.** *BBC Radio 4 Front Row* [online], 16 May. [Accessed 17.05.11]. Available on: http://www.bbc.co.uk/iplayer/episode/b01132zj/Front_Row_Germaine_Greer_reviews_Tracey_Emin

Guba, E.G. & Lincoln, Y.S., 2005. **Paradigmatic Controversies, Contradictions, and Emerging Confluences.** In Denzin, N.K. & Lincoln, Y.S. (Eds) *Sage Handbook of Qualitative Research,* (3rd edn): 191-215. Thousand Oaks, London, New Delhi: Sage

Hadley, T., 2010. **Author, author.** In *Guardian Review*, 6 November: 15

Hakim, C., 2011. **Feminist Myths and Magic Medicine: the flawed thinking behind calls for further equality legislation.** Centre for Policy Studies paper [online], January. [Accessed 01.06.11]. Available on: http://www.cps.org.uk/cps_catalog/Feminist%20Myths%20and%20Magic%20Medicine.pdf

Hanson, M., 2009. **Women.** In *Guardian G2,* 25 March: 16, 17

Harman, C., 1991. **Sylvia Townsend Warner: a biography.** London: Minerva

Haug, F. et al, 1999. **Female Sexualisation: a collective work of memory.** Translated by Carter, E. London, New York: Verso Classics

Hen Co-op, 1993. **Growing Old Disgracefully: new ideas for getting the most out of life.** London: Piatkus

Hertz, R. (Ed), 1997. **Reflexivity and Voice.** Thousand Oaks, London, New Delhi: Sage

Higgins, C., 2009. **Ours for 600 bottles of sherry: Carol Ann Duffy becomes first woman poet laureate.** In *Guardian,* 2 May: 3

Houle, K., 2009. **Making Strange: deconstruction and feminist standpoint theory.** In *Frontiers: A Journal of Women Studies,* 30 (1): 172-93

Hudston, J., 2011. **Praise for history of Bridport rope and net making.** *Real West Dorset* [online], 24 January. [Accessed 25.01.11]. Available at:
http://www.realwestdorset.co.uk/wordpress/01/2011/bridport-rope-net-and-twine-book-praised/

Imagine: Louise Bourgeois, 2007. [BBC1 TV]. Alan Yentob, 13 November

Itani, F., 2008. **Remembering the Bones.** London: Sceptre

James, N. & Busher, H., 2006. **Credibility, authenticity and voice: dilemmas in online interviewing.** In *Qualitative Research,* 6(3): 403-420

James, N., 2007. **The use of email interviewing as a qualitative method of inquiry in educational research.** In *British Educational Research Journal,* 33 (6): 963-976

Jennings, L., 2009. **Obituary: Pina Bausch.** *The Guardian* [online] 1 July. [Accessed 13.05.11]. Available on:
http://www.guardian.co.uk/stage/2009/jul/01/pina-bausch-obituary

Jha, A., 2011. **The only real truth is that there's doubt, say scientists.** In *Guardian,* 15 January: 7

Jolly, M. & Stanley, L., 2005. **Letters as / not a genre.** In *Life Writing,* 2(2): 91-118

Kristeva, J., 2001. **Hannah Arendt: Life is a Narrative.** Toronto, Buffalo, London: University of Toronto Press

Kvale, S., 1996. **InterViews – an introduction to qualitative research interviewing.** Thousand Oaks, London, New Delhi: Sage

Lather, P., 2007. **Getting Lost: feminist efforts towards a double(d) science.** Albany: State University of New York Press

Lessing, D., 1983. **The Summer Before the Dark.** New York: Vintage Books

Levitas, R., 2011. [Seminar]. **Heretical Academic Identity and Utopia as Method.** Graduate School of Education, University of Bristol. [Verbatim notes]

Lively, P., 2009. **A Life in Books.** Interview by Crown, S. In *Guardian Review,* 25 July: 10,11

Louise Bourgeois: The Spider, the Mistress and the Tangerine, 2008. [Film]. New York: Zeitgeist Films. [Written and directed by Marion Cajori and Amei Wallach]

McAfee, N., 2004. **Julia Kristeva.** New York, Oxford: Routledge

McIntyre, I., 2008. [Talk]. **Dear Mistress.** Bridport Literary Festival. [Verbatim notes]

McNicol, J., 2008. **WOW! Wild Old Women!** Exhibition at Novas Gallery, Novas Contemporary Urban Centre, London 14 November 2008-3 January 2009. [Exhibition publicity and catalogue]

Mair, M., 1989. **Between Psychology and Psychotherapy: a poetics of experience.** London, New York: Routledge

Marcus, G.E., 1994. **What comes (just) after 'post'? The case of ethnography.** In Denzin, N.K. & Lincoln, Y.S. (Eds), *The Handbook of Qualitative Research*: 563-574. Thousand Oaks: Sage

Mantel, H., 2004. **Eight months on Ghazzah Street.** London: Harper Perennial

—. 2007. **Ghost writing.** In *Guardian Review,* 28 July: 4,5

—. 2008. **Author, author.** In *Guardian Review,* 24 May: 15

—. 2009. **Women.** In *Guardian G2,* 4 August: 9

—. 2010. **Author, author.** In *Guardian Review,* 6 March: 15

Metta, M., 2010. **Writing Against, Alongside and Beyond Memory: Lifewriting as Reflexive, Poststructuralist Feminist Research Practice.** Bern: Peter Lang

Millay, E. St. V., first published 1922. **A Few Figs from Thistles: poems and sonnets.** In *Poets' Corner – Bookshelf* [online]. [Accessed 21.12.08]. Available on: http://www.theotherpages.org/poems/millay02.html

Miller, L., 2007. **Mother complex.** In *A life in writing, Guardian Review,* 7 April: 11

Moi, T. (Ed), 1986. **The Kristeva Reader.** Oxford: Blackwell Publishers

Moore, S., 2011. **All this polite and smiley feminism is pointless. It's time to get angry.** In *Guardian,* 15 January: 33

Morris, F., 2000. **Louise Bourgeois.** Installation at Tate Modern Gallery, London 12 May-17 December 2000. [Exhibition catalogue]

—. 2007. **Louise Bourgeois.** Retrospective at Tate Modern Gallery, London 10 October 2007-20 January 2008. [Exhibition catalogue]

Morris, M. (Ed), 1996. **The Virago Book of Women Travellers.** London: Virago

Munro, A., 1985. **Something I've been meaning to tell you.** London: Penguin

Myerhoff, B., 1986. **"Life Not Death in Venice": its second life.** In Turner, V.W. & Bruner, J.M. (Eds), *The Anthropology of Experience:* 261-288. Urbana and Chicago: University of Illinois Press

Mykhalokvskiy, E., 1997. **Reconsidering "Table Talk": critical thoughts on the relationship between sociology, autobiography and self-indulgence.** In Hertz, R. (Ed), *Reflexivity & Voice:* 229-251. Thousand Oaks, London, New Delhi: Sage

New Cultures of Ageing, 2011. [Conference]. Brunel University, West London. 8, 9 April. [Verbatim notes]

Number Our Days, 1977. [Film]. Los Angeles: KCET. [Produced and directed by Lynne Littman]

O'Hara, M., 2010. **Raging Grannies light up the age with rage.** *The Guardian* [online] 13 January. [Accessed 15.01.10]. Available on: http://www.guardian.co.uk/society/joepublic/2010/jan/13/raging-grannies-older-people-activism

Oakley, A., 1981. **Interviewing Women: a contradiction in terms**. In Roberts, H. (Ed), *Doing feminist research*: 30-61. London, Boston, Melbourne: Routledge & Keagan Paul

Oliver, K. (Ed) 2002. **Portable Kristeva.** New York: Columbia University Press

Padel, R., 2010. **Darwin: a life in poems.** London: Vintage

Personal Narratives Group, 1989. **Interpreting Women's Lives: feminist theory and personal narratives.** Bloomington, Indianapolis: Indiana University Press

Pina, 2011. [Film]. London: Hanway Films. [Produced and directed by Wim Wenders]

Polanyi, M., 1967. **The Tacit Dimension.** London: Routledge & Kegan Paul Ltd

Pollitt, K., 2005. **Invisible Women.** *The Nation* [online] 4 April. [Accessed 09.09.07]. Available on: http://www.thenation.com/doc/20050404/pollit

Poirier, A., 2011. **Romcom-free zone.** In *Guardian Film,* 25 March: 8

Prendergast, M., 2009. **Poetic Inquiry is ... 29 Ways of Looking at Poetry as Qualitative Research.** In *Educational Insights,* 13(3) [online] 2009. [Accessed 16.02.10]. Available on: http://www.ccfi.educ.ubc.ca/publication/insights/v13n03/intro/pre ndergast.html

Poustie, S., 2010. **Re-Theorising Letters and 'Letterness'.** [Online]. [Accessed 27.05.11]. Available on: http://www.oliveschreinerletters.ed.ac.uk/PoustieWPLetterness.p df

Reed, M., 2006. **A Perplexed Story.** In *Changing English: Studies in Culture and Education,* 13(2)

Redfern, C. and Aune, K., 2010. **Reclaiming The F Word: the new feminist movement.** London: Zed Books

Richardson, L., 1990. **Writing Strategies: reaching diverse audiences.** Newbury Park, London, New Delhi: Sage

—. 1997. **Fields of Play: constructing an academic life.** New Brunswick: Rutgers University Press

—. 2000. **Writing: a method of inquiry.** In Denzin, N.K. & Lincoln, Y.S. (Eds), *Sage Handbook of Qualitative Research,* (2nd edn). Thousand Oaks, London, New Delhi: Sage

—. 2005. **Qualitative Writing.** In Denzin, N.K. & Lincoln, Y.S. (Eds), *Sage Handbook of Qualitative Research,* (3rd edn): 959-967. Thousand Oaks, London, New Delhi: Sage

Richardson, L. & St. Pierre, E.A., 2005. **Writing: a method of inquiry.** In Denzin, N.K. & Lincoln, Y.S. (Eds), *Sage Handbook of Qualitative Research,* (3rd edn): 959-975. Thousand Oaks, London, New Delhi: Sage

Rowe, D., 1994. **Time On Our Side: growing in wisdom, not growing old.** London: HarperCollins

St. Pierre, E.A., 2000. **Nomadic Inquiry in the Smooth Spaces of the Field.** In St. Pierre, E.A. & Pillow, W.S. (Eds), *Working the Ruins: feminist poststructural theory and methods in education:* 258-283. New York, London: Routledge

—. 2005. **Writing as a Method of Nomadic Inquiry.** In Denzin, N.K. & Lincoln, Y.S. (Eds), *Sage Handbook of Qualitative Research,* (3rd edn): 967-975. Thousand Oaks, London, New Delhi: Sage

Saner, E., 2010. **Too old for TV?** In Guardian G2 'Women', 5 February: 18

Scott-Maxwell, F., 1979. **The Measure of My Days.** Harmondsworth: Penguin

Shaw, M., 2011. **A Branch from the Lightning Tree: ecstatic myth and the grace in wildness.** Ashland, Oregon: White Cloud Press

Shilling, J., 2011. **The Stranger in the Mirror: a memoir of middle age.** London: Chatto & Windus

Sparkes, A., 2002. **Autoethnography: self-indulgence or something more?** In Bochner, A. & Ellis, C. (Eds), *Ethnographically Speaking: autoethnography, literature and aesthetics:* 209-232. Walnut Creek, CA: Altamira Press

Speedy, J., 2004. **Living a More Peopled Life: definitional ceremony as inquiry into therapy outcomes.** In *International Journal of Narrative Therapy and Community Work,* 3: 43-53

—. 2005a. **Writing as Inquiry: some ideas, practices, opportunities and constraints.** In *Counselling & Psychotherapy Research,* 5(1): 63-64

—. 2005b. **Failing to Come to Terms with Things: a multi-storied conversation about poststructuralist ideas and narrative practices in response to some of life's failures.** In *Counselling & Psychotherapy Research,* 5(1): 65-73

—. 2005c. **Collective Biography Practices: collective writing with the unassuming geeks group.** In *British Journal of Psychotherapy Integration,* 2(2): 29-38

—. 2007. **Constructing Stories: Narrative interviews and conversations with Donald.** In Speedy, J., *Narrative Inquiry in Psychotherapy:* 115-158. Basingstoke: Palgrave Macmillan

Stanley, L., 2009. **Introductory comments.** [Online]. Centre for Narrative & Auto/Biographical Studies, University of Edinburgh. http://www.sps.ed.ac.uk/NABS/LizStanley.htm

—. 2010. [Conference session]. **Olive Schreiner and company: Letters and 'drinking in the external world'.** IABA Life Writing and Intimate Publics Conference, University of Sussex, 28 June-1 July. [Verbatim notes 29.06.10].

Steiner, C., 1990, 2nd edition; first published 1974. **Scripts People Live.** New York: Weidenfeld

Steinman, M. (Ed), 2001. **The Element of Lavishness: Letters of Sylvia Townsend Warner and William Maxwell 1938-1978.** New York: Counterpoint

Steinmetz, M., 2009. **Pina Bausch, she who made dance speak.** *L'Humanité in English* [online] 2 July. Translated by Henry Crapo. [Accessed 13.05.11]. Available on: http://www.humaniteinenglish.com/spip.php?article1270

Stensrude, J., 1995. **The Invisible Woman.** [Online]. Unpublished academic paper. [Accessed 14.04.09]. Available on: http://www.stensrude.com/invisible.html

Stronach, I., 2002. **This Space Is Not Yet Blank: anthropologies for a future action research.** In Day et al (Eds), *Education Action Research,* 10(2): 291-307. Oxford: Symposium

Take my eyes, 2003. [Film]. Madrid: La Iguana & Alta Produccion. [Directed and co-written by Icíar Bollaín]

Tan, A., 2003. **The Opposite of Fate: a book of musings.** New York: Putnam

The Brain: a secret history (part two), 2011. [BBC4 TV]. Dr. M. Mosley, 13 January

The Concise Oxford Dictionary, 1991. Allen, R.E. (Ed). London, New York, Sydney, Toronto: BCA (with Oxford University Press)

The F Word [online]. [Accessed 30.05.11]. Available on: http://www.thefword.org.uk/

Tomalin, C., 1974. **The Life and Death of Mary Wollstonecraft.** London: Weidenfeld and Nicolson

Toms, K., 2010. **UK Feminism: a review of the last decade.** [Online]. Article 31 March. [Accessed 30.05.11]. Available on: http://www.tmponline.org/2010/03/31/noughties-uk-feminism/

Turner, V., 1982. **From Ritual to Theater: the human seriousness of play.** New York: PAJ Publications

Vygotsky, L., 1986; first published 1934. **Thought and Language.** Kozulin, A. (Ed) [revised and edited translation]. Cambridge, MA: MIT Press

Walby, S., 2011. **The Future of Feminism.** Cambridge: Polity Press

Walter, N., 2010. **Women have gone missing, and new sexists are dusting off old theories.** In *Guardian,* 28 April: 36

Watts, J., 2010. **Obituary: Dame Beryl Bainbridge.** In *Guardian,* 3 July: 39

Wild Old Women, 2009. [Exhibitions]. **WOW!! Wild Old Women.** [Online].   [Last   accessed   18.05.11].   Available   on: http://www.wildoldwomen.info/index2.php

Winterson, J., 2001. **The Power Book.** London: Vintage

—. 2004. **Lighthousekeeping.** London: Fourth Estate

Wright, J.K., 2004. **The Passion of Science, the Precision of Poetry: therapeutic writing – a review of the literature.** In Bolton, G. et al (Eds), *Writing Cures*: 7-17. Hove, New York: Brunner-Routledge

Wright, K., 1991. **Vision and Separation: between mother and baby.** London: Free Association

Young-Eisendrath, P., 2000. **Women & Desire: beyond wanting to be wanted.** London: Piatkus